Baby Boomers and the Big Society

Wally Harbert (signature)

by

Wally Harbert

Grosvenor House
Publishing Limited

This book is published by
Grosvenor House Publishing Ltd
28-30 High Street, Guildford, Surrey, GU1 3EL.
www.grosvenorhousepublishing.co.uk

A CIP record for this book
is available from the British Library

ISBN 978-1-908596-92-5

For Sue

Also for
Alison
Gillian
Josephine
Richard
Stephen

Acknowledgements

Among the national organisations I encountered when I joined Help the Aged in 1991 was the Retired and Senior Volunteer Programme (RSVP) of Community Service Volunteers. From a passing interest in volunteers and volunteering I became enthused by the passion and skill displayed by RSVP's staff and volunteers. I wanted to learn more about the huge potential of volunteering to change lives.

This book is a tribute to staff and volunteers at RSVP with whom I have worked for over twenty years. Many of them have, unknowingly, contributed ideas and given me the motivation to write it.

Bill Kerry from the Equality Trust kindly made some helpful suggestions about chapter one. Denise Wilkinson OBE shared with me her wisdom and knowledge of volunteering. Others, who have commented on draft material, helped to fill gaps in my knowledge or supplied examples of volunteering projects, include:

Doug Adams
Margaret Dexter
Dame Elisabeth Hoodless
Peter Hay

Muriel Jennings MBE
Rob Lever
Carol Reynolds
Lesley Welch
Jon Westoby

I am grateful for all the advice I have received, without which the book would be much poorer but I alone take responsibility for the views expressed.

The cover was designed by Simon and Jacob Burton to whom I am greatly indebted.

Glossary of terms

There is no agreement on terminology about volunteering. "Volunteer Manager" may describe a paid member of staff who manages volunteers, a volunteer who manages other volunteers or someone who serves as a Trustee

In this book, paid staff are referred to as managers. Volunteers who have executive functions over colleague volunteers are referred to as volunteer organisers and volunteers who are legally responsible for the work of an organisation are described as trustees.

The word "manager" does not adequately describe the functions of staff who supervise volunteers. "Community worker" is a far better description but, to avoid confusion, I have generally followed convention.

In the context of volunteering an *Intermediate Body* is an organisation that deploys volunteers on tasks presented to it by another organisation. For example, a hospital that arranges for the WRVS to provide canteen facilities. This is the volunteering equivalent of outsourcing.

Contents

Preface

In July 2010 the Prime Minister, David Cameron, told an audience in Liverpool that his great passion was to build the Big Society. He went on to say that this was not a new concept but encompassed what some people would call liberalism, empowerment, freedom or responsibility. He called it a powerful idea that encompassed a huge cultural change

It was, he said, characterised by people, in their everyday lives, in their homes, in their neighbourhoods and in their workplaces not always turning to officials, local authorities or central government for answers to the problems they face but instead feel both free and powerful enough to help themselves and their own communities. He called it the biggest, most dramatic redistribution of power from elites in Whitehall to the man and woman on the street.

He said there had been a basic assumption at the heart of government that the way to improve society was to micromanage from Westminster and to pour money down the throat of wasteful, top-down government schemes. But this demonstrably did not work and had led to the biggest budget deficit in the G2 as well as a steady worsening of pressing social problems.

He thought that the way government had worked – top-down, top-heavy and controlling – had the effect of sapping responsibility, local innovation and civic action. It turned many motivated public sector workers into disillusioned, weary puppets of government targets and turned capable individuals into passive recipients of state help with little hope for a better future. Lively communities had been turned into dull, soulless clones of one another.

"We need to turn government completely on its head", he said. "The rule should be, if it unleashes community engagement – we should do it. If it crushes it – we should not." His government would decentralise power to communities, neighbourhoods and individuals including budgets devolved to street-level.

This is not the place to debate whether politicians and the bureaucracies through which they operate are ready to reduce the extent of their power and authority. Cynics are doubtful. As Jack Straw pointed out in 1995, "Democracy is about conceding power to those with whom you disagree not to those with whom you agree[1]." In a society which is so unequal with many divergent interests is the Big Society just a sentimental journey back in time to the primitive tribe where the interests of the individual were the interests of all and where key decisions were made by villagers sitting together under a tree?

But a more important question is whether communities are ready to accept the challenge implicit in David Cameron's rhetoric or will the most articulate members of society drown out the others? And if front-line professionals are given more power, who will ensure that they wield it in the interests of the people they serve?

Local people who volunteer to serve their communities are too often presented with tasks and targets determined by people at a distance and volunteering activity is judged by criteria that place quantity above quality. If they are to become more central to community life volunteers must be valued because of their capacity to bring about social change. For this to happen there needs to be a more equitable distribution of power between volunteers and the bureaucracies that loom over them or well-meaning organisations will usurp their authority.

For the Big Society to reach its full potential we need to capture something of the spirit of the Arts and Crafts movement of 130 years ago. John Ruskin and William Morris were concerned that machine-made factory goods stifled the individuality and creativity of the workforce. They sought to show that human aspirations, fulfillment and personal satisfaction could be achieved by emphasising quality in design and production and by giving work-people a sense of ownership in the end-product of their labours. They regarded the process of production as of equal importance to the finished product.

In the twentieth century, revolutionaries in Germany and Russia claimed to represent the ordinary men and women in the street but were careful not to concede any power to them. They soon lost touch. That is the challenge of the Big Society – to redistribute power downwards, not to appointed apparatchiks who claim to represent the best interests of the people but to ordinary men and women who represent themselves.

Accountability for community services is widely dispersed among quangos, local government, government agencies, trusts and private sector organisations. Accountability to the people being served is at best tenuous. Through government funding, the voluntary sector is seen to have largely lost its independence. As a result, in the words of Margaret Simey[2], the citizen "is a pawn in the scramble for power".

Despite the UK's long history of voluntary activity the sector has not universally adapted to a post-industrial society. Lessons learned in the war were soon forgotten. Too few volunteer managers, even at senior levels, are appropriately trained and, as we shall see, "managing volunteers" can become a euphemism for controlling them. Too often, volunteering is an add-on, sustained by a few individuals. It collapses when a key player withdraws or short term funding is cut. The secret of successful volunteering is to embed it in the communities it serves so that it becomes self-sustaining. That requires both statutory and voluntary agencies to examine how they empower local communities.

Unleashing community engagement is not a simple process. It entails allowing volunteers to dance to their own tunes. Many community organisations need considerable help to rise to the challenge. The government intends to train and deploy a cadre of community workers to spearhead the Big Society. How, and to whom they are to be accountable will determine whose agenda they promote. If they are appointed by the government they will be perceived as government agents. Ill thought-out volunteering projects can disempower local residents and volunteers.

Fulfillment has become the driving force behind much human activity in western countries and it has the potential to unlock talents and enthusiasms to build healthier communities. This is at the heart of the Big Society. Unfortunately, ideas that are promulgated and supported by government tend to lose their lustre and are viewed with suspicion. The Big Society promises to break with the past and to revitalise British society. It is important that it is not held back by its association with government policy. The notion is good in itself, regardless of whether it is championed by a particular political party or none but it is good to have the government of the day espousing the cause.

The Big Society has proved to be an elusive concept. It is best understood as a direction of travel rather than an end product; as a way of thinking about the manner in which services are controlled rather than a code of practice. Too often public bodies make a series of pragmatic decisions only to realise as the years go by – usually when an outsider points it out – that they have created an unwieldy, centralised and unresponsive structure. It takes strong nerves and courage to decentralise power.

Britain is an ageing society. As in most of Europe, the birth rate increased substantially between the end of the Second World War and 1964. It peaked in 1947 and again in 1964. These cohorts – the baby boomers - are now becoming pensioners. Each succeeding cohort of older people is healthier than the last and lives longer. 30% of the UK population is aged over 50 years and numbers continue to rise. By 2031 nearly a quarter of the population will be aged over 65 years.

Older people represent an enormous power for good if ways can be found to nurture their talents. They play an important role in charities. There are over 800,000 charity trustees in the UK with an average age of 57 years. Two thirds of them are aged over 50 years[3]. Many older people therefore already play leadership roles within their communities. Their potential for providing leadership in the Big Society is huge.

This book explores the background to volunteering in the UK with particular reference to men and women over the age of fifty years. It examines some of the social problems that beset the country and asks questions about the values that underpin voluntary enterprise. It suggests that current organisational and management systems inhibit some older people from volunteering leading to a higher than necessary scale of disillusionment among them and a wasteful rate of attrition.

I am not a baby boomer and therefore have nothing to defend. But I have observed their behaviour and understood their aspirations as they came of age and, eventually, took political control. Some social changes can only be understood in the context of social conditions at the time. Personal anecdotes are included in footnotes to illustrate some of these changes.

This book is intended for policy makers and managers in the public and voluntary sectors but also for the indefatigable army of volunteers because, without pressure from them, essential change will come about more slowly. Too many publications, research studies and conferences about volunteering fail to include the voice of volunteers. This book is intended to redress the balance.

Wally Harbert
Frome.
October 2011.

CHAPTER ONE

The challenge

The relations between the individual and society
are like a roulette table. Society is the banker.
Individuals sometimes win and
sometimes lose; but the banker wins always.
W. Somerset Maugham

The UK and its component countries are distinguished by being top of many European league tables for failure. Whether it is the number of children living in broken families, teenage pregnancies, alcoholism, drunken teenagers, drug abuse, rates for divorce, obesity, eating disorders, self-harm, rates of imprisonment for men, women and children, violence, crime, burglary, assaults, road rage, common psychological disorders or inferior child care we are number one in the European Union and, for some, in the whole of Europe, including ex communist countries in the East.

The UK has one of the highest incidences of sexually transmitted disease in Western Europe. It is on the edge of having the highest European rates for abortion and stillbirths. We also score badly for the proportion of young people not in school, training or work.

Scotland is top of the European league for murder and deaths from cirrhosis of the liver. Parts of Scotland have the lowest life expectancy for males and the highest rate of violence in Europe. Figures for Scotland may skew the UK figures but Scotland makes up less than 12% of the UK population and in many measures the figures are similar.

But worse, these problems are steadily increasing. If our financial position were as grave the International Monetary Fund would, long ago, have laid down strict conditions to HM Treasury and the Bank of England. If the UK were a football team it would dismiss its manager every week. Each statistic, on its own, has little meaning but taken together they reveal a cluster of serious social problems indicating an alarming deterioration in the quality of our lives.

How bad is bad?

Life and Death

Rates for **infant mortality[4] and premature births[5] in the UK are the highest in Western Europe.** Apart from Austria and France the rate of still-births in the UK is the highest in Europe – on a par with Belarus and Estonia[6]. Scotland has a particularly high rate of stillbirths[7]. Experts agree[8] that birth outcomes are related to poor lifestyles including smoking, substance abuse, poor nutrition and poor prenatal care. With death visiting so many foetuses and babies it is reasonable to suppose that some who survive may be weakened by their early experiences and succumb more readily to illness and disease.

Figures published by *The Lancet* in 2008 show that women's life expectancy in the UK is sixteenth out of 25 European countries[9]. The Chief Medical Officer for Scotland reports[10] that **Scotland has the shortest life expectancy of any Western European country**. Men in Scotland can expect to live four years less than Swedish men[11].

Of 38 European countries, the UK has the highest abortion rate apart from Sweden and France[12]. It has one of the highest rates for sexually transmitted disease in Western Europe with Wales doing particularly badly[13]. UK rates for sexually transmitted disease doubled between 1991 and 2001[14].

The UK has the highest teen birth rate in Europe[15] - more than double the rate in ten other western European countries[16]. After the United States it has the highest rate of teen births in the industrialised world[17].

Health
"UK and Spain top league for common psychological disorders in European study". This was the heading of a press release issued by the Royal College of Psychiatrists in 2008. It went on to explain that the prevalence of psychological disorders in both men and women was significantly higher in the UK than in five other countries studied[18].

The UK has the **highest mortality rate due to drug abuse** of all 28 countries studied by the European Monitoring Centre for Drugs and Drug Addiction[19]. Brighton & Hove records the highest annual drug related deaths in the UK with one death per 6,200 residents[20]. This compares with Slovakia's one death per 216,000 residents[21]. **Young people in the UK are more likely to take cocaine, ecstasy and amphetamines than in any other European country** while the use of cannabis is just behind that of Denmark and France[22].

Alcohol-related deaths in the UK rose from 6.7 per 100,000 population in 1992 to 13.6% in 2008[23]. Scotland has the eighth highest alcohol consumption in the world – more than double Scandinavian countries[24]. **The death rate for cirrhosis of the liver in Scotland** has risen sharply in recent years and **is now the highest in Europe**[25] at more than double the European average[26]. In four years prescriptions for alcohol dependency in England rose by 31%[27] and rose by 12% in 2009[28]. Over half of woundings and minor injuries caused by violent attacks in England are believed to arise from the influence of alcohol[29]. 40% of patients presenting to hospital accident and emergency departments have alcohol-related problems; on Saturday nights this rises to 70%[30].

We are the fattest people in Europe and just behind the USA and Mexico in the world obesity league[31] - at more than twice the rate of France, Sweden and Denmark and more than seven times the rate for Japan[32]. **The UK is the biggest consumer of crisps and nuts in Europe** at double the rate of our nearest rival, Germany[33].

The UK has the highest rate for eating disorders in Europe[34] Over-eating can be a reaction to depression, boredom, stress or anger. A long-term study of 6,500 children in the 1970 British Birth Cohort found that those with low self-esteem worried more and were heavier than others. They were also more likely to gain weight over the next 20 years. 10 year olds with low self-esteem tend to be fatter as adults[35].

The UK has the highest rate of self-harm in Europe[36], Manchester[37] being the European capital of self-harm. This is contested in a report claiming Scotland to have a higher rate. A study in Edinburgh among 14 and 15 year old pupils found that one in three girls and one in eight boys had self-harmed. One in 20 girls said they had attempted suicide. Contributing factors were said to be depression, social deprivation, drugs and bullying[38]. Suicide is the most common cause of death in men under the age of 35 in England.[39]

Crime and Punishment
"Britain top of European Crime League", screamed headlines in the Daily Telegraph[40]. It went on to report that Britain was the **most burgled country in Europe,** that it had the **highest level of assaults** and above average rates of car theft, robbery and pick pocketing.

Figures[41] gathered in 2001 show that **England and Scotland jointly head a list of 18 European countries for violent crimes**. A study in England suggests that children in deprived areas are five times more likely to require hospital admission for assault than children from prosperous areas[42]. **Assaults leading to death, are more than double among Scottish men than for their counterparts elsewhere in Europe.**

Physical and verbal assaults on NHS staff in Britain have been increasing and have now reached 95,000 each year causing stress, sickness, low morale and problems in staff recruitment and retention[43]. Alcohol is a common cause. In Scotland,[44] over 28.000 assaults take place every year on public service workers.

A study by Gallup International of 10,000 motorists in 16 European countries found Britain to be the **road rage capital of Europe**. A key factor behind aggressive driving is said to be the congested road network in Britain which is the most heavily used in Europe. We have an average of 67 vehicles per kilometre of road, compared with 34 in France[45].

The UK has the highest proportion of its citizens in prison in the EU[46] with nearly three quarters of prisoners reconvicted within nine years of their release. Reconviction rates are higher for prisoners who have been excluded from school, been received into care or witnessed violence in childhood. Those with problems related to alcohol or drug abuse are also more likely to reoffend[47]. **England and Wales have the highest number of life sentences in Europe** – more than Germany, France, Italy and Turkey combined[48].

England and Wales imprisoned the highest number of women ever in 2008. Numbers increased by 50% in ten years[49]. **England and Wales have the highest rate of imprisonment for women in the EU** and are fourth in the world after the United States, Thailand and Russia[50]. The Howard League for Penal Reform report that half of women in prison are held on remand awaiting trial of whom 60% are subsequently found not guilty or receive a non-custodial sentence. More than 17,000 children are separated from their mothers each year as a result of imprisonment[51].

England and Wales have more than three times the number of suicides among women in prison than the combined total for Belgium, Canada, Denmark, Ireland, New Zealand, Norway and Sweden[52]. Total suicides among male prisoners in those countries do not reach the total for England, Wales and Scotland.

Domestic violence represents almost a quarter of all violent crime in England and Wales although it is the least likely crime to be reported to the police. Violence has been shown to be a prime cause of miscarriage, still-birth, maternal deaths and suicide at child birth. 30% of domestic violence starts in pregnancy. Children who live with domestic violence have an increased risk of mental health problems in adulthood[53].

Child Wellbeing

The UK was bottom for the social wellbeing of children in a UNICEF study in 21 industrialised countries including 19 in Europe – well below that of Poland[54]. Between 2000 and 2009 the achievement of UK children fell from 4th to 16th in the world league table for science, from 7th to 25th place in literacy and from 8th to 27th for mathematics[55]. The UK also scores badly in an OECD study for the proportion of young people not in school, training or work[56].

69% of UK children report that they have been bullied at school and 87% of parents report bullying in the previous 12 month[57]. When children in seven countries were asked whether bullying was a problem in their school, children from the UK gave the highest response at 48% with Portugal (35%) second[58]. It is estimated that 31 million school days are lost each year in England as a result of bullying[59]. About 150,000 children are educated at home with bullying at school the most commonly quoted reason given by parents[60].

More British children are overweight than children in other Western and Northern European countries, apart from Spain[61]. Obesity among children has been rising although it varies in different parts of the country. In Stockton-on-Tees where 31% of the population is obese, one in six children is obese in reception classes. At the end of their schooling this rises to one in five[62]. Nearly 10% of children in England's reception classes are obese and by the end of their final year of primary education this almost doubles[63].

In the ten years 1995 – 2005, the number of children admitted to hospital in England arising from a diagnosis relating to alcohol rose by a third[64]. **Drunkenness among teenagers in the UK is the highest in the OECD** which encompasses thirty four countries, including 24 in Europe[65]. It is no accident that heavy drinking by teenagers in France is described as "le binge drinking".

The number of children sentenced to custody by the courts in England and Wales more than tripled between 1991 and 2006 and the **UK has the highest proportion of its children in custody in Western Europe**[66]. Many children in prison have not committed serious offences.

At least a third are locked-up for non violent crimes, including motoring offences and drunkenness[67].

Children with learning disabilities and other impairments are more likely to go to prison than others. 23% of young offenders have IQs of less than 70[68]. 85% show signs of personality disorder; young males in prison are eighteen times more likely to kill themselves; more than two thirds of children under 18 discharged from prison in 2004 were reconvicted within a year; 75% of 18 - 20 year old men are reconvicted within 2 years of release[69].

Of 15 European countries, the UK had by far the **highest rate of asthma among children aged six and seven.** The rate was more than twice that for nine other countries in the study. Of 20 countries, only Ireland had a higher incidence of asthma among 13 and 14 year olds[70]. Asthma is more prevalent in families where parents smoke and among children born prematurely or with a low birth weight. Lack of exercise in childhood is another factor. In an eight-year study[71], it was found that children of parents who coped poorly with the demands of parenting were more than twice as likely to develop asthma by the age of 6 -8 than others. Another study reported that children whose carers had "clinically significant levels of mental health problems" were almost twice as likely to require treatment in hospital for asthma as others. Also, children with "significant behaviour problems had significantly more days of wheeze and poorer functional status"[72].

International comparisons of data are not always reliable because definitions vary and, in some cases, information relates to different years. In some studies country-wide rates have been calculated from small samples. However, the UK's position is as likely to be overstated as understated in the figures provided. Given the range of indicators involved and the pattern revealed there can be no doubt that the UK is the sick man of Europe and one of the sickest in the industrialised world. It is urgently in need of treatment.

A Collective Unconscious?

Until the 1940's, generations of British children were brought up to believe that Great Britain was the world's leading country. We ruled the waves for four centuries, conquered lands across the world, ruled countries many times our own size, created the mother of parliaments and, for many years, our industrial output topped the world. As the Second World War ended, the self belief that this endangered came to a juddering halt. We had lost our industrial supremacy and were in the process of losing an empire. Even the most ardent nationalist had to agree that we no longer held super-power status.

The British suffered less from the two world wars than most of Europe but, from being a dominant force in the world we quickly became a supplicant nation, one of a number clamouring to be noticed. Hence the so called, "special relationship" with the United States, sentimental links with the Commonwealth and the love-hate relationship with the French and Germans. We continued to strut on the world stage but lessons were learned at the time of the Suez crisis when the United

States threatened to bring down our economy unless we withdrew troops.

Followers of Carl Jung will have no difficulty associating our social decline with our sudden and dramatic loss of status in the world. He believed that societies have a collective unconscious which is the product of shared past experiences that shape present day attitudes. On this basis we are today mourning the loss of our former greatness, snatched from us by a defeated enemy.

Perhaps this accounts for the popularity of television dramas set in the years leading to the First World War. *The Forsyth Saga*, *Upstairs Downstairs* and *Downton Abbey* evoke a time when Britain was the undisputed leader of the world. We were a country dominated by great aristocratic families who had no doubt that it was their right to rule others. Everyone else in this golden age knew their place and doffed their caps obligingly. It was a time of moral certainty which ended ignominiously in the mud of Flanders and the Somme.

The level of immigration is sometimes held to be responsible for Britain's decline but there is no evidence to suggest that it has any part to play. Out of 29 European countries, twelve have a higher percentage of foreign-born citizens than the UK including France, Germany, Sweden and Switzerland. Switzerland has double the rate of births by mothers from outside the country than the UK but its social problems are considerably less[73]. The proportion of people of Muslim faith in Britain is lower than for several other European countries including France, Germany and the Netherlands[74]. Berlin is reputed to have twice as many followers of Islam as Catholics[75].

Research suggests that poverty is far more likely to create tensions among British people than ethnic diversity. Drawing on information from government surveys of over 25,000 individuals in 4,000 neighbourhoods, one researcher observed, "Basically, it is poverty, not race that makes people uneasy and not trust each other"[76]. Other research, widely reported in August 2011 when observers were trying to advance reasons for the riots, concluded that riots in India during the 1980's and 90's were strongly influenced by economic circumstances; a 1% increase in economic growth decreased the expected number of riots by 5%.[77] An abrupt fall in living standards is likely to be a precursor of riots anywhere in the world. A study into social unrest across Europe since 1919 by the Centre for Economic Policy Research found that demonstrations, riots, assassinations and general strikes all rose in proportion to harshness of cutbacks in social spending"[78].

Yet immigration appears to create greater levels of anxiety in the UK than in other countries. It is likely that a community that is beset by acute social problems is less tolerant of immigrants than one which is more settled and sure of itself. However, a Jungian explanation would be that after generations of believing that our superior culture gave us the moral authority to govern others we now find it difficult to treat people from other races as equals.

Family and Personal Relationships

A report in 2009 claimed that the **UK had the highest divorce rate in Europe**[79]. At the time of the 2001 census

23% of dependent children in the UK lived in one parent families and 40% of live births occurred outside marriage – compared with 6% in 1960[80]. The number of children living in one parent families trebled between 1971 and 2008[81]. **Wales and Scotland have the highest proportion of children living in one parent families** of 23 European countries studied by the OECD[82].

Such children do less well at school, are more likely to play truant, be excluded from school and leave school at 16. They are less likely to gain qualifications, have a higher risk of mental illness in childhood, are more likely to abuse drugs or alcohol, have a greater chance of living in poverty, are at greater risk of physical, emotional or sexual abuse, more likely to run away from home, to become teenage parents, to offend and to smoke. In later life they are more likely to experience homelessness, unemployment, divorce and to enter prison[83].

A survey of over 200 research reports found that children in separated families have a greater risk of behavioural problems, are more likely to be admitted to hospital following accidents and more likely to suffer depressive symptoms[84]. They account for the boom in teenage pregnancies, abortion and sexually transmitted diseases which are strongly correlated with poverty and disadvantage in later life.

Research by Davos[85] shows that children with married parents, both of whom are the child's biological parent do best in wellbeing scores – they are twice as likely to be in the top 20% than children in one parent families or with a step parent. Conversely, children with married parents are half as likely to be in the bottom 20% of wellbeing scores as those with a lone parent or a step-parent. Children with cohabiting parents do worse than those with married parents but better than those with a lone parent or step-parent.

That social problems are greater among one-parent families does not necessarily mean that single parenthood causes those problems. The Baby Boomer generation and those that followed place less faith than their predecessors in the formal institution of marriage. It is unlikely that more visits to the registry office would solve family problems. The section below, "Inequalities of income and wealth" demonstrates that high levels of poverty may be a more important determinant of family instability and poor health than single parenthood. This helps us to understand how many one-parent families seemingly rise above the challenges that face them

A common thread running through the failings listed above is unsatisfactory personal relationships. We learn to relate to others from the day we are born and our growing personalities are largely shaped by our relationships as we develop. Bad, inconsistent parenting or traumatic events in our early lives can leave an indelible mark.

Relationship problems are at the heart of eating disorders. Human relationships begin with feeding and the most intimate relationship between mother and child is expressed by the provision and consumption of food. Later, unsatisfactory relationships including perceived rejection, a sense of unworthiness or dissatisfaction with body image are commonly revealed in eating disorders. Anorexia nervosa and bulimia are associated with low self esteem, depression and obsessive-compulsive disorder. There is no doubt that the quality of personal relationships in early life and the quality of nurturing provided influence subsequent levels of self esteem.

Experiences in teenage years and early adulthood sometimes serve to heal early psychological wounds but where this fails, professional help is expensive and success uncertain. Anger-management courses for young adults are no substitute for good parenting earlier in life.

At first glance, incidents of domestic and street violence may appear random. Closer examination usually reveals that attacks are a response to an intense feeling of humiliation. The man who beats his wife when he returns from the public house may resent her real or imagined criticism of his drinking habits. A fatal stabbing, widely reported, occurred when a man was excluded from a public house. He returned later and stabbed a teenager in a nearby street. Another young man was stabbed through the heart on a train because his killer thought he had smirked at him on the station platform. When his partner told him that a man had pushed in front of her in a supermarket queue, the man punched him so hard that he died as he hit the floor. It later transpired he had hit the wrong man.

These incidents demonstrate a similarity. The perpetrators were consumed by anger because they felt humiliated and wanted revenge. We have all felt sufficiently humiliated to wish the ground would quietly swallow us but, thankfully, few of us are so enraged that we kill. We are not accustomed to thinking about aggressive, violent and threatening young men as delicate flowers who have a desperate need to be seen in a good light by those around them. But they are often hyper-sensitive and will go to extreme lengths to protect what remains of their sense of self-worth. Seeking in vain for the respect of others, they settle for revenge.

It takes very little for a smouldering sense of humiliation to become an outburst of despair, anger and violence in a poor community. Civil unrest in deprived areas of the United States and UK has sometimes been triggered by single acts of thoughtlessness by the police towards a member of a minority group.

In clinical experiments it is possible to identify the kind of situations that lead to anxiety and stress. When we are faced with perceived threats, cortisol is released into the blood stream to prepare us physiologically for fight or flight. Levels of cortisol in the blood and saliva can be measured. A study of 208 experiments[86] where cortisol levels were measured indicated that the most stressful events were those in which people felt humiliated or ashamed or suffered a loss of self-esteem or status.

There are important lessons here for social policy. The more social miscreants feel humiliated the more they are likely to react with more of the same. Some try to escape from the reality of their position by becoming part of an elite band revelling in anti-social activities, gaining satisfaction by being looked up to by their friends and colleagues for their extremes of bad behaviour. For most of us, committal to prison would be a humiliation but for some it is a sign of achievement for which they expect respect from friends. The reality of their situation may be too devastating for them to acknowledge.

Inequalities of income and wealth

We all understand that people living in disadvantaged areas have a lower quality of life and lower life expectancy than average. We are apt to blame this on the individuals concerned and may believe that the reasons are to be found in their mental make-up. When we hear that in these areas, crime, alcoholism, unemployment, drug taking and abortions are high we shudder and strengthen our belief that bad or inadequate individuals sink to the bottom of society. But can this really explain why two children born in different districts of Glasgow have differences in life expectancy of 28 years?[87] We cannot blame children for choosing the wrong parish in which to be born. There must be something else at work.

Wilkinson and Pickett[88] demonstrate that countries with more equal incomes have a much higher quality of life, better levels of health and less crime. The United States, UK and Portugal, the most unequal societies in the developed world, are, almost invariably, high in the failure league while more equal nations such as Japan and Scandinavian countries consistently score better. Figures from Wilkinson and Pickett, together with those from Eurostat suggest that wellbeing is more closely linked to equality than to income or membership of the Catholic or an orthodox church.

The authors argue that life expectancy, the quality of life and a sense of wellbeing improve dramatically as poor countries begin to move out of abject poverty but there comes a point when further increases in average incomes no longer make a measurable impact. They argue that high levels of inequality within a population condemn both rich and poor to lead lives that are shorter, unhealthier, unhappier and more violent than their counterparts in poorer countries where income is shared more equally.

Countries in which people are most likely to feel that others cannot be trusted are those with the greatest income inequality. Scandinavian countries score high both on trust and equality. Putnam noted that in the US:

> "States whose residents trust other people, join organisations, volunteer, vote and socialise with friends are the same States where children flourish: where babies are born healthy and where teenagers tend not to become parents, drop out of school, get involved in violent crime or die prematurely[89]."

As already indicated, the United States, UK and Portugal imprison large numbers of young men who fail to benefit from education and have missed their chance to find a satisfactory niche in the employment market. All three countries have an alarming rate of mental ill-health. The sense of alienation, frustration and humiliation experienced by young persons from knowing they are among the have nots while being painfully aware of the plenty enjoyed by others sparks a bitterness and a rage that infects their behaviour, their ability to make choices and mental stability. Society's response is almost exclusively directed towards punishment and little is done to address the underlying low self-esteem. Gilligan[90], a prison psychiatrist in the US argues that inequality makes people more sensitive to experiences of inferiority such as disrespect, loss of face and humiliation which are amongst the most common triggers for violence.

Scrutiny of rates for homicides, robbery and violent crime in up to fifty countries, shows that they are higher in unequal societies; also that a small fall in income inequality leads to significantly lower rates. Furthermore, an increased rate of murder in Britain during the 1980's and 90's coincided with dramatic increases in inequality. Japan became a much more equal society in the second half of the twentieth century and homicide rates fell by 70% but, in England and Wales, they doubled between 1967 and 2001 alone[91].

Despite leading more comfortable lives than previous generations our levels of anxiety, depression and stress have been rising. We have become safer from serious disease, natural predators and murderous neighbouring tribes but have become more prone to a loss of self esteem. Wilkinson and Pickett[92] show how 269 similar studies in the USA demonstrate an upward trend in anxiety levels over a period of 40 years. By the late 1980's, the average child was more anxious than child psychiatric patients in the 1950's.

Low-income parents facing social and financial pressures often have difficulty setting and enforcing rules for their children[93]. Parents who feel they are failures have little respect for themselves and have difficulty gaining respect from their offspring. Children in these families often have diets that are high in fats, sugars and processed foods; hence the high obesity levels. Poor diet in the first three years of life has a profound effect on a child's development that is reflected in behaviour and school performance later in life as well as in a lower level of intelligence – perhaps by five points. This arises because the brain is growing at its fastest rate in the first three years of life. More worryingly, subsequent improvements in diet do not reverse the effects of poor diet in the first three years; the damage is permanent[94].

As these parents struggle to pay their bills and keep their children out of trouble their more affluent neighbours embark on courses of retail therapy, buying goods they do not really need. As we shall see, there is enormous pressure, aided by the advertising industry, to make us dissatisfied with our lifestyles and to spend money we do not have. Meanwhile, concern is expressed about the impact of over-consumption on the environment.

Professional football is almost a religion in some parts of the country but it is now priced out of the reach of low income families. A season ticket at Liverpool, where one in three households has no one in work, costs £725, a single ticket, £39. This is caused directly by the way top salaries have escalated, marginalising low wage-earners and those on benefits. It would be instructive if researchers could tell us what excluded young men in Liverpool think when they gather on street corners on Saturday afternoons and hear the roar of the crowd.

Economic growth has been a powerful mobilising force in society. It is a basic human instinct for families to protect themselves from hunger, thirst and threats to their existence. Survival depends on it. We are so programmed that even when we can comfortably meet all our material needs, like children who break into in a sweetshop, we continue to want more until we become ill. We overeat, drink more than is good for us and rely on drugs – prescribed or otherwise. When frustrated, like children, we can turn to antisocial behaviour and self harm.

There is growing awareness of the effects of gross inequality on society but pay ratios in Britain's largest companies are increasing. At Marks and Spencer it is estimated to be 1:656[95], a figure that is difficult to defend.

It might be supposed that the National Lottery would have the effect of redistributing funds from rich to poor areas but the reverse is the case. Research[96] shows that the poorest spend more on lottery tickets as a proportion of their income but are least likely to benefit from its funding. In parts of West Yorkshire the average spend per person in a year is £591 and the area receives one penny for each pound spent[97]. The lottery is a tax on poor people to benefit the middle classes. This could easily be reversed if there was a political will.

A key question for policymakers is whether the UK's social decline has been primarily caused by the increase in single parenthood or by the gross income inequalities across society. Wilkinson and Pickett are in no doubt. By comparing the UNICEF index of child wellbeing with the proportion of one parent families in each of twenty one countries they conclude:

There is no connection between the proportion of single parents and national standards of chid wellbeing. This contrasts sharply with the strong relationship between child wellbeing and income inequality[98].

There is a link between the dismal social failure that abounds in England and the social discontent that manifested itself in the August 2011 street riots. Unlike the disorder in Greece the riots did not arise from demonstrations against public service cuts that got out of hand. These were people who felt that the consumer society had passed them by and that they had no stake in the future of their communities. They were determined to draw attention to what they saw as the hopelessness of their condition. They did not attack public offices but took retribution from shops, both great and small. Many theories have been advanced about the causes and, doubtless, there will be some new government policies but, unless there is a fundamental change to the way in which income and power are distributed we can be sure that there is worse to come.

Conclusion

It is clear that conventional ways of tackling the problems described in this chapter are failing. Huge sums are spent annually to deal with symptoms of social malaise but the situation worsens. Health, education and justice services spend record amounts of public money on services but have failed to prevent a steady deterioration. Solutions are to be found, not in an extension of traditional public services to tackle symptoms but in local neighbourhoods by seeking to change inappropriate lifestyles and to build on the strengths of families and communities. The Big Society embraces the concepts needed to build a healthier society.

Yet some social problems are felt to be so severe that neighbourhood resources that could be used to improve community life are used instead to protect it from the anti-social behaviour of the few. If this continues we shall become a nation of gated communities protected by vigilantes.

The nuclear family is under pressure. Ways are needed to harness the power of local communities and extended families to enhance the quality of life by establishing good role models and providing support. That is why care in the early years when most learning occurs is important. Frank Field MP was asked by the government in 2010 to examine, how to extend the life chances of children brought up in poor households. He reported[99] that the government should endorse policies that improve the lifestyles of families in what he called "The Foundation Years".

There are no quick fixes but the sooner we address severe deprivation among young children the sooner we can expect to reduce the appalling catalogue of failure that currently characterises the UK.

Field did not envisage early years' services being monopolised by professionals. He drew attention to the role of volunteers, many of whom have successfully brought-up families and have skills and practical knowledge to impart to others. Formal and informal arrangements at neighbourhood level can help to fight the social exclusion that blights the lives of people in need and that isolates their children from sources of help.

Of those who donate to charity, poorer donors give a higher proportion of their income than rich donors. The top 10% gives approximately 1% while the bottom 10% donates nearer 3%[100]. Some individuals are so wealthy that they buy football clubs to advertise their wealth and, presumably to add to their sense of achievement and fulfillment. If they want their communities to remain safe they should consider returning some of the money they derive from the poverty of others by supporting local initiatives to improve the life chances of deprived children and to restore some equilibrium and purpose to the lives of people who are having difficulty finding their way in the world. If they do not contribute voluntarily, sooner or later government will be forced to build and staff expensive institutions to accommodate more wayward individuals for whom the strains of an unequal society are too great.

Most of us can play our part in this endeavour by contributing to the safety of our communities through voluntary activity.

Income inequalities lead to inequalities of power. Increasingly, people in once-revered organisations have been found misusing power. Bankers, newspapers (telephone hacking), television (phone-in scandals), the Roman Catholic Church (paedophile cover ups), Parliamentarians (fraudulent expense claims) and big business (tax avoiders) have all been guilty of placing their own personal interests above those of the people they serve and, in doing so, have damaged the wider community Tighter regulation will stop the worst excesses but unless there is a change in the values of society generally, we appear to be doomed to a continual downward spiral. The values of volunteering stand out like a bright light in a naughty world.

Jenny is aged 100 years. She has three sons and two daughters from Austria, adopted during the war. After her husband died, she moved in with a friend with Alzheimer's to care for her. She now lives alone and says she knits five hours every evening, mainly children's clothing that is sent to Eastern Europe. RSVP organised her 100th birthday party and the publicity helped to recruit more knitters. She says, "Knitting keeps me active and it is nice to feel you are being useful to others. It helps to make the time fly by and stops me feeling lonely as there are days when nobody calls or comes round".

CHAPTER TWO

The elephant in the living room

*You can tell the ideas of a nation
by its advertisements*

Norman Douglas

Television and the digital age are making a significant impact on the way lives are led. Personal and family relationships, the employment market, community life and leisure activities are all changing under the influence of digital technology. Unless we appreciate the influence this is having on the use of our time and on social attitudes we will fail to understand the changing dynamics of our lives. It is not just the ubiquitous visual and sound images that confront us and new ways of communicating with one another, we are assailed by messages urging us to spend money and aspire to new lifestyles.

One of the characteristics of modern life is the pace at which it is lived. There never seems enough time to do all the things we wish to accomplish. Despite a reduced working week and the installation of labour saving devices in the home during the past fifty years, more people complain of stress and overwork. Yet, amid the pressure to fit so much into an overcrowded schedule,

Britons spend an average of four hours a day watching television. To this should be added time in front of DVD's and computer screens. What compels us to be such avid watchers? What impact does this have on other aspects of our lives? Perhaps, most importantly, what have we stopped doing to find the time to sit in front of a box?

Of fourteen European countries studied, the UK had the highest level of television viewing at 28 hours a week. The lowest were Finland, Norway and Sweden at 18 hours. Searching for firebrands to man the barricades, Karl Marx might have said, "Television is the opium of the people". If the British people spent as much time volunteering as they do watching television, society would be transformed.

In the 1950's, television in the home was rare and there were few programmes. Now, television sets are more common than the kitchen sink. There are hundreds of channels to choose from throughout the day, each using all the tricks of the trade to attract our attention. Television sets are bigger, brighter and more colourful. From being discreetly enclosed in polished wooden cabinets they now nakedly dominate most living rooms, replacing the traditional fireplace as the focal point of the seating arrangements. The language of television has become more direct and scenes of sex and violence that would have shocked the nation in 1960 now go almost unremarked.

Many of the things we enjoy are bad for us if indulged in to excess. Taking drugs, smoking, drinking alcohol, eating chocolate and fast food or sitting in the sun all have their downsides. Is it the same with television? If so, what are the negative consequences of watching television and how much is too much?

In a seminal book[101], Aric Sigman has gathered a vast amount of information about the impact of television on human behaviour and presented it in a readable form. It contains extensive references to source material. If this chapter whets your appetite for more information you are advised to read it. Unless otherwise indicated, references in this chapter are to Dr Sigman's book.

There has been sporadic public debate about the impact of violent television programmes on children and young people but scientists have known for a long time that watching television has a negative influence on children irrespective of programme content. Speeding images and bright colours designed to capture children's' attention work too well making it difficult for them to pay attention to lessons or books without the bells and whistles of television. One consequence is that less time is spent reading books and England slipped from third to nineteenth place in an international literacy league table between 2001 and 2006. In Scotland it fell from 14th to 26th place during the same period.[102] Moreover, more than a third of 14 year old boys have a reading age of 11 years or less while more than one in five has a reading age of 9.[103] It is reported that 18% of five year old children have fallen behind expected levels of speech development for their age and that, in some areas, 50% start formal schooling unable to link words together or even understand simple instructions[104].

More than one third of children live in homes where the television is switched on throughout the day (p 29). This appears to interfere with the thought processes of very young children who, as a consequence, are less likely to read at the age of six years. It is estimated that half of all main meals are eaten in front of television sets (p 321). As tele-addiction enters its fourth generation, it is no surprise that some teachers report that young children are less able than in former years to communicate with adults and, increasingly, they start school without knowing how to use a knife and fork (p 42).

Researchers are in no doubt that a developing young brain has difficulty processing images received from television and that early exposure is associated with subsequent problems of maintaining attention. Flashing lights and moving images captivate even babies who are placed within sight of a screen. The American Academy of Paediatrics recommended in 1999 that children should not watch television until the age of two (p 4). There is general agreement about this among experts and that, after the age of 13, children should be restricted to a maximum of 1½ hours a day. Very few families attempt to restrict viewing in this way and those that do are widely regarded as freakish.

Three and four year olds watch television for an average of five hours a day and half of three year olds have a set in their bedrooms; this rises to nine out of ten for sixteen year olds. (p 50) Children aged 11 to 15 are thought to spend 53 hours a week watching television or computer screens (p 2). Some spend more time watching screens than sleeping.

Studies into childhood obesity show that it is linked directly with the extent of television viewing (p152). Experts are clear that reducing viewing by children would be the most effective way of helping them lose weight. Huesmann and Eron[105] reported that excessive television viewing at the age of eight years increased the likelihood of being arrested and prosecuted for criminal acts in adulthood.

Children with a set in their bedrooms score worse than other children in school tests, they sleep less and are inclined to be drowsy and irritable (pp 29 & 38). A longitudinal study in Britain found that children between 5 and 15 years who watched television more than two hours a day increased the risk of ill health in their mid twenties; researchers calculate that 15% of high cholesterol levels, obesity, smoking and poor cardio-vascular fitness are linked to television viewing in childhood (p 42).

One researcher is confident that, not only do young children who watch excessive television have an increased risk of developing attentional problems by the age of seven but that, for every hour of television watched each day there is a 9% increase in attentional damage (p 15). The most common behaviour disorder among children in the United States – affecting 7% of children - is Attention Deficit Hyperactivity Disorder (ADHD). This is characterised by impulsive behaviour, an inability to concentrate and needing constant rewards to retain attention. Brain imaging work in London confirms that these symptoms have a biological base and that young boys with ADHS are four times more likely to develop mental illness ten years later (p 15).

Programme makers have responded to the reduction in attention spans of viewers. To maintain interest and excitement in dramas, cameras do not remain in position long but take a scene from several positions. Over a quarter of a century the number of editing cuts in Sesame Street, a children's educational programme, have doubled (p 24). This may make for easier viewing by today's children but panders to their increasing inability to concentrate.

The attention span of the average viewer is short so the story is told in sixty-second bites. We are all treated like children with ADHS. Although there are frequent complaints about the dumbed-down content of television programmes, the dumbing-down in the editing room probably does as much damage.

In his influential book, *The Uses of Literacy* written over fifty years ago, Richard Hoggart drew attention to the way in which the popular press tended to restrict itself to no more than three-syllable words and seven word sentences. He added, "All premasticate their material so that it shall neither bore nor tax anyone…. New sensations have to be found daily". He was uneasy about "the extraordinarily low level of the organs of mass communication".[106] More recently he has castigated television programme-makers for the "rampant, immature cupidity of some game shows".[107]

The flickering screen appears to replace the real world for some children and young people. In busy families it is tempting to sit even quite small children in front of the screen to keep them occupied while parents do other things. Unsupervised, they often spend a greater part of the day with computer games or watching television, even viewing programmes aimed at children much younger than themselves.

In a world where much paid work is not intrinsically interesting or demanding, we have created a leisure industry that is a mirror image, pandering to the lowest common denominator, making little or no demand on the intellect. Entertainment programmes and football viewing are essentially passive, requiring nothing from the viewer except that he or she should be at least half awake. Computer games are little better except they sometimes involve hand and eye coordination. Neither necessitates the level of personal involvement required in discussion or playing card games.

Television and video addiction are not problems solely of the young. Professor Van Cleave has written an account of his personal battle against addiction to video games, describing how he watched them for 60 hours a week and, sometimes for 18 hours without a break. He learned to eat meals using only one hand to prolong his time in front of the screen. Only when his work and family life were in tatters and he was near to suicide did he find a way out[108].

An increasing number of countries have addiction recovery clinics to help young people and adults with an Internet and/or computer based behavioural addiction. Organisers claim that television and computer addicts have a heightened sense of euphoria when involved with the small screen, crave to spend more time watching and feel restless when they are no longer engaged with the screen. They neglect friends and family, their schooling and their jobs. They commonly feel guilty, ashamed, anxious or depressed about being unable to control their behaviour.

Britain's first computer rehabilitation clinic opened in 2009 with publicity about the harmful addictive effects of computer games which were leading some young people to become aggressive with irregular eating and sleep patterns. The computer industry responded by denying that its games could lead to addiction and claimed that they had a positive effect on the people playing them. This is reminiscent of the tobacco industry that protected its commercial interests for many years by denying that smoking was harmful – despite contrary evidence. With cross-ownership of television and newspaper companies it is rare to find a newspaper dealing impartially with the subject.

Television programmes propagate social norms. Aggressive outbursts, casual violence, intemperate language and straightforward bad manners are daily fare in children's cartoons and in many other programmes. Lack of self-restraint is not a good role model but makes for high television ratings. Instead of being socialised by loving parents, children now copy anonymous people with agendas that are far removed from the personal care and concern for young minds that good parenting requires. Socialising children was always a complex task. It has been made infinitely more difficult now that parents must overcome the negative influences of television. Moreover, in our television age there is less face-to-face communication between children and parents, making it more difficult for children to absorb parental values.

It can be demonstrated that television viewing causes anti social behaviour. Bhutan is a small Himalayan mountain Kingdom that was isolated for centuries and, even now, has few outside influences. In 1998 the King lifted a ban on television and, in the space of a few months several dozen channels were bombarding the country. The result was dramatic. Violence in school playgrounds, crime and family breakdown became more common. One study found that some children watched television for twelve hours a day and that conversation between parents and children was greatly reduced (p 63).

Other studies examining the effect of the introduction of television to previously tranquil and isolated communities as far apart as Canada and Turkey have similar findings. Increased violence among children, including bullying is common. In British Columbia, two years after television was introduced to a remote village, violent incidents among children increased by 160% whereas nearby towns with no television experienced no increase (p 122). In Tonga, three years after American television arrived, crime by young men increased dramatically, particularly house break-ins. The police were convinced that the methods used had been learned from American DVD's (p 69).

One reason for the unpopularity of the United States across the globe is that it is, unwittingly, imposing its brash and idiosyncratic culture on countries that have deep and lasting traditions of their own. By watching US television programmes and, more recently, imported DVD's, young people are picking up the exaggerated mannerisms, phrases and customs that characterise American television. This threatens traditional cultural values and lifestyles, creates new norms for personal relationships and challenges cherished religious beliefs. Many community leaders across the world are dismayed at the weakening social stability of their communities brought about by alien forces they cannot control. Deep religious convictions motivate them to resist change by all possible means. They face colonisation without a shot being fired; it brings an added dimension to misunderstandings and tensions between East and West.

Yet there is a positive side to international television. The velvet revolution in Eastern Europe in 1989 became inevitable because local populations could see for themselves on their television screens that Communism was not delivering the advantages of non-communist states

In the United States, as in the UK, a typical child watches 28 hours of television each week and by the age of 11 has seen 8,000 murders. In New York a correlation was found between the number of hours children watched television and their likelihood of being involved in violent behaviour in adulthood (p 123). The obverse is also true. After dramatically reducing the number of hours children watched television, researchers noted that their physical violence and verbal aggression reduced (p 125).

Anderson and Dill[109] have found that playing violent video games can increase aggressive thoughts, feelings and behaviour. They believe interactive video games are more harmful than television because they require the player to identify with the aggressor. Another study suggested that if TV had never been invented there would be 10,000 less homicides each year, 70,000 fewer rapes and 700,000 less assaults causing injury (p 120) in the United States.

The beautiful people displayed on television tend to make the rest of us dissatisfied with our appearance. British girls as young as six have been found to dislike their body shape, some are on diets and others are already anorexic (p 203). Across Asia, following the introduction of television, women want to look more western and sales of skin whitening creams are increasing. Self-induced vomiting among teenage girls in Fiji has been reported since television arrived in 1995. Interviews have confirmed that this is because Fijian girls, whose bodies are traditionally full, want to look like the western women they see on television (p 69).

In one UK study, nine out of ten general practitioners said that large numbers of patients consulted them about symptoms they shared with television characters. A serious illness like cancer or a brain tumour depicted in a soap opera is likely to convince large numbers of viewers that they have similar symptoms and need treatment. Similarly, suicide by a well known figure or in television soap is likely to lead to others taking their lives. (p 102).

Television has spawned the celebrity culture in which people with dubious talent are fêted simply because they appear on television screens. A book with a television personality pictured on the front cover is virtually guaranteed to make the best seller list however badly it is written and however uninspiring the story. Celebrities appeal to young people because of the lifestyles they appear to enjoy. Anyone can become a celebrity if television producers promote them. Celebrity has become a religion and the small screen its pulpit.

Young people are encouraged to believe that there is no connection between educational achievement and a successful career; they envy individuals who have been plucked from obscurity to perform in a reality show and become instantly recognisable to the general public. This points to the possibility of untold wealth and fame for people who lack the ability or determination to learn a skill. They await a mystery caller who will recognise their untutored talents and scoop them up into stardom. It is not until they leave school and are expected to study for a skill or earn a living that they realise that the dreams they have nurtured through childhood, in the words of one teacher, "can't come true". (p 117).

Concerns have been raised about the impact of text messaging on children. A study at Monash University, Melbourne concluded that the use of mobile telephones with predictive text – that is to say, where a single key press enters common words – makes children more impulsive, even reckless. They regularly make the fastest response to test questions but their answers are less accurate. For them, an instant response is more important than a considered reply. Researchers believe that predictive texting damages children[110].

Modern technology helps us understand how other people lead their lives and can increase the number of people with whom we interact but the technology creates ephemeral and shallow relationships divorced from personal face-to-face contact. Social networking internet sites create the illusion of intimacy and a wide circle of friends but, in reality, are products of solitary individuals interrogating a screen. As we move to a greater use of computers for viewing television we are probably moving towards greater solitary viewing.

The use of both the Internet and television reduce communication between neighbours and between family members and, to that extent, damage family and community cohesiveness. Happiness and contentment are associated with good and fulfilling personal relationships. Individuals who spend much of their waking life in front of a screen cannot nurture these. On the positive side, social networking sites promote connectedness, freedom of expression and creativity. The question remains as to whether these benefits are nullified by the growing absence of real human contact.

On holiday, some adults of all ages, even those normally living alone, retire to their rooms early to watch their favourite television programmes, ignoring evening entertainment provided. Their favourite soap opera is more real and more comforting than the people with whom they share a meal. Popular newspapers recognise this by carrying news stories about "celebrities" and the characters they play on television as though they were of equal importance to real news stories.

A 2008 study into fear of avian flu in 23 European Union countries concluded that television viewing accounted for 52% of the variation in anxiety levels and that each average additional hour of viewing increased the likelihood of being worried about the virus by 15.6%[111]. Meanwhile, television reporters tell us what to believe in a way that is easier to absorb than studying the facts to reach our own conclusions.

Advertising

The impact of television on the behaviour of viewers is significant. If this were not so, why would commercial companies spend billions of pounds advertising their products on television? Advertisers of such products as anti-wrinkle cream and sleek cars are not so much trying to sell a product as a lifestyle and a sense of happiness. You may believe that a wrinkled face is a natural consequence of growing older but advertisers try to convince you that wrinkles are unnatural and preventable; moreover, they demonstrate to others that you do not take care of yourself. Car advertisements tell you that you should judge yourself as you will be judged by others - on the look and performance of your car. To be successful you need the latest limousine that looks more expensive than it is. Advertisers want to make you disenchanted with what you have so that you buy a new product which, they tell you, will instantly improve your life.

In the US, it is estimated that advertisers spend $12 billion each year on advertising to the youth market. It is known that television advertisements about food have a marked effect on children. A study at Liverpool University concluded that children between the ages of 9 and 11 increased their consumption by around 100% after watching food advertisements on television.[112] The impact on overweight children was greater than for those of normal weight while obese children were affected most of all. Research at Yale University[113] showed that children aged seven to eleven years who watched a television cartoon that included food commercials ate 45% more snack food than children who watched the same show with non-food commercials. What other subliminal messages are children absorbing from their screens?

There is no place for the innocence of childhood in modern society. Children can be confused by brash advertising campaigns and find it difficult to distinguish between truthful, unbiased statements of fact and the persuasive intent of television advertising. They must learn at an early age to grow a protective shell if they are to avoid the depredations of television advertising. So strong has been concern in Sweden that, in 1991, it banned television advertising aimed at children under the age of 12.

In April 2007 the Office of Communications (Ofcom) introduced a total ban on television advertisements for high fat, salt and sugar food and drink (HFSS) aimed at children between 4 and 9 years. This was extended in January 2008 to 15 years and further strengthened in January 2009.

Television viewers are bombarded by advertisements stressing the attraction of immediate pleasure. The value of investing in activities that take time for payback are underplayed. So great is the impact of advertising in western societies that it can be argued that it had a direct bearing on the disastrous financial failures of 2008. It is common to blame the bankers and politicians for these events and they must take some responsibility but it takes two people to make a financial transaction.

It is reported that 93% of house repossessions in the United States in 2007 occurred when low initial interest rates came to an end[114], typically after the first two years. In other words, house purchasers were lured into debt they could not afford by short-term low interest rates which they knew would be increased. It is a similar story with the credit card debt mountain. Those who took out loans they could not repay must take some blame along with television presenters who traded on their popularity by masquerading as financial experts and fronting advertisements aimed at parting people from their money. They profited from the calamities they helped to heap upon others by assuring them that if they were overwhelmed by debt, a kind person, dedicated entirely to their welfare would solve the problem painlessly by the simple magic of "consolidating your debt". The cost of this "kindness" was not disclosed in the advertisements.

Whatever attempts are made to increase levels of public understanding about financial products, without substantial changes in attitudes and lifestyles they are doomed to failure. Personal debt in the UK is still one of the highest in the world, representing almost one year's economic output. That is not sustainable. Like overeating, over-drinking and smoking, dependence on the small screen and an uncritical belief in what they see and hear leads some people into an unsustainable way of life. To reap, you must first sow. This is a fundamental law of nature that our ancestors knew well. If they ignored it they and their families were liable to suffer a slow and painful death. The "credit crunch" merely confirms that the law still applies.

In grossly unequal societies like the USA and UK, the have-nots can boost their self-esteem by using credit to pursue the same lifestyles as their more affluent neighbours. If they are lucky, inflation and rises in income will get them through. Otherwise, they risk a catastrophic fall in living standards.

The immense power and brashness of television has led to a sharpening of messages right across the public relations industry. New goods and services are not presented to the public until they have been scrutinised by public relations experts who focus, not on the product but on the vulnerability of consumers.

A shopping experience is not complete unless it involves an assault on all our senses – distorted music echoing in the rafters, bright lights and gaudy signs, the smell of freshly baked bread or ground coffee and offers of free tastings. There are even opportunities for customers to caress their food as they slip it into the trolley. This technique of total sensory immersion has been used by the Christian church for centuries to secure the engagement of its adherents - the dazzling priestly robes, the profound music, the incense, the taste of wafer and wine and the clasping of the bible all combine to heighten the senses. There is even a loyalty card that promises a future reward for the faithful.

Television advertising has conditioned customers to suspend their critical faculties when they collect their supermarket trolleys. The extent of alcoholism and obesity is a measure of television's success. More customers attend cathedrals of consumerism on Sunday mornings than any denomination of the Christian church.

Moreover, strident music has become an accompaniment to many public activities, invading shops, bars, restaurants, trains and doctors' surgeries - anywhere that people congregate. Unlike television, the on/off switch is not available to the consumer who must endure whatever sound is offered. For those with even a mild hearing loss, it drowns out the spoken word.

The extent of the virtual world that is now available damages family life and the health of communities by stimulating behaviour that reduces opportunities for personal relationships with family and friends. It is a contributory factor to the growth of obesity in industrialised countries. At its extreme it is addictive but even at its best it tends to make us dissatisfied with our way of life and to consume more than is good for us.

In future we need to encourage activities that lead to personal interaction within and between families and which lead to healthier lifestyles. Volunteering is an inexpensive option but sports, hobbies, discussion groups and other events in the real world bring people together in a positive way. It is a reflection of our disconnected society that, during street parties to celebrate the wedding of the Duke and Duchess of

Cambridge, some families met their neighbours for the first time.

In the Tees valley eight volunteers provide a lunch club for older people serving freshly cooked meals to over 30 older people each month. Trips out are also organised.

Marjorie, aged 83, one of two volunteer organisers for the project says the lunch club helps to reduce social isolation. She says, "I like to be busy. I cannot be doing with sitting at home. I need to be useful. It does no one any good to stay within the four walls of their homes. Also, it is awful eating on your own. We want everyone to go out with a smile on their faces". Another member said, "I enjoy having a home-cooked meal – but also enjoy the chatter before, during and after lunch."

Another said the social exchange was a welcome change from the television set which played such a large part her life.

CHAPTER THREE

The volunteering industry

It is impossible to enjoy idling thoroughly
unless one has plenty of work to do
Jerome K. Jerome

Volunteering is a broad church with a varied liturgy embracing all faiths and none. Perhaps the most succinct definition is contained in the *Volunteering Compact of Good Practice*[115] that describes volunteering as,

> *......an activity that involves spending time, unpaid, doing something that aims to benefit the environment or individuals or groups other than (or in addition to) close relatives".*

The brevity of this definition makes it particularly useful as long as we remember that volunteering is as much about the impact it has on volunteers and on the health of communities as on recipients of services. Understanding this is key to the successful deployment of volunteers.

There is room to dispute what activities come within the definition of volunteering. Few of us would classify amateur dramatics as volunteering but if performances are given in residential homes or proceeds are given to charity we might feel differently. Similarly, knitting is not generally regarded as a voluntary activity but many thousands of knitters produce articles that they donate for premature babies as well as for people living in disaster areas across the world.

Social action, by which people agitate for social change properly belongs to the field of volunteering. But those who spend their time volunteering are not always clear about the definition. An electrician asked whether he did voluntary work replied scornfully, "No I haven't time for that kind of thing. I am too busy running a youth football team".

Volunteering is encouraged or discouraged by the actions of public bodies, by structures that advance or regulate the work, by the way services are funded and by the extent to which volunteers feel fulfilled.

Large numbers of volunteers are engaged in work to relieve suffering among disadvantaged people. That is not to deny the importance of those engaged with animal welfare, improvements to the environment, conserving heritage sites or those engaged promoting political parties or the work of faith groups. Benefits for the volunteer and the local community are similar for all types of volunteering and management issues are the same. This book is written from the perspective of volunteers in the field of health, welfare and community activities because they are closely allied to the concepts behind the Big Society.

Types of Volunteering

The word *volunteer* is sometimes reserved for people who offer their services through an organisation but a great deal of care and support is provided to vulnerable people by friends and neighbours outside any organisational structure. This is usually described as "informal volunteering".

The government's definition of volunteering includes both formal and informal arrangements but some researchers exclude information about informal work because it is notoriously difficult to measure. Perhaps holding open a door to allow a disabled person to pass through is an act of volunteering. The bus driver who waits for passengers to be seated before pulling away from the bus stop might be cited as an informal volunteer; on the other hand, some would claim that to be part of his or her job. Saxton and Baker[116] suggest that someone giving directions to a lost driver would, under the government's definition, be classified as a volunteer. The definition also encompasses neighbours who look after one another's pets during holidays and parents who drive groups of children to a school sports match or stand on the touchline, cheering-on their child's team. Saxton and Baker recommend that informal volunteering should be re-christened, "neighbourliness," "community spirit" or "social capital".

To draw attention to the absurdities created by sloppy definitions of volunteering, a not-for-profit research organisation, nfpSynergy paid its staff to watch the 2010 football World Cup in a local public house and claimed that this was within the government's definition of volunteering[117].

Formal organisations usually have a chairman, a secretary, a constitution and a membership list but an informal group is more amorphous. It may not have a recognised leader and membership may vary from week to week. Recent research[118] has found that informal groups exceed formal volunteering by as much as 4 to 1 in some areas but they are largely hidden from researchers and other outsiders. Some issues surrounding informal volunteering are discussed in chapter nine.

Many challenges apply equally to formal and informal volunteering but formal volunteering has a framework and an organisation that accepts responsibility for the quality of the work undertaken. The volunteer can opt out at any time and the organisation takes responsibility for work left undone. Informal volunteering, on the other hand, carries a greater moral commitment. Providing a mid-day meal for a disabled neighbour carries an obligation to ensure that alternative arrangements are made if you are unable to fulfil your promise. Formal volunteering carries a limited obligation and may be less onerous than informal arrangements. Ironically, looking after your granny can be more difficult than looking after someone else's.

In many ways, formal volunteering has replaced informal networks made by the tribe, the family and the local community in former societies for protecting weak and vulnerable members. One of the aims of public services and of volunteering should be to strengthen informal networks. This must be remembered when attempting to compare the extent of volunteering in different communities or at different times. A decline in formal volunteering may be a matter for congratulations if it arises from increased informal activity. Inferences drawn from figures showing a decline in volunteer numbers may also be wrong if the average time contributed by each volunteer is left out of account.

Formal volunteering defies neat classification. Two main strands are sometimes recognised. Firstly, philanthropy in which an organisation recruits volunteers to meet an identified need: secondly, mutual aid or self help, in which volunteers join together to benefit their local community or to help people with common characteristics such as cancer sufferers or families with young children. These volunteers may be motivated at first by a desire to help themselves or their families but their energies may be channelled wider by the organisation they join. One of their strengths is that they bring an understanding of the issues from the users' perspective.

As we shall see in later chapters, these two volunteering strands were firmly established by the nineteenth century and nearly every organisation today that deploys volunteers can be classified as a philanthropic or mutual aid organisation. Philanthropic bodies tend to be centralised in character with hierarchical structures whereas mutual aid bodies are generally smaller with power and authority more evenly dispersed. Many mutual aid bodies serve local communities and are more likely to be run by volunteers. The Institute for Volunteering Research found that voluntary organisations in health services were nearly four times more likely to have over one hundred volunteers than community based organisations[119].

Volunteering should not be confused with State schemes in which "volunteers" may choose to carry out unpaid work as a means of satisfying the government about their desire to be good citizens. Community orders enable offenders to undertake community service for a specified number of hours in place of punishment; about 130.000 orders are made in England and Wales each year. Plans to implement a scheme which would enable immigrants to undertake voluntary work to reduce the length of time they must be in the UK before being eligible for citizenship were abandoned by the new government in 2010.

Whatever the merits of such arrangements it is important that there is no confusion in the public mind about volunteering. Fundraising and the recruitment of genuine volunteers could be affected if it were widely believed that volunteers were part of a state scheme of social engineering.

Numbers of Volunteers

A Home Office survey suggests that 28% of adults in England undertake formal volunteering once a month and 37% volunteer informally[120]. The Scottish Household Survey, using a different definition, concludes that 28% of the adult population provides unpaid help to organisations or individuals in a 12 month period[121].

It is a sign of the importance of volunteering in national life that a number of esteemed organisations regularly conduct surveys into the number of volunteers. This leads to erudite debates about why there have been marginal shifts in overall numbers and why numbers in certain age groups are increasing or decreasing. However slight the changes between different studies, pundits surface to explain the probable causes, sometimes ignoring the fact that the explanation lies in different sampling methods, definitions and sample sizes.

Under the eye-catching title, *Damn lies and volunteer statistics*[122], Das-Gupta has drawn attention to three surveys showing rates for formal volunteering in England as respectively 19%, 44% and 59%. The wording of a question influences the response. Asking, "Do you give unpaid help?" is said to be more likely to be answered by "yes" than the question, "do you volunteer?"

Both the Home Office and the Scottish Household Survey appear significantly to under-report informal volunteering. Even if the term is restricted to those outside the immediate household it is difficult to believe that so many people have no impact on the lives of those living around them.

The Conservative Party has drawn attention to the conflicting results of volunteer-counts, saying,

....the Citizenship Survey found that women were only a little more likely to volunteer than men while the Charity Awareness Monitor found that women were almost twice as likely to volunteer. As for age, the Charity Awareness Monitor found that volunteering among the older age groups was more common than among the younger. However, this was not found by the Citizenship Survey which, if anything, suggests the reverse. [123]

The 2011 Citizenship survey[124] published as this book went to press indicates that twenty-five per cent of people in England reported volunteering formally at least once a month in 2010-11, a lower rate than at any point between 2001 and 2007-08 when it ranged between 27% and 29%.

The Third Sector Research Centre examined a number of surveys and concluded that adult volunteering is within the range of 20% -50% for those who volunteer at least once a year and 10% -30% for those who volunteer on a monthly basis[125]. Given the wide disparities in findings and the conclusions of the Third Sector Research Centre it appears that a lot of money and effort is being spent on research of dubious value.

It is not just the UK that is battling to quantify the extent of volunteering. Following the 2001 International Year of Volunteering the United Nations urged governments to build a knowledge base of voluntary work[126]. This led to the International Labour Office preparing a manual on the measurement of voluntary work to enable countries to collect comparable data[127].

The term *Older Volunteer* is usually applied to people over the age of 50 years. The extent of formal volunteering by older people in England has been found to be 29% between the ages of 50 and 64, 31% between 65 and74 years and 24% over 75 years[128]. Informal volunteering in England is said to vary little between age groups except that it falls away in the late 70's[129]. This is likely to arise from growing infirmity and from the loss of a spouse. Also, a higher proportion of people aged 75 and over are in hospitals, nursing homes and residential care where research into the many kindnesses between residents are less likely to be charted.

Volunteer activities may be undertaken on a long term basis or as "a one off'. Helping a child to read or supporting a patient who has suffered a stroke are activities that are best undertaken by someone who commits time over an extended period but other tasks, such as marshalling cars at a car boot sale or stuffing envelopes as part of a fundraising appeal are time-limited. The challenge for organisers is to attract volunteers for casual work thereby capturing them for long-term commitments.

A study of volunteering opportunities created by the youth charity v found that more than half were on one-off placements, typically lasting for half a day[130]. This is valuable but to add the numbers involved in this kind of volunteering to figures from charities where volunteers commonly offer three or more hours a week throughout the year produces meaningless statistics. The only safe conclusion is that surveys of volunteering should be treated with extreme caution.

The Citizenship Survey report, calculated that at the national average wage, the hours spent volunteering formally and informally in England and Wales was equivalent to about two million staff or £45 billion per annum[131].

Surveys tell us a lot about numbers but very little about the content and quality of voluntary work. As a consequence volunteering is too often depicted in two dimensions and measured by inputs rather than outputs.

The 2003 Citizenship Survey showed that young Asian people had one of the highest rates of formal volunteering of any group. The report went on:

> Active community participation is not the preserve of white people – Black Africans were as likely as White people to have volunteered informally and formally and mixed race people had the highest rate of civic participation; among people born in the UK, Black and Asian people had similar rates of active participation to White people.

One of the largest informal volunteering networks in the UK is composed of off-duty home helps and their families. They are more aware than most of the deficiencies of public services. They visit disabled and disadvantaged people in their own homes and recognise that, for most of the time, very vulnerable people are left to fend for themselves. Often, their clients are socially isolated as well as frail and poor. Many have no one to help them when an appliance fails to work, a window will not close, the curtains need changing or the garden becomes overgrown.

It is often not possible for a home help to locate someone who will carry out such tasks at minimum cost so they return outside their working hours to provide the much-needed service themselves. Sometimes they cajole their husbands to attend at weekends to decorate, put up shelves or undertake gardening. They do this willingly, out of a sense of duty because they know that they are the only people who care enough to make a difference.

Hunt[132] found that 15% of home helps undertook laundry work and nearly 14% undertook ironing for their clients in their own homes. A survey by Avon County Council[133] showed that 10% of home help clients received one or more unofficial visits from home helps within a seven-day period. If we take the lower figure of 10% as representing the proportion of home help clients currently provided with a weekly voluntary service from home care services, over 40,000 households in Britain are benefiting. Not only do staff give their time freely but, as informal volunteers, they have no insurance cover and do not recoup their expenses.

Other public servants also work beyond the call of duty. Teachers, doctors, nurses, medical auxiliaries and social workers frequently face the dilemma of leaving work on time or staying to resolve a crisis. That is one reason why the Parliamentary expenses scandal in 2009 touched a raw nerve with members of the public. Low-income public servants know that they carry the burden of under-funded services. When the expenses scandal was revealed they were appalled that comparatively well-paid public servants had betrayed the trust that they and their clients had placed in them.

A Changing Consensus
Until the 1980's there was general agreement that welfare services represented a good investment for the country and that successive governments would ensure they continued to grow as public funds became

available. Now there was a wish to shift away from collective and universal provision towards services that ensured the empowerment of individuals, self-determination, independence, variety, choice and flexibility. The principles of decentralisation and diversity began to replace predictability, standardisation and State control. Decades of new legislation designed to re enforce and develop State responsibilities were now being called into question.

Great liberal movements earlier in the century had sought to create a compassionate society by bestowing power and control on the State but compassion without freedom of choice was now seen to be humiliating and stigmatising. There was a desire to empower service users. This could not be achieved within the framework of current legislation which guaranteed care of a kind but was constrained by cost, bureaucracy, social control and the need for conformity at the expense of sensitivity and flexibility.

We had learned from Eastern Europe that a society that places excessive power with politicians and professional carers becomes a conspiracy against the laity. It puts parameters round self determination and freedom of choice. Whatever the benevolent intentions, State power tends to be seen as inflexible, even unaccommodating and malevolent. People prefer the tyranny of self government to the implied generosity of colonial rule. In democratic countries it is seen as more important to cherish individual liberties and freedoms than to maintain a universal and consistent pattern of services.

The importance of these changes in thought can be seen across Western Europe in countries as diverse as the UK, Sweden, Norway, The Netherlands, Germany and Italy where a greater variety of providers were sought. In The Netherlands, the Dekker Report[134] described health and care services as virtually autonomous and uncontrollable. In countries that made extensive use of voluntary organisations to provide services there were complaints of the absence of accountability and the inflexibility of provision. When a huge proportion of the electorate had an income bordering on subsistence level they were grateful for what they received. Now they expected health and care services to offer the same kind of variety and choice that they had in other areas of their lives.

Perhaps these faults would have been less evident or would have caused less concern if public services were seen to be achieving their aims but, as indicated in chapter one, from 1970 onwards, social problems of every kind began to escalate. Services were increasingly expected to demonstrate their value to attract funding and some of them could not do so.

The changes that were brought about were not primarily intended to promote voluntary organisations but to create a greater diversity of services enabling users to have choice. But some voluntary organisations seized the opportunity to embrace the new contract culture and changed their mission and structure to make it easier to win contracts in what has become known as "the mixed economy of welfare". Some of the consequences of these changes are discussed in chapter twelve.

Volunteering in the UK

The World Values Survey[135] provides information about the active membership of voluntary organisations in six European countries and the United States. The European countries are Great Britain, France, Italy, Spain, Poland and Germany. Membership of church and religious organisations is higher in the USA than Europe but Great Britain easily leads the field in respect of organisations concerned with sport, recreation, art, music, environmental issues, professional associations and organisations concerned with charity and humanitarian issues.

Volunteering was known in England during Saxon times. In the ninth century local traders formed guilds described as "something between a chamber of commerce and a friendly society". The rules of one of these guilds stated, "If any member fall ill within sixty miles we are to provide fifteen men to fetch him and thirty if he be dead[136].

While in most of Europe, reliance on wide kinship networks was the norm, a greater reliance on the nuclear family by the English encouraged – even necessitated – the creation of formalised arrangements to protect trading interests and for providing mutual support to families in time of need. A society based on the nuclear family has a greater requirement to band with others for protection than one served by an extended network of family obligations.

Partly because of this, England developed a robust civil society and created commercial and financial institutions ahead of other European countries. It was therefore quick to exploit the benefits of the industrial revolution and expanding markets. In medieval England craftsmen formed guilds of protect their interests. They have been likened to small business associations, regulating training and standards of work. They also assisted members and their widows and orphans in distress.

We like to believe that England's ascendancy as a great power from medieval times was due to superior genes or a reward from heaven for our piety but it is far more likely to have arisen because of our powerful navy, our system of primogeniture and by an accident of our social organisation.

Nuclear families look beyond their own kith and kin for alliances and have more incentive to create partnerships with others. In some European and Middle Eastern countries the family is still the kingpin of commercial life. In such countries it is normal to employ and promote family members above strangers. In the West we regard this as at least undesirable nepotism and at most, illegal. But in other countries it is a natural thing to do; looking after family members is more important than adhering to an abstract philosophy about fairness to outsiders and equal opportunities.

Behind every revolution lie lively minds that come together to resolve what they see as injustices. Volunteers sent by the barons to plead with King John knew they risked their lives. It was a close-run thing but they came away with Magna Carta and power structures changed. Neither the monarch nor the barons now threaten volunteering. As we shall see, however, the freedom of volunteers is under insidious threat from elsewhere.

The Putney dialogues, the Swing riots, the Levellers, the Chartists, the Suffragettes, the trades unions and a host of other organisations sprang from a belief in the power of voluntary action. That these organisations thrived is a tribute to generations who fought for the liberties and freedoms enjoyed in the UK and for its tradition of toleration of dissent. The Wat Tyler rebellion and the massacres at Peterloo and Bristol demonstrate that dissent could have uncertain, even dangerous, outcomes. The policing of public demonstrations continues to be a hot political issue.

As we shall see, a key lesson from the Women's Voluntary Service and the Home Guard during the war was that volunteer recruitment largely takes care of itself when people recognise a need to band together to protect their common way of life. This is also seen in the formation of local organisations to fight unwelcome planning decisions and in groups, such as Mencap and the Alzheimer's Society in which patients and their families pursue common goals. Self-interest and the recognition that groups can be more effective than individuals working alone are strong motivational factors. The same mechanism is at work in the formation of teenage gangs.

Instant communication is changing the nature of protest. A small core of activists is now able to mobilise thousands of demonstrators to descend on a hundred sites across the country without the need for an elaborate and costly infrastructure. Moreover, as Alinsky[137] pointed out, the mere threat of a campaign can be enough to change the balance of power. Nowadays it is not even necessary to assemble large numbers of people for a successful protest. By marshalling new technology like-minded people can exert considerable pressure for social change on issues about which, as individuals, they can make little impact. A warning that consumers will boycott the goods or services of a company with a high pay ratio for its staff or that engages in large-scale tax avoidance will be enough to curb some excesses of multi-national companies. There is greater scope than ever before for trades unions and consumers to work in partnership for their mutual benefit.

Volunteering far and wide

Volunteering is such a familiar part of the local scene that we barely stop to think about its make-up or characteristics. The UK has a long history of voluntary action but not all countries are so fortunate. Totalitarian regimes find it difficult to permit volunteering. Like religious belief, it thrives even when repressed and without adequate funding because it is borne and sustained in hearts and minds, making it difficult to stamp out. Governments can discourage volunteering by making certain actions illegal or by over-regulation. They can also promote it by providing funds.

Hitler was aware of the power of voluntary associations to influence attitudes. In 1936 he began systematically to destroy the Catholic Youth Movement in Germany – his greatest rival in the fight to influence young people. Negotiations with the Catholic church centred on confining church groups to religious study and banning them from other activities such as camping holidays. Eventually, Hitler lost patience, arrested 150 leaders and murdered the Director of the Catholic Youth Sports Association. Membership of the Hitler Youth became compulsory.

Freedom of association is taken for granted in many western countries but, in most cases, it has been a long, hard struggle to wrest power from people with privilege. In countries with a recent history of excessive police power this freedom is still not fully understood or accepted. In the sixth century BC, countries outside Greece had no words for "democracy" or "citizenship". After the fall of the Berlin Wall over two and a half millennia later, western observers discovered that some European countries had no word for "volunteer". Where there is an absence of words we can be sure the concepts are not understood, let alone respected.

In some countries, even now, voluntary groups are required to register with the police. In Azerbaijan, some activities that are lawful when carried out by individuals become unlawful when practiced by two or more people acting together. In Belarus the law forbids informal associations and the official address of a voluntary organisation cannot be a private address; it must be in a formally recognised office and not shared with another legal entity[138].

In Russia[139], volunteering virtually disappeared under Communism and any attempt to resuscitate it, however modest, was likely to lead to a visit from the political police. The problem was compounded because obligatory activities were labeled as voluntary. A day of unpaid work was known as a "subbotnik", derived from the Russian word for Saturday. Work was usually carried out to support a public works project. This became an obligatory event in the Soviet Union and its satellite countries with "Lenin's Subbotnik" held round about the time of his birthday each year. Membership of the Communist Party youth wing, the Komsomols, was compulsory from the age of 9 years. Since the mid 1990's, new legislation has radically changed the position and there is now a vigorous voluntary movement in Russia and a new understanding of the word, "volunteer".

Yet older volunteering in Russia, as in other ex-communist countries is precarious. Not only have older people learned to distrust volunteering throughout their lives but chronic disease takes a heavy toll on their health, reducing their capacity to expand their horizons. Life expectancy in Russia has fallen in recent years to less than 60 years for men[140]. Lucky is the man who lives long enough to volunteer after retirement.

Throughout the world, political instability has led to restrictions on freedom of association. Emerging from the turmoil of its Revolution, France and its leaders were wary about organisations that were beyond state control. Napoleon wanted to minimise opportunities for opponents to organise themselves and to contain the clergy. Associations of more than twenty people had to be approved by the police. Controls over the formation of voluntary associations remained in place for a hundred years.

That voluntary organisations now thrive in France is a tribute to the genius of the French and their democratic institutions. Liberty, Fraternity and Equality have served them well for over 200 years. Between 1789 and 1959 insurrection was never far away. During this time France had five republics, two empires, three monarchies, three invasions and an army of occupation. At the siege of Paris in 1871 severe food shortages led to people eating rats. Thousands died before the city fell to the Prussian army. In the chaos that followed Parisian workers took control and declared the city a Workers' Commune. The Prussian army stood aside and French soldiers slaughtered 30,000 Parisians. The carnage was greater than in the French Revolution 80 years earlier. It is claimed that the Paris Commune was the first working class uprising in Europe. The slogan, "Vive la Commune" was daubed on walls during the 1968 disturbances. Radicals have long memories.

In contrast from the fraught politics of France and most other European countries little has disturbed the stability of the British political system during the same period. The British Press still describes the abdication of Edward the seventh as "a constitutional crisis" - much to the amusement of the French who, in each generation, have experienced constitutional crises of catastrophic proportions.

In democracies, protest and volunteering are important mechanisms for challenging government and altering the distribution of power. Politicians are understandably reluctant to concede power to people who have opposing views but, if there is no tension between politicians and organisations representing volunteering, alarm bells should start to ring.

David is now 71. He enjoyed being a school volunteer with RSVP Wales when, in 2004, an opportunity arose for him to visit a school in Accra to help children with their reading. He says, "I had no idea this visit would completely change my life. Six years later, after four more visits, I have just finished my 194th fund raising talk about the school and its needs."

On his first visit, David found the school in very poor condition with few facilities. But the children were full of energy, curiosity and an eagerness to learn while staff rose above the conditions in which they taught. He had filled a suitcase with paper, pens, pencils and used books and was deeply touched by the gratitude of the teachers.

Due to his efforts and the £25,000 he has painstakingly collected, the school has since been almost rebuilt and now has toilets, running water and electricity. With the help of a grant from Sainsbury's and volunteers from RSVP Wales, David has sent out a ton of books, clothes, equipment, knitted hats and jumpers. Unsurprisingly, he is now an Honorary Chief.

CHAPTER FOUR

Two centuries of volunteering

*Those who cannot remember the past
are condemned to repeat it.*

Santayana

As the new century was being celebrated in 1800, three social and economic movements were fundamentally changing British society. The population was exploding; it would double in the next fifty years. There was a rapid expansion of manufacturing industry which was to revolutionise not only the way people lived but change relationships between different segments of society. Thirdly, there was a growth in urban settlements; industry drew its workforce away from the countryside and into hastily built towns to work new machinery.

In the first 50 years of the new century the proportion of the British population living in towns rose from 20% to 50%. The 1881 census shows that of every 1,000 residents in West Ham, London, 384 were born in Essex, 298 in London and 318 were born elsewhere. In the seven largest Scottish towns, nearly half the population was born elsewhere[141]. London attracted immigrants from across Europe and beyond throughout the century.

By far the largest number came from Germany. In the 1880's there was a large influx of Jews avoiding persecution, firstly from Russia, then from Poland. The social upheaval was unprecedented. The framework of government was not prepared for what was happening. Local solutions, outside government jurisdiction, had to be found to respond to the social problems that emerged.

Lady Bountiful

At that time the social lives of middle and upper class ladies were seriously curtailed by social conventions. They served as adjuncts to their husbands and were expected to create an aura of opulence in the family home. This was not a fulfilling role. Many yearned to do something about the poverty, squalor and human misery they saw around them. They wanted to contribute something positive to the vibrant society that was developing beyond the domestic scene that enveloped them. Volunteering could provide an outlet for their frustrations.

It was not lost on some that their good fortune arose from the economic conditions that ensured a supply of cheap labour for the farms and factories that fed their wealth. Others recognised the physical dangers of leading comfortable lives adjacent to pockets of poverty where families were literally suffering from starvation. Well into Victoria's reign the spectre of the French Revolution continued to haunt the rich and powerful. Volunteering was acceptable to them because it posed no threat to the social order. Acting the Lady Bountiful helped many ladies to free themselves from the tedium of domesticity and gave them a satisfying purpose in life.

The social status of middle and upper class wives made it unacceptable for them to perform paid work; their mode of dress was carefully designed to demonstrate that they could not undertake physical labour and this differentiated them from the lower orders. Religious certainties strengthened their belief that they had a right, even a duty to reform the attitudes and behaviour of people down the social scale and they had no compunction about telling the working classes how to behave. In an age of deference and doffed caps, this probably made them more acceptable to the people they sought to help. There could be no Lady Bountiful without the Grateful Poor. They each played their roles in a rigidly divided class system.

The original Lady Bountiful was a character in the 1707 comedy *Beaux' Stratagem* by George Farquhar. The character Will Boniface describes her as,

> One of the best of women. Her late husband, Sir Charles Bountiful, left her with £1000 a year; and I believe she lays out one-half of it in charitable uses for the good of her neighbours. She has cured more people in and about Lichfield within ten years than the doctors have killed in twenty.

Thus, Lady Bountiful began life as a respected philanthropist but soon became a caricature for ladies who enjoyed their wealth and status and who engaged in ostentatious acts of charity. But a brief study of her activities during the nineteenth century demonstrates that her work helped to revolutionise perceptions about the poor and led to changes in the way in which society responded to destitution.

Lady Bountiful was rarely a lone operator. She joined with like-minded people to discuss ways of identifying the most effective means of meeting needs. This emboldened her to look beyond conventional volunteering and to consider how changes in public policy might reduce poverty and suffering. Numerous voluntary societies and associations were formed to press for policy changes, some with ponderous, even pendulous names. These organisations became vehicles through which reformers tested their theories and broadcast their ideas.

In 1813, Elizabeth Fry began a voluntary visiting service for women prisoners. At that time, prisons were bedevilled by corruption, squalor and poor administration. She saw prison visiting as a means of ensuring that outside influences were brought to bear on management arrangements. In 1816 she formed the first society for voluntary visitors in an English prison - the *Ladies Association for the Improvement of the Female Prisoners in Newgate*. The association opened a school for prisoners' children and provided food and clothing for prisoners on their discharge. The association was soon followed by the *British Ladies Society for the Reformation of Female Prisons*.

There were few opportunities for women to have a direct voice in corridors of power. Like many ladies undertaking charitable work Elizabeth Fry was well-connected and lobbied Parliament through her brother–in-law, Thomas Foxwell Buxton MP. In 1818 he told the House of Commons that there were 107,000 prisoners in British prisons – "a greater number than all the other kingdoms of Europe put together[142]". Nearly two hundred years later the UK still has a higher proportion of its citizens in prison than any other EU country. Florence Nightingale was another reformer who used her family connections to good effect. Her brother-in-law, Sir Harry Verney MP became known as the "Honorable Member for Florence Nightingale" because he raised so many issues in Parliament due to her prompting.

Throughout the remainder of the nineteenth century, voluntary organisations headed by passionate volunteers spearheaded the movement for prison reform. An Act of 1862 enabled charities to be attached to individual prisons and for local justices to pay £2 per prisoner to help with their resettlement.

Other reformers concentrated their energies on young offenders. *The Society for Investigating the Causes of the Alarming Increase in Juvenile Delinquency in the Metropolis* was formed in 1815. Later, Mary Carpenter was to open a reformatory school in Bristol.

The Manchester and Salford Ladies Sanitary Reform Association was formed in 1852 to popularise sanitary knowledge. Volunteers visited the poor, to advise on the care of children, the prevention of infection and ventilation. Ten years later it began to employ staff. This was the forerunner of Health Visiting. At the end of the century the Sickroom *Help Society* in East London provided domestic assistance for mothers who were confined or sick. This was the beginning of the Home Help Service.

By the middle of the nineteenth century concern was being expressed about the sheer number of individuals and organisations vying with one another in large cities to assist the poor. Some referred to the evils of promiscuous, indiscriminate and sentimental giving. The clergy were particularly concerned about the "lady brigades" and "rival charitable eagles" that swooped on their parishes although others complained that some churches attempted to swell their congregations by the provision of soup and food vouchers.

An average of 56 new charities was created in London during each of the first five decades of the nineteenth century. This leapt to 144 between 1850 and 1860 – a sign of growing affluence in the capital. In 1861 the aggregate income for London charities was said to be nearly £2.5 million whereas the total poor rate was less than £1.5 million[143].

The Charity Organisation Society, created in 1869 set itself the task of regulating charitable giving in the capital. The Society was greatly influenced by three strands of thought which were, closely related. Firstly, there was concern about the corrosive effect of charity on the self-esteem of recipients and their willingness to work. C. S. Lock, who became the Society's secretary in 1875, said charity "infests the people like a silent working pestilence"[144]. For a long time, givers had seen charitable giving as a road to personal salvation. Questions were now being asked about its impact on the poor. The Society's principal aim was to prevent dishonesty among applicants. Indeed, in the first year its name was, *The Society for Organising Charitable Relief and Repressing Mendacity*.

Secondly there was a growing interest in the scientific analysis of social problems and a belief that careful enquiry would find a solution to even the most intractable social ills. Charitable giving might solve a short-term emergency but there were concerns that it could create more long-term problems. By studying the epidemiology of infectious diseases and improving sanitary arrangements in the capital, Victorians had made a profound impact on public health. They now sought to apply the same careful scientific observation to social problems. Octavia Hill who deployed numerous volunteers in the management of housing projects for poor families greatly influenced the work of the Charity Organisation Society. She was herself influenced by her grandfather, Dr Southwood Smith, a pioneer of improved public health. Her mother, Caroline Hill became secretary of the Co-operative Women's Guild.

Thirdly, religious thought was changing emphasis from serving God to serving humanity. Lock, a deeply religious man wanted to create a "great army" of well-trained volunteers to create, "the religion of charity without the sectarianism of religion"[145]. The religious basis of much volunteering activity with its multiplicity of faiths and sub-faiths had fragmented effort, established rivalries and created costly overlaps.

The Charity Organisation Society emphasised the importance of a full enquiry into a family's circumstances so that any help provided would be part of a long term plan to ensure that the family became self supporting. In doing this, it rejected applications from those whom it deemed to be the authors of their own misfortune and, therefore, undeserving. Financial help was regarded as only part of the solution to a problem and volunteers were required to work with families to ensure that they budgeted sensibly and maintained good standards of household management. The Society ensured that its volunteers were trained to a high standard. The quality of volunteers was seen as the key to its success.

The social theories embraced at that time assumed social evils arose from individual weaknesses and that solutions were to be found, not through social action or collective endeavour but by bolstering the knowledge and moral fibre of the poor. Diligent work by volunteers of good character (and private incomes) was seen as the key to tackling poverty.

The principles behind the Charity Organisation Society were widely accepted by charities across the country and, by 1894, it was estimated that there were 85 similar organisations in the UK. Its influence was also felt abroad. In one year alone it reported contact with 111 towns in twenty-four countries[146].

The Charity Organisation Society was composed of people who were not afraid to face facts. They wanted to help poor people but not on any terms. Lock opposed the introduction of old age pensions on the grounds that they would weaken family responsibility. Octavia Hill told a Parliamentary enquiry in 1884 that, in some circumstances, it was preferable to spend ten shillings a week to keep a pauper in the workhouse than to pay a smaller sum to keep him or her outside[147]. On the other hand she was not sure that it was worth the expense of putting a water tap on every landing in a tenement block.

Many decisions about the provision of financial assistance to needy families were made by committees containing no women; they could be very judgmental and particularly harsh on unmarried mothers. Where there was uncertainty about need or the veracity of applicants, enquiries were sometimes made among third parties such as neighbours and local shopkeepers. Poverty trumped confidentiality.

Children soon understood that it was an accident of birth whether their family was a giver or a receiver of charity. It is a matter of speculation how far the rise of socialism in Britain in the twentieth century was due to successive generations of children seeing their parents humiliated by charity workers and Poor Law relieving officers when the economic system failed them. For those brought up in or on the edge of long term poverty, any proposal to change the power structure of society could be seized upon as an opportunity to release the economic chains that enslaved them. Some working class families were ready to follow any leader who promised a social order that would end the unfairness they endured.

Until the nineteenth century, children commonly worked long hours in inhuman conditions in mines, factories, workshops and as chimney sweeps. Tens of thousands of them lived on the streets of London alone but their lives were slowly improved by reformers such as Lord Shaftesbury, Dr Barnardo and Mary Carpenter who demonstrated what could be achieved by voluntary action. They led campaigns to change the law and galvanized the country to re-examine attitudes towards children.

Settlements, often sponsored by new universities, enabled professional and academic people to live in poor areas while continuing to pursue their own occupations. As well as providing opportunities for practical social work, they were intended to bring culture and enlightenment to poor people and stimulate a greater understanding of social issues among those who might become leaders in society. Settlements were unique among philanthropic organisation inasmuch as they endeavoured to inculcate a spirit of equality between helper and helped.

The first Settlement, Toynbee Hall in East London, was opened in 1884 and by 1903 there were at least twelve in London. Others were opened in a number of provincial cities. Settlements were less wary about expressing controversial views than many other organisations and claimed the need for academic freedom if under attack. George Bernard Shaw opened a debate at Toynbee Hall by moving, that *the Working Classes are useless, dangerous and ought to be abolished*. It would be difficult to debate such a subject without making controversial political comments.

Settlements enabled potential political leaders to examine at close hand the working lives of poor people. Clement Attlee became secretary and William Beveridge became Warden of Toynbee Hall. Their experiences profoundly influenced their understanding of poverty and gave them confidence that ways could be found to combat it.

Mutual Aid
Another strand of volunteering was greatly developed in Victoria's reign. Mutual aid and self-help organisations

can be traced back to the medieval guilds and beyond when groups of likeminded people came together to mobilise their resources and skills for the collective good. Nineteenth century industrialisation led to a phenomenal growth of a variety of self-help organisations. Friendly societies, trades unions, the Co-operative movement and working men's clubs developed strong welfare roles, collecting small weekly sums which were disbursed to members encountering hard times. Free medical attendance for the breadwinner and a subsidised service for their families were important benefits for working people. At Christmas, coal and food were distributed.

Many of these organisations had friendly visiting services run by volunteers to keep in touch with their members who were sick or otherwise incapacitated. Funeral benefits were often included to avoid the need for a pauper's funeral – the prospect of which created great anxiety. Some of the societies became quite wealthy and were able to offer bursaries enabling poor children to be educated.

Self help groups provided entitlements or offered assistance without requiring recipients to demonstrate absolute poverty. They were therefore free from the taint of charity which worried a great many people in need[i].

---

[i] In the early 1940's, after several weeks of illness, my father was admitted to hospital with peritonitis. Insurance met the medical bills but sickness benefit was meagre. A visitor from the women's Co-operative Guild, of which my mother was a loyal supporter, came to commiserate with her. As she left, she pressed half a crown (12 1/2p) from the Guild's welfare fund into my mother's hand. The relief on my mother's face was palpable. She

Friendly Societies were reluctant to pay economic rents for their premises as this would reduce the sum available for benefits. Members were mainly weekly wage earners, sharing the wealth they created with middlemen, entrepreneurs and businessmen. Their forbears in medieval craft guilds retained the full value of their labours and could afford to own premises including magnificent guildhalls of which some still remain.

As champions of the strength and independence of the workingman, even if an employer or charity were willing to provide premises rent free, Friendly Societies did not wish to accept charity. Mostly they established their headquarters in public houses, which led some observers to believe that they were little more than drinking clubs for the working classes. But this was far from the truth. They performed a valuable function in the lives of local people, including lobbying for improved public services. They were sustained by countless volunteers who expressed pride in their organisation and who were no less committed to social betterment than Lady Bountiful.

It was reported in 1849 that the Manchester Unity of Oddfellows had 250,000 members[148] - more than the number of households in the city. Seebohm Rowntree, in his monumental study of York published in 1901[149], identified that the City had 54 registered Friendly Society lodges and numerous unregistered societies. He estimated

had already sold one easy chair and was considering selling other items. She would have felt humiliated had she been cross-examined about her income and budgeting or worse, told to sell the rickety piano in the front parlour.

that, allowing for the fact that some men were members of more than one society, 7,000 men in York were in membership of a Friendly Society or paid for sick and funeral benefits through a trades union. That suggests that almost half the households in York were covered.

It is remarkable to discover that, at the same time, life insurance offices in York employed 75 agents full time and ten part-time to collect weekly life insurance premiums from city wage earners. Mostly they were employed by the Prudential Assurance Company which continued for another sixty years to be the major UK player in this branch of life insurance. The extent of philanthropic activity should not blind us to the degree to which working people made sacrifices to protect themselves from the ravages of boom and bust. They knew that Lady Bountiful had a hard edge to her skirts and could not be relied upon for sustenance.

In 1898, the Chief Registrar of Friendly Societies reported that the membership of registered friendly societies in Great Britain and Ireland was over 11 million[150]. At that time the population of Great Britain and Ireland was about 46 million. This suggests that, as in York, half of households were covered.

Yet the prevailing view among upper and middle class families was that poverty largely arose from fecklessness and moral failings among the poor and could not be resolved by State intervention. But as Rowntree demonstrated, many families made considerable sacrifices to protect their interests in the event of unemployment or sickness. However, if they were unable to work, the benefits they could afford were usually insufficient to keep them above subsistence level for more than a few weeks. For the vast majority, poverty was structural. It could not be blamed on weakness of character. It could only be solved by channelling more money to the poor.

The Great War and its aftermath

The Great War brought huge social changes making it acceptable for middle and upper class women to work. In some cases, arrangements were made for volunteers to replace workingwomen for weekends, "an admirable device to use the superfluous energy of the leisured so as to give the workers time for rest and recuperation"[151]. The Prime Minister's daughter, Cynthia Asquith, described how she undertook two-hour shifts making respirators. She said she was fascinated by manual labour and thought it would be exciting to do piecework for money but that a 12 hour day would be tiring[152].

The number of domestic servants dwindled as 400,000 of them flocked to munitions factories where, despite the tedium of repetitive work, the atmosphere could be less repressive than that in domestic service.

Wealthy families were hit by high taxation and death duties. A premature death on the battlefield leading to the death of two generations in quick succession could impoverish a wealthy aristocratic family. This hastened the demise of landed estates in private hands. Lyme Park, in Cheshire had been gifted to Sir Thomas Danyers in 1346 for his service to the Black Prince at the battle of Crecy. Exactly six hundred years later his descendants gave it to the National Trust because, ironically, taxes levied to fund two world wars had depleted the family fortune.

For one hundred years there had been more women than men in the population but as a consequence of wartime slaughter the gap increased.[i] Many women were deprived of a conventional family life or found their expected inheritance greatly diminished. Those who, twenty years earlier might have been in a position to be Lady Bountiful now had to find paid work

After the Great War a number of professions were opened to women for the first time, notably barristers, solicitors, auctioneers, surveyors and architects. Women could now stand for Parliament, become judges, serve as jurors and be admitted to universities. The professions of teaching, medicine and nursing expanded rapidly and absorbed large numbers of women.

In the first sixty years of the twentieth century single-wage households were the norm, enabling married women to engage in voluntary work. Even in the 1960's, less than half of married women were in paid employment.

In the rigid class system before the Second World War, philanthropic organisations sponsored by both the landed gentry and the new manufacturing classes had little or no contact with self-help groups created by the

---

[i] I had five childless, maiden aunts born between 1895 and 1905. When sorting through a cupboard with one aunt when she was 90, I found a faded photograph of a young man in army uniform. She said, without emotion, "This was taken in London when he was on leave. We were going to get married but he went back to France and was killed."

poor yet their objectives were the same – to reduce the impact of poverty. In a prescient report of 1928, Frederic D'Aeth, Secretary of the Liverpool Council for Voluntary Aid drew attention to the way in which residents in new housing areas created after the Great War were seizing the initiative:

> "In the old areas it was usually the social worker from outside who voiced the needs and endeavoured to meet them. In the new areas it is the residents themselves who are alive to the situation and are taking appropriate action by means of tenants' associations"[153].

This was an early sign of a challenge to the paternalism of philanthropic action and a growing belief that, given the opportunity, local communities had the capacity to find solutions to their own problems. But, as we shall see, over eighty years later, the dividing line remains intact; there are very few organisations that combine the best of both philanthropy and community action.

The first record of a local authority directly deploying volunteers was in 1898 when Margaret Frere, a Member of London County Council's Education Committee established a committee of volunteers to ensure that children were not prevented from taking advantage of education through lack of food, clothing or medical attention[154]. This was the forerunner of the LCC Children's Care Committees, started in 1909, in which groups of volunteers were supervised by paid Council staff. By 1911 they had become an important adjunct of the school health service. Dr Moxon reported[155] that children treated at Moorfields Eye Hospital were routinely referred to children's care committees to ensure that parents were advised about on-going treatment.

Until the twentieth century, voluntary organisations and volunteers were key service providers but, as public services developed they changed to complement the work of the State. By the second half of the century they had changed again to supplement statutory services.

The expansion in social worker training after the Second World War owed much to the pioneering work of the Charity Organisation Society which, in 1946, changed its name to the Family Welfare Association[i].The new profession of social work profoundly influenced the structure and the nature of public services. Newly trained social workers of both sexes gradually replaced the Lunacy Man, the School Board Man and the Cruelty Man with their threatening overtones.

The Seebohm Committee[156], reporting on the reform of personal social services in 1968 argued for the maximum participation of individuals and groups in the planning, organisation and provision of services. It also sought a more active role for consumers of services.

The Aves Committee[157] which reported the following year said that until the 1960's volunteers tended to be members of voluntary organisations even when they worked in a public service such as a hospital. It cited School Care Committees as

---

[i] In another change of name it became *Family Actions* in 2008.

an exception. The Committee suggested that, in future, it was likely that local authorities would find it more convenient to recruit, select and train volunteers directly. There was no discussion about the advantages and disadvantages of such arrangements but reference was made to the importance of volunteers feeling part of an organisation and to have opportunities to discuss their work. The Aves Report was well received and had a significant influence on the development of volunteering not just in the UK but in other parts of the world. It was translated into Dutch and German and published separately in the US.

Some voluntary organisations ensured that their volunteers were represented on the executive and other committees of the organisation although, as Dorothy Keeling, General Secretary of the Liverpool Personal Service Society from 1919 to 1940 pointed out in her autobiography,[158] "It would have been better still if we had had representatives of the consumers". That the daughter of the Headmaster of Bradford Grammar School, herself a magistrate was prepared to contemplate being responsible to an executive committee containing poor and needy people illustrates the levelling effect of the war and the shift in thinking that took place between 1940 and 1960.

In Barton Hill, a poor district of Bristol, there was a direct clash between members of the local residents association and an advisory body mainly composed of professional staff who worked in the area but lived elsewhere. After considerable tension, the two organisations eventually came together in 1959. Under the impetus of this new body, a Community House was opened the following year with a full time warden[159]. Under the influence of the Second World War, philanthropic and self-help groups had learnt a new respect for one another.

Wider society was not sure how to value paid social workers. Low salaries, especially in health services and voluntary organisations deterred potential recruits in the 1950's and 60's. Career-minded social workers tended to favour local government and the probation service where salaries were higher. Some public service administrators found it difficult to think of social work as a profession and tended to regard them as volunteers earning pocket money.

Despite the fact that the caring professions developed out of volunteering, professionals have been uncertain about the value of volunteering and wary about endorsing a close association that might seem to imply that that some of their work could be performed by volunteers. But, over the years, doctors, nurses, social workers, teachers and a variety of therapists have learned the value of working with volunteers and, from a wariness in the 1950's there are now many examples of close partnerships between volunteers and professionals. Indeed, the concept of voluntary organisations and volunteers as supplementing the work of statutory services is fast losing hold. Partnerships, service agreements and contracts are the new currency which, as we shall see, is changing the nature of volunteering.

Lady Bountiful's Legacy

Well into the 1950's it was possible to encounter social workers who, without embarrassment, would say, "Of course, I could not afford to do this job without a private income". Some social workers reported that requests for a pay rise were met with the response that higher pay would attract, "the wrong kind of staff". The concept of Lady Bountiful lived on long after her demise.

What have we lost and gained as a society by her passing? There are discernable links between voluntarism in the nineteenth century and the present day. She can be detected in philanthropic organisations in which power is centralised and volunteers are allocated tasks from the centre. As in the nineteenth century, much prevailing literature on volunteering is derived from staff in these organisations. They may regard themselves as the forerunners and flag-wavers for the Big Society; however, it is from the mutual aid tradition of small, locally-based organisations where power and authority are more evenly distributed that we must look for the inspiration behind the Big Society.

The Government's White Paper on Open Public Services[160] is unequivocal. It seeks to delegate functions to local people – not to organisations controlled by managers. The document refers to "democratic accountability at the most local level" and seeks to ensure that neighbourhood councils have more control. It would be a travesty if power and control were transferred to non elected managers.

Later chapters show how Lady Bountiful's legacy still casts a long shadow over volunteering. There is considerable pressure from funders for self-help groups to abandon their localism and morph into centrally controlled philanthropic organisations. Where power is held centrally it is counter-intuitive to disperse it. Professionals, managers, accountants and politicians find it easier to relate to organisations with philanthropic aims. As we shall see, organisations with immense influence over volunteering policy and practice have, unashamedly, adopted Lady Bountiful's vision and values. She continues to dominate literature about volunteering and training programmes for managers.

Some sociologists believe that Lady Bountiful left a legacy that not only persists in the voluntary sector but still taints public services. A United States author[161] argues that her image is still deeply embedded in popular culture making it difficult to address issues surrounding white supremacy and social class in teacher training programmes.

Volunteers deployed in philanthropic organisations have relinquished some of Lady Bountiful's qualities for those of her self help brothers and sisters. Lady Bountiful was happy in the company of the Relieving Officer and members of boards of guardians. She shared their values of hard work, thrift and moral rectitude and believed in the social system. She was as much part of the Establishment as members of the clergy. In contrast, many of today's volunteers identify closely with the poor and needy. They search the small print of legislation and official regulations to obtain every ounce of benefit from the system for them, and are willing to challenge authority if necessary. They stand alongside their clients – not over them – and many feel more comfortable talking with the needy than to those in authority.

On the other hand, the late Margaret Simey[162] reflected that State services dispensing benevolence by contract replaced the sense or reciprocal obligation that accompanied charity work. Thus, opportunities for us all to feel part of a lively community have been reduced. A gift, freely given, may evoke gratitude and a feeling of connection and belonging that cannot be replicated by the recipient of State social security benefits.

Concerns currently expressed about benefit scroungers arise from widespread disquiet that moral judgements no longer play a part in determining responses to financial need. Where rights and entitlements do not involve reciprocal duties the nature of community relationships change profoundly.

Nineteenth century volunteers and relieving officers combined their giving with a moral judgement and advice. The personal relationship between giver and receiver was important. By providing entitlements to benefits we have largely stripped volunteering of the role of deciding who gets material help and how much. This has reduced the social stigma surrounding poverty and reliance on others but, at the same time, it has reduced the sense of personal responsibility and obligation that shapes relationships between families and the communities in which they live. Moral judgements are out of fashion but the residual functions of Lady Bountiful of compassion and advice in a supporting relationship are desperately needed to tackle many continuing social problems.

Len worked in the building industry and became a volunteer ambulance driver when he retired. At the age of 70 he was told he was too old for this work and joined RSVP where he drives for patients in a GP surgery. He is proud of his role, realising as he does how difficult life can be without a car. "Going to the GP or hospital can be stressful," he says. "It is nice for them to go with someone they know will not let them down and with whom they can have a friendly chat. I have always liked to be responsible for something. There is a real satisfaction in making someone happier."

The volunteer who began a bicycle recycling scheme in Dudley says, "If I was a realist this would not be here. Dreams and aspirations are what move things on".

He and fellow volunteers repair and refurbish bicycles that have been abandoned or unclaimed after being stolen and are made available to poor families and childrens' homes.

CHAPTER FIVE

Lessons of war

Keep the home fires burning
A patriotic song by Ivor Novello
and Lena Gilbert Ford, 1914.

When war threatens, men and women of all persuasions have a strong desire to show their solidarity with fighting men at the front. In the First World War many organisations were established to support the war effort. Among them was the Womens Institute movement which held its first meeting in September 1915 in Anglesey. Its birthplace is visited by countless tourists each year, not because of its association with the Women's Institute but because the little village is called, Llanfairpwllgwyndrobwillantysillogogogoc. The aim was to help revitalise rural communities and to encourage women to become more involved in producing food for the war effort. Since then, Women's Institutes have played an important role in the life of rural communities.

The Women's Voluntary Service
With the prospect of war becoming more certain, in 1938, the Home Secretary Sir Samuel Hoare recognised

the enormous disruption that would be caused by air attack and decided to establish a national voluntary organisation of women to respond to the needs of bombed-out families. On 16 May, the *Women's Voluntary Service* was founded with The Dowager Marchioness Lady Reading as chairman. Queen Elizabeth and Queen Mary, the Queen Mother became joint patrons. By the outbreak of war in September 1939 the WVS had a membership of 165,000.

Lady Reading brought with her considerable experience of charitable work. She was chairman of the Personal Service League which had been created in the early 1930's to assist unemployed men and their families. She was determined to take the best that Lady Bountiful could offer and democratise it so that the most humble of women could make their contribution. Every woman could become her own Lady Bountiful.

During a recruitment drive early in 1939, Lady Reading said that the motto of the organisation was *flexibility* and that the work undertaken would depend on local people and local circumstances. She was determined not to superimpose a common approach across the country. She instinctively knew that volunteers could be led but not directed and preached the cause of decentralisation. She set out to identify women with flair, resourcefulness and capacity irrespective of social standing, to serve as organisers.

It was a shrewd decision to put the word *women* in the title rather than *lady*, which would have confused, if not alienated, many of the women whom it was hoped to recruit. This was one of the first organisations recruiting volunteers that set out to welcome women of all creeds and background, ignoring class distinctions. It accepted that every woman had something to offer the community. This was many years before the terms; *inclusivity, equal opportunities* and *non-rejection entered* the lexicon of social policy. More than seventy years later, some organisations have still to catch up.

Membership of the *WVS* reached a peak of a million and a quarter volunteers during the war, responding to emergencies across the country. It was volunteer-led insofar that it was local volunteers, in consultation with statutory services, who decided where and how to apply their efforts - to serve members of the forces, homeless families, children, hospital patients, evacuees or others groups in need.

A government document, *National Service Handbook*, published in January 1939 stated that women over the age of 50 years had nothing to offer. When confronted by this, Lady Reading said a man wrote it. The *WVS* was ahead of its time in so many ways. But the suggested age limit should not surprise us. The life expectancy of a female at birth did not reach 60 years until the mid 1920's. In 1939 it stood at 67 years.

Volunteers were encouraged to wear uniforms but no badges of rank were allowed. All volunteers, from the wife of the squire to the servant girl were equal. They bought their own uniforms, utilising their own clothing coupons to do so. The absence of insignias of rank sometimes led to misunderstandings. Lady Reading told the story of when she visited a canteen in her uniform and asked what she could do to help. You can wash these dishes, came the reply, so she did. When she once told a group of people that she worked in the WVS headquarters she was asked whether she had ever met, "the old cow in charge".

The British class system showed through in places. An American visitor to London noted that a temporary hostel in which he was housed was managed by WVS volunteers "of the upper middle class and by one or two titled ladies". He went on to describe the contemptuous way in which the ladies spoke to serving staff. He found this to be in marked contrast to egalitarian attitudes in the United States.

Although the WVS *was* a national body, real power was held locally. Local volunteers determined where needs were greatest and set up services to meet them. Canteens organised by the WVS were among the earliest services to be outsourced by hospitals. Local leaders sometimes emerged in unexpected ways. It was not uncommon for volunteers to be thrust into positions of great responsibility a few weeks after joining because they demonstrated abilities to organise others. A woman might be a team leader one week and find herself part of a group the following week working on an entirely different project.

Training was provided wherever possible by local authority staff, the Red Cross, Civil Defence experts and health service personnel. Courses in Civil Defence were common, including anti-gas measures; first aid courses were particularly useful for volunteers working in and around casualty stations where bombing was a frequent occurrence.

In wartime, very little went according to plan. In some areas the WVS was asked to take part in the evacuation of women and children from large cities. Trains often ran late and did not always arrive at the expected destination. Volunteers learned to improvise as trains arrived unexpectedly with hungry and tired children who had to be fed and accommodated. About 1.5 million people, mostly children, were helped to leave big cities in the first month of the war alone. Many of them returned home after a few weeks or months only to dash to the countryside once more when air raids became particularly fierce.

Whenever there was a huge movement of troops the WVS was on hand. During the Dunkirk evacuation volunteers provided food, drink, clean clothes and blankets to returning soldiers. Their biggest complaint seems to have been that soldiers fell into a deep sleep before they had finished their mugs of tea. Volunteers also issued post cards so that survivors could let their relatives know they were safe – there were no mobile telephones or emails to keep in touch. WVS volunteers were active again in the build-up to the D Day landings.

The new organisation worked in every town and city during the Blitz setting up mobile canteens and field kitchens in areas where power was interrupted. Lady Reading asked volunteers to ensure that food provided to bombed out people was easy to eat because, "the first thing people lose is their spectacles and the second, their teeth."

Refreshments were supplied to rescuers and the rescued. WVS volunteers helped over 10,000 people every night running advice services and rest centres. They were enjoined to be vigilant about improvised sanitary arrangements in building with poor ventilation where hundreds of people of all ages were huddled together night after night to escape bombs and rockets. At the peak of the London blitz, the WVS provided services for 180,000 people in London Transport's underground stations[i].

Several deep underground shelters were built by the government in London in the early part of the war. They were constructed in such a way that they could later be used as by-pass tunnels for the Northern and Central lines. As well as being extensively used by civilians they

---

[i] One of my most vivid recollections of the war was when, late at night and with my parents, I changed trains at Charing Cross underground station. We carefully picked our way along the platform edge to avoid the mass of humanity sprawled across the platform. Some spread their possessions as widely as possible to maximise personal space. Cardboard or cushions were used to ward off the cold from the hard concrete beneath; a lucky few had manhandled mattresses down the escalators. I felt like an interloper in this private world. Babies cried, old men coughed, mothers bellowed at their children to stop shouting or to keep still. By comparison, our garden Anderson shelter was a quiet, snug, haven.

accommodated many thousands of troops. The WVS were largely responsible for domestic arrangements. They are now largely used for data storage[i].

The bombing inevitably led to casualties to *WVS* personnel who worked in dangerous situations. Nearly 250 *WVS* members were killed by enemy action and many more were wounded. 25 *WVS* offices were destroyed by May 1941.

Incident Inquiry Points were opened by volunteers so that families that had been split-up by the bombing could be reunited. This included men returning on leave from the forces whose family homes had been bombed and children who had been separated from their families in the rush to enter shelters. The *WVS* also provided information about people who had been killed and injured. Volunteers sometimes had the task of helping distraught parents sift through the debris of a bombed school to identify the remains of their children.

Each *WVS* centre had its own Salvage Officer, Clothing Officer and Food Leader. The Food Leader did whatever was required locally to assist the authorities in the

---

[i] At the end of the war I joined a tour of the shelter at Clapham South when it was being used as emergency accommodation. It was a drab and cheerless tunnel lined with beds. The only thing to raise the spirits as underground trains rattled overhead was the presence of the WVS who seemed unaffected by the gloom and kept us happy with refreshments.

complicated task of food rationing. They also helped with the distribution of emergency food supplies. After the Coventry Blitz one food convoy organised by the *WVS* enabled 14,000 meals to be served. The first Meals on Wheels service on a regular basis started in 1943.

Volunteers learned to be self-reliant; if their own knowledge and common sense did not help them find an answer to a problem they knew they were held in sufficient esteem to turn to statutory services for help and advice. The camaraderie between volunteers sustained them through the hardest of times and the cruelest of disappointments. The brand of volunteering they experienced was empowering.

From the beginning, some men were involved in the *WVS*. They were particularly engaged as drivers as there was a shortage of women with driving experience. However, there was an expectation that men would join the Home Guard, become firewatchers or Air Raid Wardens and they were reluctant to be seen as part of the *WVS* for fear of being considered as shirking their responsibilities.

The government expressed gratitude for the work of the WVS throughout the war but believed that, in peacetime, volunteers would not be required in significant numbers. Beveridge had outlined a plan which, many thought, would ensure that all needs were met by the State. By September 1945, the Home Office, which funded the *WVS*, wanted it to run down and announced that it would continue for "possibly" two years more.

But while the Home Office was contemplating ways of disengaging from the *WVS* the harsh winter months in1947, which included extensive flooding, demonstrated once again the value of a flexible voluntary organisation that could be mobilised in an emergency to work alongside statutory services. In April 1947 the Home Secretary announced that the government would continue to support the *WVS*. After some icy blasts from the cold war its position was further consolidated.

In 1962, the Ministry of Health recognised the value of peacetime volunteers and issued a circular recommending that the health service and local authorities should encourage volunteering. Four years later the *WVS* became the *Royal Women's' Voluntary Ser*vice, confirming that it was here to stay.

In 1968 a Home Office circular advised Probation Committees to consider the direct recruitment of volunteers by probation officers as well as working through voluntary organisations. Later, a Home Office Committee chaired by the Dowager Marchioness of Reading urged probation services to appoint their own volunteers to assist where long term personal relationships were likely to be forged with offenders. Volunteering had become an integral part of public services.

Without doubt, the *WVS/WRVS* has been one of the most successful voluntary movements of all time, galvanising the efforts of over one million women for a common purpose. Much of the activity undertaken by its members during the war and after required no special abilities beyond those of life experience. Some volunteers had valuable managerial and administrative skills which were put to good use. Flexible managerial arrangements enabled women with a variety of experience and skills to find fulfilling roles. Self-motivated volunteers were welcomed and their skills put to good use. Those with nursing experience were eagerly sought.

Guidance was provided from the centre but establishing control, direction, targets and standards were largely the responsibility of volunteers at local level. Arrangements were flexible and largely informal and they worked.

Whatever their experience and social background, volunteers worked as equals. Any deference between volunteers arose out of personal respect and not through a system of rank imposed by the organisation. If there was animosity between local organisers and their volunteers they had to patch up their differences or find other roles. Rank and file volunteers were king (or queen) and there was plenty of work to do without tolerating displeasing behaviour from others.

Two features of the WVS structure that helped to make it such a success were its loose organisational framework, which promoted flexibility and a management hierarchy that included volunteers at all levels. This was an organisation of volunteers – not of managers deploying volunteers. Local volunteers were an essential part of the decision-making machinery, helping to ensure that decisions were heavily influenced by people with experience on the ground. If necessary, they could explain decisions to volunteers who might feel their viewpoint was being ignored. There are lessons here today for some national organisations in which there is conflict between the centre where policy is decided and the localities where it is put into effect.

Propaganda from the *WVS* and the Home Office at the time, understandably, glossed over problems. Some would-be recruits found their local WVS office leaderless with no one able to give advice about how to join. Before enemy action made itself felt, a number of recruits felt deflated because no tasks were assigned to them. During such periods of inaction, women would seek other outlets for their enthusiasm such as the Air Raid Precautions Service or ambulance driving.

The fact that the *WVS* had a strong national identity and sense of purpose meant that it was a recognised brand and was trusted by the public. This was helped by the fact that key decisions were made by people who lived in the neighbourhood and were approachable. Staff in public services soon gained a clear idea of how the *WVS* could help them achieve their objectives and knew to whom they should turn if difficulties arose. Volunteers could move between different parts of the country or ask for assistance from another area and be sure that their needs were understood.

This was achieved at a time when less than one household in twenty had a telephone and the Internet had not been invented. Ownership of motorcars was at a low level while petrol rationing kept most cars that existed off the road.

The breadth of opportunities available through the *WVS* and the range of different responsibilities undertaken enabled volunteers to find their own niche and to move to different or more complex tasks if and when they felt ready. The organisation provided a broad framework; volunteers filled it out, gave it character and ensured it responded to local needs. Nowadays there is a tendency for voluntary organisations to specialise in specific needs. This can mean that their volunteers must more often move to another organisation if they feel unfulfilled; some are lost in the transition.

WVS gave volunteers a sense of empowerment. They could make a real difference to local services by their own efforts. There was little of the "we – they" problem which bedevilled so many organisations at a time when class differences were more marked than they are today. All shared in the joys, frustrations, sorrows and disappointments in equal measure. Volunteers felt that they were an important part of a team giving them a strong sense of belonging.

Volunteers were not shielded from the realities of war. The organisation depended on the inventiveness, enthusiasm and problem-solving ethos of its volunteers. Of course, there were tensions between personnel at the centre and those working in the localities but records suggest they were less virulent than in many national organisations today.

Although, increasing numbers of women entered the labour market between the wars, many, like teachers, left employment when they married. The WVS provided opportunities for tens of thousands of women to experience the challenge of important work which used their talents more fully. When the war ended they were in no mood to return to a life bounded by domesticity. The family with two wage earners gradually became the norm, particularly when labour-saving home appliances greatly reduced the drudgery of housework.

It is comforting to know that the aims of the WRVS today, as displayed on its official website are not strictly accurate. Under, "Our aims" it says it wants to make Britain a great place to grow old and to help older people get more out of life". It does not refer to children, families or people with disabilities; nor does in mention fire, flood and civil emergencies. But it provided emergency assistance in London following the bombings of 2005 and deployed emergency teams of volunteers to run more than a dozen rest centres during severe flooding in 2007. Old habits die hard.

The Home Guard

On 10th May 1940, Neville Chamberlain's administration was defeated in the House of Commons. Winston Churchill formed a new government as the German army raced through Holland and Belgium. By the end of the month they would reach Dunkirk. On 14th May, Anthony Eden, Secretary of State for War, announced the creation of a new force – *The Local Defence Volunteers* whose task it would be to prepare defences against possible invasion. All men between the ages of 17 and 65 years were invited to register with the police.

In practice, men over the age of 65 year were welcomed if they had military experience – and many of them did. Those registering were asked what experience they had with firearms and whether they were willing to serve away from home. They were not required to state their age or date of birth. It had been common in the First World War for young men to overstate their age in order to enlist; now there was an incentive for some to stay silent on the subject to get into the new defence force. Others made no secret of their age. A recruit in Crieff, Perthshire, was aged 80 years. He had been part of the force sent to relieve General Gordon at Khartoum and had served in both the Boer War and the Great War.

Eden's announcement was made just in time. Already there were rumours of enemy agents in the country and fears of parachutists falling from the skies as well as of sea-borne invasion. Civilians were arming themselves with shotguns and staves to patrol the beaches and the countryside. Over a quarter of a million men registered to become *Local Defence Volunteers* in the first 36 hours.

These new volunteers were impatient for action and, without waiting for instructions, began patrolling villages and towns. At this stage there was no organisational structure; nor were there arms and equipment. Some men – and their wives – improvised their own uniforms or searched in attics for old World War One tunics. They also devised LDV armbands[i]. They built up armouries from old guns smuggled home

---

[i] In June 1940 I won first prize as a Local Defence Volunteer in a children's fancy dress parade. A Box Brownie photograph shows me pushing an old bicycle with a World War One helmet over the handlebars. I was wearing a cut-down army battledress, a railway porter's peaked cap and a homemade

from the First World War, from theatrical props and even, in at least one case, the Boys' Brigade. But suitable ammunition was in short supply. Some units had rifles but no ammunition while others had ammunition and no rifles - the fortunes of war.

Eventually, the War Office provided some elderly rifles from the US and Canada but improvised weaponry continued in use, including Molotov Cocktails and a grenade firer which made use of a toy pistol cap. Gas pipes with bayonets welded to them were used as pikes leading to cries of "Gadzooks" from unkind bystanders as platoons passed by.

Local Defence Volunteers was not a good name. It did not easily roll off the tongue. Its members were soon lampooned as the *Look, Duck and Vanish Brigade* and the *Long Dentured Veterans*. At Churchill's insistence its name was changed in July 1940 to the Home Guard.

Many recruits remembered the excitement in 1914 when volunteers from across the country marched behind town bands to the local railway station on their way to war. They recognised that, whatever they were required to face could be no worse than that of their fathers, uncles and brothers before them. Some were probably

LDV armband. Apart from my ill-fitting cricket trousers, the ensemble was probably an accurate representation of local defence volunteers at the time. It is a snapshot for the archives. The LDV existed for only ten weeks from 15th May before its name was changed to the Home Guard.

hoping to avenge the death of close relatives in the earlier conflict.

A few retired soldiers welcomed the opportunity to march in their old uniforms. Society was still very class-ridden. Ex officers could demonstrate their superiority over other ranks in a way that was not possible in civilian life. In some parts of the country there was a surfeit of senior officers volunteering their services. East Sussex had six generals. A squad in London is said to have been composed of eight uniformed and bemeddled generals plus one civilian. Another had no one beneath the rank of major. The War Office estimated that 40% of the membership were veterans of the Great War but it was no easy matter to create a fighting force out of randomly recruited men.

By November 1940 the War Office overhauled the recruitment system by creating independent selection boards but the Home Guard was still bedevilled by the old boy network. Officers who did not like decisions that were made locally were inclined to raise their complaints directly with the War Office or with politicians – echoes of Lady Bountiful. The rank and file were more likely to be loyal to their commander but even they sought out local dignitaries like doctors, solicitors and councillors to argue their case.

Gradually standard uniforms were issued and parades began to look like the real thing. Predictably, under the War Office, red tape gradually grew. One volunteer complained of too many written instructions. "There seemed to be," he said, "a paragraph and sub paragraph to cover every tiniest event which could possibly happen, not only to every man, but to every buckle and bootlace.....many a man felt encouraged to take shelter behind an appropriate regulation rather than think and act for himself".

Discipline was difficult to enforce. If a farm labourer said he was needed on the farm during the lambing season he missed parades. Whatever the chagrin of officers, there was little they could do about it. Attempts by retired drill sergeants to improve performance on the parade ground had mixed results.

Mostly, local commanders knew that over-regulation would demoralise their men and sap individual initiative. A pragmatic view was taken of regulations about age limits and, despite the rules, men joined the *WVS* and women worked alongside men in the Home Guard as clerks, typists and cooks. Local groups took up Home Guard duties before they received authorisation to do so and, when the emergency had passed, forced the government to disband the organisation to avoid being faced by mass absenteeism. Volunteer power was a force to be reckoned with.

The War Office in Whitehall made the rules but local people decided how and to what extent they would be implemented. Much was left to local initiative. Instructions passed down the chain of command were interpreted to take into account local circumstances. Improvisation was encouraged and innovation rewarded. Receiving the King's shilling took away the civil rights of army recruits. Home Guard recruits did not take the shilling and their civil rights gave them a strong bargaining position. When services are donated, not bought, the donor holds most of the aces. These were civilians serving part time in the army – not soldiers serving as part time civilians. The result was a martinet's nightmare but, provided instructions were consistent with the purpose of the Home Guard, they were obeyed. An organisation that is volunteer-led can still behave responsibly.

Wise commanders took full advantage of the individual skills and aptitudes of their men when allocating responsibilities. They also understood that not every recruit found it easy to work as part of a team. Private Godfrey was affable to everyone but Private Frazer could be tetchy and domineering and felt that Godfrey was, "as soft as a cream puff". Even Captain Mainwaring knew that sending these two septuagenarians on a joint mission would end in disaster.

A major change in June 1942 meant that the Home Guard was, strictly, no longer a volunteer force. All men between the ages of 18 and 51 could be ordered to join and were liable to prosecution if they did not do 48 hours' training or guard duty each month. Once a member, they could not leave until they reached the age of 65 years.

In April 1943, *Women's* Home Guard *Auxiliaries* were created, recognising that if the rules prevented women from joining they would join anyway. But women were not provided with uniforms, helmets or respirators despite facing the same dangerous situations as men.

The force was never required to respond to an invasion but, during air raids, assisted with extinguishing incendiary bombs, clearing streets of rubble, guarding damaged buildings, redirecting traffic, undertaking rescue work and first aid. By 1944 its men were manning anti-aircraft guns and coastal batteries. It was sufficiently powerful for the army to take it into account when deciding how many men it could send abroad.

The potential dangers for recruits were not merely the possibility of hand-to-hand fighting following an invasion but a threat issued by the Third Reich that "civilians who take up arms against German soldiers are, under international law, no better than murderers, whether they be priests or bank clerks". Members of the Home Guard had no option but to be on the winning side.

About 1,000 members of the Home Guard were awarded medals and commendations, including four posthumously.

A small number of able Home Guard recruits were selected for one of the most secret and potentially dangerous tasks of the war. About 6,000 men and women were recruited to serve in small, heavily armed, guerrilla groups to operate behind enemy lines in the event of an invasion. Their official name was "Auxillies" but insiders called them "Scallywags" after the name given to white southerners who supported black emancipation during the American Civil War. Each group of Auxillies was allocated a one gallon jar of rum which could be consumed only to relieve pain in the event of injury or if capture was imminent, the notion being that this would help them resist interrogation or torture for a few hours.

As the threat of invasion receded it became increasingly difficult to keep up spirits and absenteeism became a problem. Men wanted to be with their families who were being harassed by flying bombs and V2 rockets. In September 1944 all parades were made voluntary again and the force was disbanded two months later. The War Office had doubtless learned lessons from the shambles in 1919 when thousands of soldiers refused to obey orders because their demobilisation was delayed after the cessation of hostilities. Members of the Home Guard were willing to work hard and to make sacrifices but only if there was a clear relationship between the sacrifices they were asked to make and the war effort. At its peak, the Home Guard had over 1¾ million men. More than 1200 were killed on duty or died from their wounds and nearly 600 were seriously wounded.

The spirit of comradeship and solidarity was important in ensuring cohesion but, beyond that, the Home Guard had a clear purpose. As soon as that purpose no longer existed there was nothing to galvanise men into action and other priorities in their lives took over. Doubtless, many friendships continued in the local pub and elsewhere but the Home Guard was more than about friendship; it was about a shared mission.

In the event of a new emergency it was clear that most of these men would willingly return to serve their country.

Both the WVS and the Home Guard were volunteering organisations but they operated in different ways. The Home Guard, through its military connections was more authoritarian but the end product was much the same. Home Guard discipline was more apparent than real. Men had responsibilities towards their families and employers as well as to the Home Guard. Morale would fall if men felt that unreasonable demands were being made upon them. They could only be governed by consent.

Men and women in the WVS and Home Guard were striving for ideals beyond themselves and their families. They made sacrifices. They put themselves in great danger for the common good. That was in the best traditions of volunteering. Some of the lessons learned before baby boomers were born are still being ignored by voluntary organisations and need to be rediscovered to revitalise voluntary effort.

Material in this chapter has largely been drawn from:
Bentley Beauman, Katherine. *Green Sleeves*. Seeley Service.1977.
Graves, Charles. *Women in Green*. Heinemann. 1948.
McCann, Graham. *Dad's Army*. Fourth Estate. 2001
Mosley, Leonard. *Backs to the Wall*. Random House. 1971.
Parker, Peter. *The Last Veteran. Harry Patch and the Legacy of War*. Fourth Estate. 2009.

Judith has volunteered all her life. She says, "one of the main benefits is the amazing people I have met and friendships forged over the years". During the war she was a bicycle courier carrying messages from Air Raid Wardens to the Town Hall (no mobile telephones then). She was also a Red Cross Nurse and then worked for the Citizen's Advice Bureau for 20 years, also becoming a bereavement counsellor. Now at the age of 81 she volunteers with RSVP because, she says, she wants to put something back into the community and it helps to keep her young. She says, "helping children to read is immensely satisfying and it is wonderful when they discover they can do it".

When Doris' husband died seven years ago she tried to fill her time by helping neighbours. Then a social worker introduced her to RSVP. She says, "I do befriending, look after disabled neighbours and generally help wherever I am needed. I enjoy the company. It's the kind of companionship you would get during the war. I don't have time to feel sorry for myself and I think I am really lucky".

CHAPTER SIX

The changing lives of older people

Grow old along with me; the best is yet to be
Browning

The ageing population impacts on families, communities, jobs and public services. Inevitably, there is a time lag between changes in social reality and society's response. The task is to shape public policy to respond to the material and social needs of an older population that is more sophisticated and more demanding than at the time the Welfare State was founded. A great deal can be achieved by changing attitudes and by mobilising the huge resource that large numbers of active older people represent.

Government advisers on the needs of older people have tended to be professionals from health and caring services. Their training and experience is based on identifying problematic behaviour and offering treatments to remedy it. That works well for major health and care problems but older people have other needs - to be needed, to be creative, to relate to others, to be personally fulfilled.

If their needs are studied mainly through the prism of caring professionals there is a danger that expensive and invasive remedies are applied before more straightforward solutions are tried and that older people unnecessarily surrender their independence to become patients and clients.

There is little pretence that health and social care providers work with users of their services on equal terms. Although many practitioners strive to do so, they carry too much real or imagined power. There is still concern about medical models of care for disabled people in which therapists concentrate on that part of the patient that is malfunctioning rather than on working to strengthen the part that is well.

In recent years, both at Westminster and in the devolved governments there has been a growing interest in developing holistic strategies for responding to the needs of disabled and older people. This has increasingly led to strategies using the older person as the frame of reference rather than service provision. Strategy documents now encompass health, social care, housing, environmental, transport and leisure services and refer to the need to assist older people retain their independence so that they play an active role in society. This has been a greatly encouraging development, brought about in part by intensive lobbying from voluntary organisations...

The terms, "older person" and "elderly" are often used to describe anyone over the age of 50 years - a period of up to sixty years. It is difficult to divide older people into neat categories. What they have in common is that they have passed their prime and are likely to become increasingly dependent on others. But some people are older at 50 than others are at 80. Ageing strikes us in different ways and over different timescales. At one extreme are healthy and active people in their 50's who have retired early on a good inflation-proof pension and, at the other, are those made unexpectedly redundant on a basic State pension and with failing health.

The home circumstances of older people have been improving but much unfit housing is still occupied by older people. Compared with fifty years ago, many more have hot water systems, central heating and labour saving devices for cooking, cleaning and laundering. This greatly assists self-care and facilitates support from family and friends.

In William Shakespeare's day older people usually carried on working until they were physically or mentally incapable of continuing. It is not surprising therefore that, in *As You Like It*, Shakespeare identified just two of the seven ages of man that related to old people – the active and the inactive. In the sixth age, he tells us, man becomes lean and shrunken with ill fitting clothes and a thin voice, liable to become the butt of jokes. In the seventh age he enters second childhood – "mere oblivion; sans eyes, sans taste, sans everything."

Most of us retain reasonably good health and an active life well into our seventies. Some active people are playing squash one day and are dead the next but, as body and minds age, for most of us, tasks that were once simple and straightforward slowly become more difficult. We all age in different ways but, if we live long enough, we are likely to be confronted by a range of disabilities, one at a time or in concert.

On retirement many people feel a sense of loss – of status, purpose and friends. Income is likely to be reduced – often severely – and adaption to a new lifestyle is required. New domestic routines and a new relationship with a spouse develop. People who regard themselves as experts and as important in the lives of those around them may suddenly feel, after retirement, that they are novices. The sense of loss may be so severe as to induce clinical depression.

Hearing loss may make us decide to withdraw from meetings. In pubs and restaurants, hearing aids pick up the sound of music and laughter from the other side of the room but not the conversation of members of the group round the table in front of us. Air conditioning that no one else seems to notice drowns out the man on the platform at formal meetings. Telephone conversations with insurance companies and the bank become arduous – why do call centre staff all have strong and unfamiliar accents?

After a traumatic episode like a stroke or broken bone we may return to near-normality but lose confidence in our abilities. The death of a partner is likely to require a significant change in lifestyle. When they outlive many friends and family older people are prone to loneliness and depression. The number of single person households in western countries is increasing. Much of this increase relates to older women. In Great Britain 30% of women over 65 years live alone. This rises to over 60% for women over the age of 75 years[163]. As we age we become frailer we are more likely to live by ourselves.

People living alone have a higher rate of heart attacks than others and have higher levels of coronary artery calcification. They have an increased risk of death from cardiovascular disease[164]. Most human beings thrive best when they share their lives with others.

Over one million older people in the UK go for a month without seeing any friends or family[165]. Nearly half a million older people tell researchers that they leave home once a week or less[166]. Clinical depression among older people is rising. One in five older people living in their own home suffers from depression; this rises to two out of five for those living in institutions[167].

Although many voluntary organisations offer befriending scheme, one or two visits each week still leave long periods of isolation for those who are immobile and live alone. Also, such visits do not necessarily appeal to people who have led active social lives hitherto. Many older people want to feel they are in charge of what happens to them and are unhappy to be on the receiving end of help.

Amid this gloomy portrayal of life in old age stand out two positives. Free bus passes widen opportunities for those who otherwise lack the funds to travel and encourage greater mobility. Secondly, for those with adequate incomes, recent years have seen a steady growth in the number of cafes, restaurants and gastro-pubs. At off-peak times they are often crowded with pensioners claiming age-related discounts. Perhaps eating-out has replaced the cinema-going of their youth. But this starkly reveals the importance of sufficient income to enjoy changing lifestyles.

One third of us are likely to develop problems of incontinence at some point in our adult lives[168]. At first, it may seem a minor problem but it can become increasingly embarrassing. Surveys have found that more than half of older people say that the lack of public toilets stops them going out as often as they would like[169]. 15% of men and women over the age of 65 years living at home have faecal incontinence[170] and incontinence is second only to dementia as the reason why older people enter residential care[171]. Nevertheless, incontinence is not an inevitable consequence of ageing and medical intervention can reduce some problems.

With a growing loss of independence the outside world may seem too terrifying to contemplate. Friends you have known for 60 and 70 years pass away and you are not well enough to travel to their funerals. You rely on others for shopping and preparing meals. Dementia may be closing in but, if you are fortunate, it will not affect your mood and life will not seem too bad as long as there are no surprises. But you may not be aware of the strain that is being put on your carers. On the other hand, if you suffer from agitated depression, you may be so heavily drugged that you are barely aware of what is happening around you.

The ageing process leads our relationships increasingly to revolve round our dependency needs. Reciprocity is replaced by obligation and enjoyment by gratitude. The simplest problem can present the most serious challenge; arranging a complex psycho-geriatric assessment or intricate and costly surgery may be easier than the collection of a prescription.

As our lives take us through this cycle of change fewer opportunities are presented for us to make and sustain mutually satisfying relationships. Physical and mental frailty focus our minds on ourselves, making us more inward-looking and less responsive to those around us. There are, of course, exceptions; some people experiencing considerable discomfort from their ailments continue to brighten the lives of those around them. That is a lesson for the rest of us.

Changing Social Conditions
Improved lifestyles, diet, hygiene and medical care enable very large numbers of older people not just to survive but to lead active and fulfilled lives for many years. There is some doubt about whether these trends will continue in an upward direction. Lack of exercise, over-eating and the impact of drink and drugs may see a downward trend in life expectancy in future years. Among people between 55 and 64 years, 76% of men and 68% of women are obese or overweight[172]. Perhaps the greatest contributions that older volunteering can make to human well being is to ensure that they remain physically active.

Neither age nor disability need be a barrier to volunteering. There are numerous examples of severely disabled people assisting others, like an 80 year old blind lady who counsels others who are becoming blind or the physically disabled man living in sheltered housing who organises a group of older volunteers in his local community.

Longitudinal studies of different cohorts of older people show that during the past sixty years they are generally fitter than earlier generations of the same age. The average 75 year old today probably has the functional ability of a 50 year old sixty years ago[173]. The bonnet-clad old ladies that we see in Victorian sepia photographs were probably aged about 45. For most people, retirement is now a time of reasonable health. Whether we die at 75, 85 or 95 it is normally only during the last two or three years of our lives that we lose our capacity for self care.

The cost of health, social care and income support for older people is a major part of the national budget. It is not surprising that the government is raising the pension age and encouraging older people to remain working longer. Coming generations of older people, will find that satisfactory pensions are difficult to achieve unless they are willing to work well into their 70's.

The proportion of men between the ages of 60 and 64 in the workforce persistently declined between 1961 and 2000 - from 91% to 47% [174].It then began to rise and was 57% in 2007[175]. In future, the proportion will depend on the availability of jobs although increases in pension age and the demise of final salary pension schemes are likely to encourage older people to work longer. But for most, retirement will not be a brief interregnum between work and death as it was up to the

1960's. For many it will represent twenty or more years of active life with new and, hopefully, exciting challenges.

Changing Community Life

But as lifestyles and expectations have changed, the communities in which older people live have been transformed. As indicated in chapter two, television is now all-pervasive, leading to more of life being led at home. More married women are in the labour force than previously, leaving fewer at home to care for older and disabled relatives. In 1900, about 6% of married women were in paid work. This rose to 42% in 1971. It is now in the region of 70% although figures are difficult to interpret because of the rise in cohabitation. However, 55% of mothers with children under five are in work as are 80% of mothers whose youngest child is 11-15 years[176]. Disabled and frail people are less likely than in previous years to have their day-by-day needs met by their daughters.

The corner shop, that social institution that once provided a venue for neighbourhood gossip and whose owner would be aware of the absence of a regular customer, is fast disappearing. In 1953, a study in an inner city area of Bristol showed that there was one shop for every sixteen dwellings[177]. Now, around 2,000 small independent shops are closing each year[178] as a result of internet shopping and the increase in the number of out-of-town supermarkets.

The number of vacant shops in high streets has increased dramatically since the credit crunch began. At the end of

2008 it was estimated that 5% of high street shops were vacant. In July 2011 the figure had risen to 14.5% with 45,000 vacant retail premises across the UK[179]. Some small market towns have become ghost towns, largely bereft of shops and shoppers. Many will never reopen. The social consequences of these changes will be significant for older and disabled people. In 2008, before the acceleration of closures, 10% of households in England containing people over the age of 75 years reported difficulty accessing shops[180]. An increase in home deliveries will mitigate some problems but people with restricted mobility will continue to lose some independence while their ability to socialise and make choices will be reduced.

Some older people remember when shop assistants in grocery stores carefully weighed and packaged produce before handing it to the customer thus allowing plenty of time for an exchange of views[i]. The personal attention could not fail to make the customer feel important. Today, anything more than a few clipped sentences between shopper and assistant is likely to lead to icy stares from impatient shoppers in a queue.

---

[i] At the village shop in Botley, Hampshire during the 1960's customers indicated the type of bacon they wanted and a joint was placed on the slicing machine. Customers would then be asked the thickness and quantity required. The sliced bacon was shown to the customer for approval and wrapped in greaseproof paper. A sheet of brown paper was then cut from a roll for the outer wrapping and tied with string before being handed to the customer.

Banks have been closing branches in great numbers. 3,000 closed their doors between 1995 and 2003[181]. The 2007 closure of post offices reduced their numbers by 2,500[182]. There are now less opportunities for postmasters and bank managers to know their customers personally and they are more likely than previously to live outside the neighbourhood of their business. About 12 small independent petrol stations close each week due to competition from supermarkets[183]. Some of these petrol outlets sell groceries following the closure of local shops. Now they are going too.

Even launderettes which replaced communal washhouses of an earlier age and served as local meeting places have passed their heyday. Public houses that have for long provided the backdrop for local gossip in soap operas have declined in numbers at an increasing rate. Gerry Sutcliffe, the then Parliamentary Under-Secretary (Sport) told the House of Commons in November 2009 that 2,377 public houses had closed during the previous 12 months.[184]

Bingo halls are also declining in number; figures are difficult to obtain but the industry reported in 2009 that numbers had fallen from more than 700 to about 590 "in recent years" with a further 100 under threat[185]. Bingo players smoke more than others in the population and the smoking ban is thought to have had an adverse effect on attendance. Reports suggest however that older people – many of whom are avid players - are greatly helped by the game. They do better than non-players in mental tests and significantly outperform younger players[186]

Increased car ownership, out of town shopping, the school run and car journeys to work have reduced the likelihood of casual meetings with neighbours in the street. Pavements which once jostled with local people going about their business are now more likely to be empty and silent. Various people whose jobs required them to knock on doors have melted away in the past fifty years. Rent collectors and caretakers with personal knowledge of vulnerable people have almost entirely disappeared. Payment of pensions and rent by direct debit reduce the chances of the death of a tenant living alone being discovered quickly.

Window cleaners are hard to find. The once ubiquitous insurance collector has become a rare species. The number of new policies in this branch of the insurance market fell by half in the early 1990's and the Prudential Assurance Society, which once visited one household in three, ceased accepting new business in 1995.

Christmas club collectors are being replaced by cheaper and more reliable arrangements. For some, household rubbish is deposited in a central place so collectors may not notice the absence of a bin. The demise of bread and milk delivery has further reduced the number of callers at the homes of isolated people. Coal deliverymen are going the same way as the rag and bone man, the knife grinder and the chimney sweep.

Gas and electricity meter readers are less in evidence than previously. One person now often carries out the functions of both and some meters can be read without accessing the premises while estimated bills are more common. Before long, technology will enable meters to be read remotely while electronic mail will threaten Postman Pat; only junk mail and the delivery of items bought on the Internet will save him. A time may come when we have the option of collecting our mail from a local depot or having it delivered for an extra charge. The growth of Internet shopping and home deliveries by supermarkets further lessen the need for frail people to leave their homes. This assists independence but further reduces social contact.

In former years, residential areas swarmed with tradesmen and public servants of all descriptions. The midwife, district nurse, health visitor, the school board man, the welfare officer, public health inspector, the probation officer and the policeman commonly travelled on foot or by bicycle, encountering customers and clients in the process. They were looked upon as part of the local community and mostly lived nearby. Now these staff often occupy offices remote from the neighbourhoods they serve and visit by car.

A veritable army of hawkers, dealers, traders and public servants have deserted the streets. Who can remember bookies' runners, lamp lighters and knockers up? Who will be next to go the same way?

The combination of these changes means that older people, especially those living alone, are more isolated than in former years. Urban life is no longer punctuated by regular calls at the door and a walk down the street no longer promises a succession of encounters with familiar faces. Largely emptied of the hustle and bustle of the world at work pavements no longer appear as safe as in former years. There are fewer pedestrians to spot and deter exuberant teenagers, vandals and criminals. Good role models are difficult to find in some residential areas. Guy Fawkes Night with its festivities round the bonfire has been largely replaced by the more boisterous Trick or Treat that can be more intimidating to those living alone. Even Christmas carollers are liable to be regarded as threatening or sinister. As a result, the environment appears less friendly and welcoming. More of life is lived behind the bolted and barred front door.

As indicated above, isolation and loneliness have become a major cause of depression and anxiety among older people. The use of new technology facilitates social inclusion and older volunteers have been at the forefront of projects encouraging older people, including those living in residential homes, to embrace the digital revolution.

Citizens Online is a national charity promoting universal internet access. In partnership with BT it is working in eight of the most disadvantaged and least connected communities in the UK. It has sponsored a number of well researched publications[187]. A government report has set out an action plan to achieve greater digital inclusion. It draws attention to a project by the Royal National Institute of Blind People Cymru (RNIB), funded by the Welsh Assembly in which "Digi Volunteers" have been recruited and trained to help blind and partially sighted people to make use of new technology. 80% of the volunteers suffer sight impairment. The report argues that:

> Digital technologies provide opportunities for new forms of volunteering ranging from mentoring to training and from home support to online shopping. There needs to be a national promotion and local campaigning to build up a cohort of digital equality volunteers which will include opportunities to

encourage children to engage in "reverse mentoring" of their parents and grandparents.

Just as neighbourhoods have undergone substantial change, medical and nursing services have been transformed. Surgeries, clinics and hospitals tend to draw on larger catchment areas than formerly making it necessary for patients to travel greater distances. Hospital stays have been getting shorter and medical interventions that once required in-patient treatment can now be undertaken by day attendance. The closure of long-stay beds means that large numbers of dependent people who would previously have lived for many years in hospital now live in the general community and risk being socially isolated. Patients with traumatic head injuries that would once have led to certain death now live a normal lifespan. Increasingly, patients with severe learning difficulties are living into old age.

As the number of people needing care increase the balance of responsibility is moving away from health and care professionals to individuals, families and communities at a time when their capacity for providing care is decreasing. Furthermore, developments in technology make it possible for patients to be interrogated by their family doctor remotely with the use of sophisticated diagnostic tools and prescribed treatments without personal contact.

These changes in local neighbourhoods can serve to isolate and marginalise older people. Just as some retirees need incentives to make financial provision for their retirement they need encouragement to enlarge the quality and quantity of their personal relationships to prepare for the future. There is a role here for voluntary organisations and local authorities. The provision of social activities, often financially supported by local authorities, has been the traditional way of responding to social isolation but this treats symptoms, not causes. One size and shape does not fit all. Volunteering projects can attract many more people to find fulfillment and lasting friendships.

With so many physically active people retiring, there is a growing pool of talent to be tapped for the benefit of the community. Nevertheless, social change is producing new generations of older people suffering from profound loneliness. There is clearly scope for baby boomers to transform volunteering and to improve their own lives by doing so. The next chapter considers the terms under which they may be expected to throw in their lot with the Big Society.

Muriel an 86 year old RSVP volunteer living in South Wales tours residential homes playing the electric organ. She bought it for her husband who was ill when he asked for something to help pass the time. However, he was too ill to make progress with it so Muriel decided to learn to play. She made her public debut at a fundraising concert for a leukaemia charity nine years ago. Her husband was present but died five weeks later.

Muriel has been on the entertainment circuit for ten years. She does not charge a fee. Sometimes, she says, concert organisers reject her offer of help on the grounds that she must be too old but she shrugs that off with a smile.

CHAPTER SEVEN

The baby boomers' life cycle

*There is no finer investment for any
community than putting milk into babies.*
Winston S. Churchill 1943.

Baby boomers are commonly regarded as those born between 1945 and 1964. They did not have an encouraging start in life. Born in the aftermath of a devastating war, many of them entered the world to live in sub standard housing. For much of the time food was rationed, fuel was scarce[i] and the world around them was drab. Clothes and toys were often hand-me-downs. In their early years there was no television and cinemas closed periodically in winter to save fuel. The wireless brought news of tensions between east and west and endlessly played the Warsaw Concerto, evocative of the recent death and destruction in that city. Children's entertainment was what they did on bombed sites. Schools were cold, dreary places. From these unpromising beginnings, baby boomers were to forge a new identity for Britain.

---

[i] In the long, hard winter of 1947 I worked in an office with no heating. I took my turn gathering wood from local common land and surreptitiously smuggled coal from home to keep the office warm.

Their parents were determined that they would have the best possible start in life and the new Labour Government demonstrated its priorities with free school milk and a burgeoning National Health Service. An Act in 1944 had already made sweeping changes to the education system, extending opportunities for higher and further education for many young people. The search for self advancement and fulfillment intensified.

Children born in the 1930's had been raised in a world where basic entitlements were limited. There was no National Health Service; a good education was chiefly the prerogative of those who could afford to pay for it; social security payments were largely discretionary and at a minimum. Employment rights were minimal and much employment was casual. Although those living in Council owned housing could usually expect reasonable standards there was a severe housing shortage and rents in the private sector were substantially determined by the market. Many dwellings were unfit; bathrooms and indoor lavatories were luxuries.

By the end of the next decade, despite a major war in the interim, baby boomers were born into a world of entitlements. For them, health, education, financial security and housing were basic human rights. The introduction of family allowances symbolised that the care of children was a shared responsibility between parents and the State. Gradually, the neglect and abuse of children was seen to arise more from failures in public services, than the behaviour of parents. The term "welfare rights" was coined in the 1960's as a replacement for "welfare benefits" to emphasise that they were entitlements while "applicants" for National Assistance became "claimants" for Supplementary Benefits.

The 1920's and 30's had been a time of perpetual mourning. Over 30% of British men aged 20 -24 in 1914 had been killed in action or died of wounds. Many others had been seriously wounded. Even happy family events were tinged with a half hidden tear. Family parties dissolved into melancholy when someone with a faraway look began singing a wartime song. In millions of homes, mantelpieces were weighed down by photographs of young men in uniform; the frames were lovingly dusted and polished every day to protect them from the smoke and soot of coal fires.

For over a century, Trafalgar Day had been an excuse to celebrate Britain's invincibility with flag-waving parades and patriotic speeches. Now the mood had changed. No more triumphalism. Every town and nearly every village had its war memorial lovingly tended by volunteers. In the inter-war years Armistice Day was rigorously observed with elaborate religious ceremonies focused on memorials. Mass Observation reported twenty years after the armistice that, overwhelmingly, the population observed the two minutes' silence. One veteran of the war related in the 1960's:

Into the 1930's, memories of the Great War remained indelibly printed in the minds of all who lived through it and the celebration of Armistice Day was very important. There was complete silence at 11am on 11th November each year. I once saw a coalman stand rigid for two minutes with a two hundred weight sack of coal on his back. Now the day is celebrated on the nearest Sunday. It has lost its meaning. Guy Fawkes Day is held on the exact anniversary but we celebrate the glorious dead of a whole generation when it is convenient[188].

Armistice Day, later renamed Remembrance Day, was and is, celebrated, not as a triumph but as a reminder of the folly of war. Reminders were continuous in the 1930's when former battlegrounds yielded up twenty or thirty bodies every week. The living were not allowed to forget. The inter-war generation was brought up in mourning and was not ready for the outburst of gaiety and exuberance of baby boomers that was to come in the 1960's.

The arrival of the baby boomer generation coincided with the publication in 1945 of "Dr Spock's Baby and Child Care" which encouraged a new approach to child-rearing. Spock urged parents to follow their instincts and encouraged them to believe in themselves. He believed that harsh discipline and didactic instruction inhibited a child's development. He was against rigid rules on matters such as feeding times but recognised that if a mother worked towards a schedule she could better plan her day. He could see no point in allowing a child to cry without offering comfort, saying that this relieved stress for the child and parent. Nevertheless, he argued for clear boundaries and a consistency of approach.

Much of this was in sharp contrast to previous expert advice. For example, Dr John Watson's guidance in a

1928 book[189] was that parents should never kiss their child, never hold a child on the lap and never rock its carriage. At that time some serious books were instructing parents on how to spank their children without leaving tell-tale marks.

Dr Spock's book sold about fifty million copies in forty two languages and is in the top ten of the world-wide best seller list. It had a profound impact on parents in the post-war years. When, later, baby boomers demonstrated against the Vietnam War, Spock's critics, including the preacher Norman Vincent Peale and Spiro Agnew the US Vice President blamed him for encouraging permissiveness in childhood. This was a misreading of his views. But if church and political leaders misunderstood the message it seems likely that many who tried to follow his guidance did so too.

Like all young people, those who reached maturity in the 1960's were rebellious. They had a lot to rebel against. Sexual repression was at its height. Donald McGill had been prosecuted in the previous decade for publishing saucy seaside postcards. It was not until 1960 that publishers risked publication of DH Lawrence's Lady Chatterley's Lover in the UK and faced a lengthy obscenity trial. Philip Larkin later captured the mood with his poem, Annus Mirabilis -

> Sexual intercourse began
> In nineteen sixty-three
> (Which was rather late for me) -
> Between the end of the *Chatterley* ban
> And the Beatles' first LP.

Young people in the 1960's were the first cohort in the western world for seventy years to reach the age of majority without being part of the grotesqueness of a major war. They could rebel without feeling that they were being unpatriotic, interrupting a process of mourning or being disrespectful to the dead. Nor were they thrust into a war to put right the errors of their grandparents. Furthermore, the absolute poverty that limited the life chances of previous generations of young people was lifting. Popular music, dance and fashion were designed specifically for the expanding pockets of the youth market, Young people were now the focus of attention and wanted to be seen and heard in what was still largely a drab post-war world.

They were no longer sure that patriotism was a good thing and were willing to say so. Articulate young people sought freedom of thought and distinguished themselves from older generations by demanding "Love, not War" and "Flower Power". This came to a head in the "Summer of Love" in 1967. They experimented with drugs and looked beyond traditional religious beliefs to Eastern philosophies and New Age practices for inspiration. They were suspicious of authority and determined to retain control over their lives. The ferment found a focus in protests against the Vietnam War where, for ideological reasons, the United States was engaged in a bitter struggle against a tiny country with a peasant economy.

It would be a mistake to believe that all young people took part in these activities. For many, life continued much as before but they could not fail to be influenced by the challenges to traditional authority that were taking place. They also shared the belief that they should wield more control over the institutions that shaped their lives.

The education reforms of the 1944 Butler Act were creating greater social mobility and higher education was expanding rapidly. New "red-brick" universities became sounding boards for ideas. New opportunities opened-up for the sons and daughters of manual workers who, while eagerly embracing a middle-class way of life wanted society to change. Young people who might formerly have concealed their working class origins obtained a certain cache by announcing what their fathers did for a living[i]. Sadly, the upsurge in social mobility was not to last.

The baby boomer generation's pursuit of rights and fulfillment was central to the student unrest that swept across Europe in 1968. They erected street barriers, had running battles with the police and occupied public buildings. They were telling the world that they were not prepared to accept what they saw as the Victorian heritage of rigid control and repression that two world wars had perpetuated. They wanted to break with the past, particularly with the kind of authoritarianism that sent so many unquestioning young men over the top to their deaths

---

[i] When I went up to university in the 1950's my grandmother asked whether anyone ever asked what my father did. It was well into the 1960's before I was happy to tell the world that he operated a bread-slicing machine at the local Co-op bakery.

in the First World War. If they were to make sacrifices they would not do so before being satisfied that it was necessary. The older generation, especially those who lived through two world wars, were not ready for the exuberance and self-indulgence of boomers as they came of age.

In Northern Ireland civil rights marches became more fervent and were taken over by hard men, rapidly developing into a sectarian conflict where it was almost impossible for citizens to remain neutral or for the voice of reason to be heard. Scottish independence is less complex than that of Ireland but it is noteworthy that the current controversy has evoked no call to arms. There will be no Black and Tans in Scotland.

The United States was also experiencing the wind of change in the 1960's. Civil rights marches, centering on racial segregation were at their height and there were clashes on university campuses as well in the streets about the Vietnam War. The half a million young people who celebrated at Woodstock in 1969 felt they were fashioning a new world and were as passionate about their beliefs as were their parents who took up arms against fascism over 25 years earlier. Young people on both sides of the Atlantic were engaged in a struggle to find an identity with which they could feel comfortable. Music festivals became, and remain, icons of youth against age.

The idealism of aspiring middle class baby boomers did not end with street demonstrations, flower power and the rock concerts of the 1960's. Indeed, these events were only symbols of a changing culture. As they matured, boomers continued to question fundamental attitudes on which society was based. As a result, most of the western world now has a widely different set of values from those that prevailed fifty years ago.

As boomers entered the workforce, growing affluence led to significant changes in social norms and values. Hard work and self-denial of earlier years gave way to a search for self-fulfillment and enjoyment both in and outside employment. This coincided with changes in employment where, with the decline of smoke-stack industries, work increasingly entailed the delegation of judgments and decision-making. More jobs required specific skills which provided a source of pride and self fulfillment for the workforce, offered challenges, personal growth, opportunities for creativity and empowerment. Yankelovich[190] believes the work-ethic in the US changed from one of stoic endurance, sacrifice and pain to satisfaction and fulfillment. The same trend can be seen across Europe.

Moreover, traditional values of loyalty to employers and respect for authority had been weakened. Baby boomers reserved their loyalty for members of the team with whom they worked. They challenged authority, believing that respect must be earned and that promotion should be based on performance – not length of service. Where they had a choice, personal satisfaction played an important part in the careers they selected.

Television was widening horizons. Informality in dress and behaviour changed relationships. Jeans became the clothing of choice. It was now respectable for men to watch Saturday afternoon football matches in leisure clothes instead of the three piece suits worn before the war.

There was greater informality in the workplace. Until the 1960's many, perhaps most male employees were referred to by surname, often without the prefix "Mr." In return, bosses were addressed as "sir"[i]. Once baby boomer bosses began addressing their workforce by their forenames justice demanded that employees used forenames in return. Staff who would previously have stood-up when their boss entered the room now remained seated and said, "Hi"[ii].

Young people set their own standards, underlined dramatically by the widespread use of the contraceptive pill. They displayed a confidence in themselves like

---

[i] In 1951 I was interviewed for a post of junior clerk in the City of London. Suddenly, the interviewer pushed back his chair and, with a look of contempt, said, "We don't want you here. Let me give you a word of advice. Next time you have a job interview try saying 'sir' a few times". I had just completed two years of National Service where I had been obliged to be obsequious to anyone with a stripe or a pip. Like returning servicemen from the war I had resolved never to call anyone "sir" again. Boomers were being taught from an early age that Jack was as good as his master.

[ii] I vividly recall an occasion in 1968 when I entered a room reserved for students. The six or seven young people looked surprised and uncomfortable; slowly, even reluctantly, they rose to their feet to acknowledge me. This was the last time anyone stood for me when I entered a room.

no previous generation. "Because I am worth it" became the justification for any extravagance. It had been common for men in some industries to refuse promotion because they did not want to be set apart from their workmates. Solidarity with and loyalty to colleagues was still prized but there was now a more competitive edge.

Until the 1950's, mental illness in the family was so shaming that many patients were locked away for twenty or thirty years even though they presented no harm to themselves or others. Some with florid symptoms now had them controlled by a new wave of drug treatments; the number of patients in long-stay Victorian mental hospitals declined sharply and the old lunatic asylums began to close.

Boomers challenged bigotry, intolerance and discrimination of all kinds. They fought for freedom of sexual expression. They ridiculed pomposity and were irreverent towards authority figures as exemplified by satirical late-night television programmes that started in the 1960's.

In 1936 it had been unthinkable for the heir to the throne to marry a divorcee. Seventy years later, the principle was barely remarked upon when Prince Charles and Camilla married. In the interval, civil partnerships and the ordination of women became widely accepted. A clear indication of differences in attitude between the generations is that most Catholics born before the 1940's still oppose the ordination of women priests whereas a large and growing majority of those born after welcome the change[191]. Papal infallibility is now barely an issue outside cloistered buildings.

With a decline in the influence of religious practices, traditional values of morality have largely been replaced by individual judgments of right and wrong. Boomers began constructing their own rules on personal conduct and it was acceptable for them to contemplate the duty they owed to themselves. Given their caution about submitting to authority it is not surprising that conventional religion has held less appeal for them. Boomers want to be members, not followers, initiators, not servants. They are uncomfortable with social hierarchies.

Father Gregory Jordan at the University of Queensland has come to similar conclusions about changing values. He has written:

> "Before the Second Vatican Council (1962-1965), Western Catholicism was characterised by the ideal of self-sacrifice, exemplified by the saints and heroes of the Catholic Tradition......The previous twenty five years had dramatically reinforced that ideal.......After Vatican 2, that ideal of self sacrifice gave way to a preoccupation with self fulfillment"

He describes this as a shift of emphasis "from doing one's duty to an insistence on rights"[192]. Other writers have identified self fulfillment as the spiritual quest of baby boomers looking for a less dogmatic approach to spirituality than conventional religions. Spiritual beliefs are now substantially personal, not institutional.

Not only did the ideal of self-sacrifice fall out of favour but admiration for ruthless, powerful men was re-evaluated. Until the Second World War, schools tended to eulogise warriors like King Richard 1st, the Duke of Marlborough and other men of action who slashed and burned their way through foreign lands. When Hitler and Stalin did the same, the appeal of such men as role models was lost. It became manly to protect the weak. Men were even seen pushing prams in the street. Social work, nursing and voluntary work were seen as worthy male occupations.

We now know that the drive for self-fulfillment during the latter part of the 60's and early 1970's was a watershed in the UK's social history. Changes in social values and behaviour coincided with a marked increase in the scale of almost every social problem described in chapter one. Baby boomers forged a new society and there was no brake pedal. Since the beginning of time, survival had depended on hard work and sacrifice. Now, self fulfillment became an important goal which, for some, exceeded all other ambitions. The big question is whether the current slide in social stability will continue or whether other values will be adopted that combines something of the old and the new.

It is not clear that the trend towards greater opportunities for self fulfillment at work continues. Businesses seek to transfer as much work as possible to machines which are easier to control than a workforce, can cost less, provide greater consistency and incorporate their own quality control. Modern technology can be far more intrusive for the workforce. Since the 1980's, the mobile telephone, the computer and CCTV have enslaved many work-people in ways that the overseer and the foreman never could and staff, such as those working in call centres now require less skill and have fewer opportunities to make personal judgments.

Baby boomers have lost none of their aspirations over the years. They have fought fiercely to personalise public services and to make them accountable to users. They have championed equal opportunities policies, the democratisation of public services, consumer power and the green movement. Freedom of expression is important to them and they have ensured that the Internet is not controlled by a bureaucracy. In retirement they expect to be in charge of their own lives and to choose their lifestyles. They are more articulate than their forbears and have better health as well as more political clout. They spend less of their time thinking about how to make ends meet and more planning life's next adventure.

Willetts[193] describes how baby boomers have gained financially at the expense of generations immediately before and after them. Some have generous pensions which, because of increased life expectancy, greatly exceed the value of the contributions made so the current working population, as well as funding its own pensions in a more realistic way, is required to fund the shortfall for baby boomers. Those pensioners whose house values increased exponentially in the boom years have, in some instances, traded down to enhance their pensions. This includes those who bought their council house at a discount. Working people today must pay high prices for houses with less likelihood of a substantial capital gain in future.

Furthermore, public debt is at its highest level ever as the boomer generation retires, leaving repayment to the next generation. Having enjoyed free university education in their youth, baby boomers are ensuring that future generations face a huge burden of debt if they decide to enter higher education. It could not have been better for them if it had been planned. But it must be remembered that these generalised statements do not apply to all baby boomers. Some missed out on the bonanza. For example, despite the boom in university education following the war, far fewer young people had the opportunity of a university education then than now.

As emotional wellbeing has come to be seen increasingly as a worthy objective, the wealthy have turned to therapists to unlock their inner strengths. But therapy is associated with illness and failure so, more recently, re-branded lifestyle gurus have emerged to persuade people with surplus income that their lives can be enhanced by physical and mental exercises. Others put their faith in making money. Those who feel left behind in the struggle for contentment sometimes turn to drugs. The number of antidepressants prescribed by the NHS in the UK doubled in the decade to 2010[194].

A striving for self-fulfillment is now universal in western societies. Success in the domestic sphere, in a career and in leisure activities are increasingly measured in terms of the fulfillment they bring to participants. There is no reason to believe this will change. Indeed, it seems likely that it will intensify and that volunteering will be an important vehicle for its expression. UK research published[195] in 2004 concluded that baby boomers were rejecting many of the traditional associations of old age by making personal fulfillment their priority. The authors thought "many will use their purchasing power, connections and self-awareness to dominate the images and rituals of popular culture".

The Tyranny of Freedom

Doing one's duty and being a good citizen require adherence to rules which have their origin in the mists of time and can generally be shown to benefit society. Self fulfillment, on the other hand requires us to make our own rules for only we can say what we find fulfilling. But the fulfillment of individuals can clash with the needs of society. Watching television game shows every evening or getting drunk on Saturday nights may feel fulfilling, even liberating for an individual but may look like damaging self indulgence to me. Who is to judge? Is the self fulfilled sinner on a par with the self fulfilled saint?

Despite rampant individualism and growing affluence providing a variety and choice of goods and services unknown in any other age we see all the signs of a collapsing society including an alarming growth in the incidence of clinical depression and other forms of mental illness. The surge away from self-sacrifice and towards self-fulfillment has coincided with increased single parenthood, family breakdown, an increase in abortions and unwanted children. These changes flow from an inability to make the sacrifices needed to ensure stability. If everything is judged merely by its impact on ourselves, society suffers. Yet if we return to the notion of self sacrifice who will prescribe the rules and what will be the sanctions for disobeying them?

We live in a culture in which self-determination and self-fulfillment are paraded as morally right and essential ingredients of a satisfactory life. We make choices about how and with whom we live that are unknown in some parts of the world. We find it difficult to understand that, in some cultures, people expect and applaud the fact that their lives are largely controlled by institutions that deny them choice.

Popular theory suggests that the more our wants and needs are met, the happier we shall become but this is clearly untrue. Perhaps, as freedom and choice are extended increasing numbers of people find the pressure of decision-making too great and break down under the strain. The accumulation of material goods has become socially important. "Keeping up with the Jones'" is a strong social and economic force and, by definition, some will fall behind to develop a sense of inferiority. The "credit crunch" of 2008 was largely fuelled by consumers over-committing themselves.

If our lives were mapped out for us so that we were not burdened with the need to work out our own choices a huge source of stress would be removed. There is support for this in research which shows that by limiting available choices it is sometimes possible to create a more satisfying experience because decision-making is made easier[196]. There seems little chance of society moving in that direction.

Erich Fromm argued that "freedom from the traditional bonds of medieval society, though giving the individual a new feeling of independence, at the same time made him feel alone and isolated, filled him with doubt and anxiety and drove him into new submission[197]". Perhaps the same forces account for the attraction of fascism in

Germany after the First World War and the growth of crime in the former Soviet Union when Communism was abandoned. It could also account for the high number of ex-servicemen in prison who are unable to adapt to civilian life. People who are used to submitting to external authority experience freedom as a tyranny.

This may explain why some older volunteers who have spent a lifetime performing routine jobs under close supervision are happy to work in organisations where they have little opportunity to make decisions. On the other hand, unless more volunteers are provided with challenging tasks we are in danger of under-utilising their potential.

The big question is whether the enormous social problems in some western countries are merely a temporary phenomenon as society adapts to a post industrial model of freedom and plenty. Japanese and Scandinavian experience suggests that choice and affluence can be achieved without the kind of tensions we see in the USA and UK.

The basic material needs of even impoverished people in western societies can now be met with little effort. A doctor's note or registration at a job centre can preserve the roof over our heads and provide a weekly income, albeit at a bare minimum. We can engage in a drunken brawl knowing that we are entitled to receive free care and treatment from the NHS for any injuries we sustain and we can get trapped in a pot-hole or stuck on a muddy beach safe in the knowledge that our rescue is written into someone's job description. These are unprecedented rights which have not been matched by increased responsibilities.

Service to others, freely given, is the basis of a civilised society and of personal fulfillment. As we have seen, volunteering does not flourish openly in totalitarian societies although it continues informally and is an important ingredient for a satisfactory and happy life. It is the task of government agencies and voluntary organisations to stimulate its development; but, as we shall see in later chapters, although volunteering can be encouraged and supported, attempts to control it render it less effective.

David, RSVP Schools Organiser in Swansea describes how, with three other volunteers, he assists slow readers at a school in a deprived area. At the end of one summer term, the volunteers were invited into the school hall for a "special assembly". After being welcomed by the Acting Head the children sang for them as a "thank-you" for their work

Each lady was presented with a bouquet and David was given a bottle of wine. They also received cards will messages of thanks from staff and children. David goes on:

"There have not been many times in my life when I have been lost for words but this was such an occasion. I struggled to pass on my thanks. In the ensuing farewells children and staff asked us if we would return. It is an 18 mile round trip for us but the distance will not influence our decision. Of course we'll go back!"

CHAPTER EIGHT

Volunteering and fulfillment

A Man's worst difficulties begin
when he is able to do as he likes,

T. H. Huxley

Researchers receive many different answers when they ask people why they volunteer but there appear to be two basic reasons. Firstly, volunteering is a means of learning or retaining skills that are necessary for the labour market. Secondly, it represents a search for fulfillment. Sometimes it is a combination of the two.

If researchers asked a random group of people why they eat, they would receive a number of different replies including, "I feel hungry", "to survive", and "because it is uncomfortable if I refrain". These replies all stem from a biological need to eat. It would be pointless to argue that, because they use different words to explain why they eat, people eat for different reasons. Similarly, if we ask people why they volunteer, some will say, "to fill my time", others, "to make new friends", "to do something useful", "to give something back to society". All these replies can be fitted into the portmanteau words, "self fulfillment".

There are several ways of describing the elusive quality of fulfillment including self-actualisation and self-realisation. It is a sense of wellbeing that occurs when intellect and emotion combine to focus intensely on achieving a goal. Fulfillment is a state of mind. People, in what may appear to be precisely the same circumstances, may feel fulfilled or not depending on their perceptions. It is largely related to feelings of contentment, satisfaction, a sense of achievement, of being needed and of optimism for the future. The absence of fulfillment is likely to induce feelings of dissatisfaction, of failure, alienation, boredom, depression and a detachment from others. There is a high correlation between fulfillment and mutually satisfying relationships with family, friends and neighbours while the lack of fulfillment is commonly associated with isolation, social exclusion and, in extreme circumstances, hostility towards others.

Our relationships with others largely determine our sense of self, of personal worth and of identity. Where citizens have little social interaction volunteering can fill a void by creating situations that promote purposeful relationships. Forty years ago, the London Borough of Hackney supported a workshop in which older people volunteered to dismantle telephones and other electronic equipment, placing components into separate boxes for future use. On the face of it this was soul-destroying work. Yet supervisors would tell visitors that a man or women who was smartly dressed and engaging others in conversation had joined the workshop a few weeks earlier in a dishevelled state, morose and unwilling or unable to converse. Working alongside others towards a common goal had transformed their lives.

Their previous employment had commonly revolved round repetitive work and familiar colleagues. Enforced retirement had led to serious depression which was only relieved when they were able to return to a similar occupation. Attendees were considered to be within the normal range of mental health. Some had become particularly vulnerable because of bereavement or impairment. They did not need expensive or invasive medical treatment but could return to a normal level of functioning and a degree of fulfillment by becoming part of a group and doing something they felt to be useful. It was not the physical activity that benefited them but the sense of belonging.

Some retirees miss the community spirit of the workplace. Those who have held responsible jobs miss the mental stimulation of their work while others who may have spent their working lives on jobs that were too small for them now have a chance to extend their horizons into something more creative.

Many older people, especially those who live alone, have few opportunities to make a positive difference to the world around them or to feel that they can contribute to the well-being of others. Consequently, they may lack a sense of self worth, withdrawing from the little contact they have with others. Opportunities for volunteering can be a great benefit to them.

In the 1950's and 60's the United States experienced a phenomenal growth in retirement villages which attracted customers by stressing the abundance of leisure facilities available. Retirement villages were sold as permitting unremitting rounds of golf, games of billiards, table tennis and shuffleboard and constant partying. Marc Freedman, who talked with some residents at the end of the 1990's concluded that a life built around activity for activity's sake could be vapid, self indulgent and boring. He found residents who clearly missed a purpose to their lives and who complained that they made little or no contribution to society[198].

This confirms the widespread belief that some men who eagerly anticipate retirement and the freedom it promises soon tire of endless rounds of golf, gardening and day time television. The human spirit needs more nourishment than can be provided by perpetual play. There is a fundamental human need to be needed, to feel that you contribute to the well-being of others and that you make a positive difference to the world around you. The more frail and dependent we become, the more these pressing imperatives determine whether our lives are endurable or unbearable, fulfilled or frustrated. Most retirees need challenges that match the intensity of the interests and relationships that surrounded their working lives. Domestic routines and do-it-yourself projects that looked so attractive as retirement loomed soon lose their lustre.

Volunteering that does not offer opportunities for self fulfillment and personal development for volunteers, that does not challenge them or explore their abilities is no more than exploitation and cheap labour. Sadly, some organisations take what is offered and give little in return. They sometimes have limited expectations of their volunteers; their priority is to make sure that the tasks assigned to the volunteer manager are carried out. Too many volunteers are kept on the treadmill of repetitive work when they have talents that could be developed. They may be excluded from tasks requiring flair and imagination in the mistaken belief that they are not suitable for volunteers, that they cannot be trusted to accept responsibility or because people in leadership positions do not understand the nature of volunteering.

Research[199] has shown that few volunteers take on more complex and responsible roles as they grow in experience and confidence. Yet in organisations that are geared to the needs of volunteers it is common for them to accept considerable responsibilities. RSVP has experience of recruiting volunteers who express dissatisfaction with the opportunities available to them in previous placements. Some transfer as a group to work within a regime which frees them to enlarge their knowledge and to develop their skills and interests.

In some organisations there is no one responsible for ensuring that the personal needs of volunteers are met or that opportunities are available for them to move to more complex work if, and when, they are ready. Many volunteer managers recognise this as their major responsibility but they must balance the needs of volunteers against the expectations of their employer. Unless, at the highest level, there is a culture of valuing volunteers for who they are as well as for what they do, unfulfilled volunteers may not stay. Ironically, volunteer managers are sometimes prevented from pursuing policies that would be more beneficial to the long term interests of their organisation than those adopted by their employer.

Organisations that fail to find ways of identifying the potential of their volunteers and releasing their enthusiasms and talents have a fraudulent prospectus and give volunteering a bad name. Volunteering will thrive only if volunteers can redefine it, shape it in their own terms and make it their own. Why would potential volunteers who are resourceful, independent, self-reliant and imaginative want to place themselves under the tutelage of an organisation that does not make use of their talents? They are the seed corn of sustainable volunteering and must be nurtured.

Employment among older people is at an all-time high and the average age of retirement is rising for both men and women. Two thirds of working pensioners are employed part-time[200] and some retired professional people have a portfolio of activities including part-time work, consultancy and volunteering. Older volunteering is competing head-on for recruits with the labour market and the leisure industry so volunteering opportunities must be tailored to suit individual needs.

Social policy documents tend to employ different terms to describe what is, essentially, the same phenomenon. When applied to social policy there is no material difference between the terms *fulfillment, social inclusion, self-actualisation* and *empowerment*. If you possess one in sufficient measure you are likely to possess all four, have a satisfactory level of self esteem and the basis for good mental health.

It is often said that volunteering, to be effective, must be fun. This is a sentiment I have often expressed but, at a training seminar, I was once rebuked by a volunteer who said she worked in a hospice where there was a great deal of suffering and sadness. She said that whatever words were used to describe volunteering, for her, it was certainly not fun. Of course she was right. Fun is a sign of engagement, of personal absorption and satisfaction. To be fulfilled we need to be transported outside ourselves; fun, enjoyment and pleasure are indicators that we are being fulfilled. Although it is usually an important ingredient of volunteering, fun is not always the most helpful way to explain why so many of us volunteer.

Volunteering can be a natural home for eccentrics and those who find themselves constantly rebelling against authority. They may find it difficult to conform to rules and the expectations of others but they can show passion, resourcefulness and unyielding attitudes. Their unorthodox views often represent a serious challenge to managers and organisers but they can bring new insights to old problems and think creatively. The world – and volunteering - would be duller without them. Research has found that eccentric people live longer and are happier than others[201].

It is not only volunteers who search for fulfillment. Many of the people volunteers set out to help seek a purpose in their lives. We all need a reason to get out of bed in the morning. People who are depressed, anxious, isolated or lonely may not have the confidence to step forward as volunteers and may need much persuasion; once enlisted they should be encouraged to lose themselves in work they find interesting.

Group bonding has been shown to be very important in time of war to keep up the spirits of combatants engaged in dangerous work. It is no accident that suicide rates in the USA and UK were at their lowest of the last century during both world wars. Physical danger could be endured if there was companionship and a sense of purpose; in war there was always something to do even if it was only queuing for food, digging for victory or boarding-up windows after a bomb blast. Inactivity, unemployment and poverty make life look a good deal bleaker than war. Doing nothing, although superficially attractive leads to boredom. Volunteering is a two way process and volunteers frequently say that they get more out of it than they put in.

Mostly, volunteers like to have personal contact with the people they help; that is why charities providing overseas aid frequently organise their fundraising to enable donors to have personal links with recipients. However, blood donors do not normally know the destination of their donation. In the UK blood donation is voluntary and the only practical reward is a cup of tea. Titmuss[202] compared voluntary and commercial blood donor schemes. He concluded that volunteer schemes were very much cheaper and were less likely to produce blood that would infect recipients. This arose because a voluntary system can be organised to provide a regular supply of blood whereas commercial systems are less predictable, relying heavily on donors in poor health whose blood is their only saleable asset and which is more likely to carry infections. He emphasised that commercial schemes, in effect, took blood from the poor and sold it to the wealthy. It was known that some donors sold their blood more than once a day when their funds were low, profoundly affecting their health.

In the year to March 2010, almost a million people pledged to help others after their death by registering their wishes on the NHS Organ Donor Register bringing the total to over 17 million. This is a very high figure bearing in mind that it involves donating an organ to an unknown person and that many of us are squeamish about surgery, even after death.

Legislation in 2006 legalised organ transplants from live donors. This commonly involves close family members but, every year, a small number of donations are made in which providers and recipients are strangers to one another. Live organ transplants are hazardous; donors risk complications from surgical procedures and become more exposed to health risks. This illustrates the complex factors behind the urge to volunteer. The common denominator is that volunteers all want to make a difference; but the conditions under which they are prepared to contribute vary.

Measuring personal fulfillment from volunteering
Fulfillment is a subjective experience and cannot be measured except in the broadest terms. However, we can rely on reports from volunteers when they indicate how volunteering has changed their lives and their mental state.

Research into the health and wellbeing of people who volunteer compared with those who do not concludes that it increases feelings of self-worth, happiness and well-being among volunteers. Those who help others catch fewer colds, have fewer migraines, eat more sensibly and sleep better than others. They have higher self esteem, a greater sense of control over their lives and improved mental and physical health. Asthma sufferers report that volunteering gives some relief from their symptoms and patients recovering from surgery do so more quickly when they help others. Volunteering strengthens the immune system and has been found to reduce symptoms of clinical depression. It significantly extends life expectancy by expanding retirees' social networks and increasing their access to resources. The happiest people have been found to be those who spend most money on others and who help others[203].

People living alone are more prone to a range of illnesses. They have fewer opportunities for social engagement, for making a positive difference to the world around them or to contribute to the well-being of others. Consequently, they may have a reduced sense of self worth, withdrawing from the few social contacts they have. Opportunities for volunteering can be a great benefit to them. Conversely, people who are socially involved with others have lower death rates. A Swedish study of 17,000 people found that those who were socially involved lived much longer than others[204]. In a study of over 400 wives and mothers in the US, those with multiple roles which included volunteering at least once a week were found to live longest[205]

In the US, researchers found that volunteering significantly reduced the chances of dying over a four-year period. The study at the University of California involved 6360 retirees aged over 65 years. Volunteering was strongly associated with lower death rates, with 12 percent of 1766 volunteers dying by 2006 compared to 26 percent of 4594 non-volunteers. Even after adjusting for numerous factors that could influence the results, such as socioeconomic status, chronic illnesses, and functional limitations, volunteering remained strongly correlated with lower death rates[206].

There has been increasing interest in the creation of volunteering opportunities for people facing challenges from physical and mental disabilities. They have the same need for fulfillment as the rest of the population but face barriers, both physical and attitudinal. Few are so frail that they can offer nothing to fellow humans.

Titmuss[207] drew attention to the fact that the exchange of gifts in primitive societies is not primarily a commercial or economic transaction. It has social, moral and religious meanings which may be far more important. Volunteering in the modern world connects us to basic human impulses to recognise and respond to the needs of others.

Hamilton examined academic research into human kindness and thought mutual trust and cooperation were "wired-into" the human brain[208]. Such a finding is not startling. From time immemorial, the family and the tribe have owed their survival to deeply embedded impulses to protect and defend the group. Paid employment tends to engage aggressive and competitive instincts to the detriment of compassion and altruism. That is one reason why, after a lifetime at the sharp end of earning a living, some older people feel they have at last found their niche in life when they engage in volunteering.

Volunteers retain a keen interest in who benefits from their labours. Titmuss[209] has shown that, where voluntary and commercial systems work side by side, the voluntary system loses volunteers. Until 1951, Japan relied entirely on voluntary blood donors. The Korean War increased the demand for blood so a commercial system was created. Within a few years the number of volunteer donors had declined and provided only 2% of the blood needed.

When local authorities transfer part of their meals on wheels service to paid staff, it becomes more difficult to sustain volunteering in the rest of the service. From discussion with volunteers, it seems that they are less willing to volunteer in a commercial residential home than in one run by a voluntary organisation or local authority. This suggests that volunteers will sacrifice time and effort to volunteer but lose enthusiasm when they know that others are paid for providing a similar service or that their endeavours could yield financial benefits to others. Privatisation and the introduction of commercial values to welfare services are almost certainly damaging altruism and voluntarism.

This should be borne in mind during the current debate about whether it is appropriate for charity Trustees to be remunerated. Representatives of all three major political parties have expressed support for payments, even suggesting that, on present trends, it is inevitable[210]. There is no record of consideration being given to the impact this could have on volunteers but it could be disastrous.

An informal (and unrepresentative) poll of baby boomer volunteers indicated that they would need persuading to offer their services to a charity that paid its trustees and would be less willing to fundraise for it. Grass-roots volunteers sometimes have more skills and spend more time on volunteer assignments than Trustees in the same organisation. They will be less enthusiastic if they know trustees are more highly valued. Researchers[211] in the United States have found that payments do not promote higher levels of engagement and that they are negatively associated with levels of Board activity in fundraising and community relations. They have concluded:

> We did not find evidence that compensating trustees help non-profits attract Board members with particular expertise. Boards that compensate were actually less likely to have members with professional backgrounds or expertise in management, law or accounting and no more or less likely to have members with expertise in the organisation's field of activity. Furthermore, compensation was not associated with achieving greater racial or ethnic diversity (P 11).

When this evidence is set against the possible impact on volunteer recruitment and retention and on fundraising it becomes clear that there are considerable risks involved in paying Trustees. It represents a threat to the current fragile standing of volunteering in philanthropic organisations and indicates a devaluing of volunteering. The values of the Big Society are already being sidelined by politicians.

John and Andy knew one another because they were both members of the local bowling league at Ypsilanti, a city with a population of 22,000 in Michigan. John was black and at 64 years, had retired from a hospital job. He had been on a kidney transplant waiting list for three years when Andy, a 33 year old white accountant, unexpectedly approached him offering to donate one of his kidneys. This occurred despite the differences in their ages, occupations and race.

Robert Putnam[212], Professor of Public Policy at Harvard University, relates this story saying that their bowling together made all the difference and that, "we Americans need to reconnect with one another".

CHAPTER NINE

Disadvantaged communities

We can scarcely hate anyone that we know
William Hazlitt

Council Housing

For sixty years until 1979, government house building programmes designed to provide quality housing for poor families, herded them together into large one-class estates. At first, they were built to a high standard and families eulogised about having indoor toilets, bathrooms and their own gardens but by the 1960's there was no pretence about the quality. Politicians, looking no further ahead than the next election, sought short-term solutions to a growing crisis. Families were decanted into high-rise blocks by local authorities seeking to maximise government subsidy that rose roughly in proportion to the height of the blocks they built. Cheap, prefabricated, tower blocks appeared across the country. They would not have been constructed for a free market because tenants did not want them but local authorities, loaded with government subsidies, stood between tenants and builders so the former had little choice.

As inner-city communities were broken-up, families were dispersed to bleak and uninviting areas with few amenities, often cut off by expensive public transport from jobs and leisure facilities. Many dwellings became damp and dilapidated through poor design and lack of maintenance. They were unfit for heroes or anyone else.

The most severe housing need was among families with children and new housing estates became notorious for their large numbers of unruly children and adolescents. Some estates had six times the national ratio of children with few facilities for them. Kirkby, a Liverpool overspill town, was the UK's fastest growing town in the 1950's and was reputed to have a higher birth-rate than Hong Kong.

The combination of poor design, low quality, high density, a lack of community facilities and a preponderance of children created a stigma that refuses to go away. Council estates (even those no longer owned by local councils) can be identified from a distance. Their drab uniformity gives the game away. As a one-time resident explained, "The privet hedges stop where the shirtless men shouting begins"[213] In the public mind, council estates are where the lifts are faulty, the rubbish chutes are blocked, the stair wells smell of urine and vomit, where there is crushing poverty and high unemployment where the use of drugs is common, where rubbish bins are used as impromptu braziers and burnt-out cars are the only public art.

Children on these estates attend local schools where it is difficult to maintain standards and discipline or to recruit teachers. Studies show that children who qualify for free school meals are half as likely to get five good GCSEs as their better-off peers[214].

Young people who cannot afford the bus fare to the city centre on Saturday evenings are likely to congregate on any available open space to "have a laugh" and perhaps deposit a few empty cider or perry bottles. Their parents are among the least likely in Europe to know where their children spend their leisure time[215].

All the indices of dysfunction described in chapter one are heightened among people living on Council estates. Furthermore, by the age of thirty years, tenants in public housing born in 1970 were twice as likely as the general population to suffer from mental health problems, eleven times more likely to be not in work, education or training and nine times more likely to live in a workless household[216].

Life expectancy on some estates is considerably lower than elsewhere. People living in the poorest neighbourhoods in England die, on average, seven years earlier than people living in the richest neighbourhoods[217] In Scotland, men in the least deprived 10% of areas live nearly 13½ years longer than those in the 10% most deprived areas[218]. Those with the good fortune to be born in Lenzie, Glasgow, can expect to live 28 years longer than those born on the Calton Estate a few miles away[219]. In parts of Glasgow, nearly six times more people die as a result of alcohol than anywhere else in the UK[220] and teenage girls living in the most deprived areas of Scotland are ten times more likely to become pregnant than those in the least deprived areas[221]. More strikingly, men living in disadvantaged areas of Scotland are 32 times more likely to die from assault than men in the most affluent areas of the country. The multiple for women is 35[222].

These figures demonstrate the powerlessness of estate dwellers to control their lives. It is no wonder that so many families give up hope. Only the most determined and resourceful find a way out. For most, the estate will dictate their lifestyle for as far as they can see ahead. Only in seriously deprived areas is the place where you are born a good indication of when and where you will die.

The Right to Buy policy under Margaret Thatcher did not have the expected impact. Dwellings were sold with up to 48% discounts against market value. Many purchasers realised their profits and moved to more salubrious locations as soon as they could. Some dwellings were snapped up by speculators who knew that political dogma forbade Councils from building new dwellings with receipts from the Right to Buy. But Councils had a statutory duty to house homeless people and eagerly rented ex Council property from speculators at inflated rents to meet the demand.

Children accept life on a Council estate as normal unless their parents provide radically different role models from those around them. If neighbouring children shout, swear, set light to recycling bins and pilfer from shops why not join them? Eventually businesses surrender and install metal shutters making the area feel more like a prison. If there is a pervading feeling of hopelessness, of failure, and oppression among adults and if they so self-evidently lack power to influence events and have no control over things that matter most, how can their children not share it?

Only parents displaying unusual strengths and values can prevent their children going with the flow. Where a child lives still determines his or her chances of educational success and the gap between achieving and underachieving areas continues to widen[223]. Education is the key to reducing poverty. Greater access to qualifications can be expected to lead to improved health, a higher income and a more fulfilled life.

It is reported that the parents of 1,100 children were caught lying in 2008 to obtain a place in the school of their choice[224]. The Chief Schools Adjudicator has estimated that this figure has since risen to 3,500[225]. How many of them came from Council estates is not disclosed but this is one of the few ways open to people living in disadvantaged areas to widen the life opportunities of their children.

Members of the political elite choose where to educate their children. Others want the same opportunities and some are willing to become involved in skullduggery if that is what it takes. What kind of person would not attempt to increase the life expectancy of their offspring by up to 28 years by seeking an education that will equip them to move out of a poor and declining area? Not to do so is close to child abuse. If large numbers of parents in deprived areas replicate the behavior of aspiring middle class parents there will be greater pressure for change.

A study by the Nationwide Building Society[226] reports that, across England, high performing primary schools add value to property in their localities. Areas with a 10% increase in SAT pass rates add a premium of between 2.6% in the south west to 3.5% in the north. In London it is estimated that buyers will pay an extra £8,000 to live in an area with a 10% increase in pass rates above the norm. One way or another, some people are priced out of a good education.

A possibly apocryphal story is told about a disadvantaged estate in the London Borough of Lewisham. A parliamentary candidate called at the house of two pensioners. "I know about your problems", he declared. "I was born on this estate and went to school here. In fact I still live here". The couple were unimpressed and, after he had gone the wife turned to her husband and said, "If he was born here and has even now not managed to get out there is not much he can do to help us".

Events in the early, formative years of life impress themselves on the psyche in a way that is difficult to shake off in later years. They create a state of mind and value systems by which we lead our lives and judge others. This has been described as "a wall within the head" in which adults live within mental confines determined by their upbringing. Those brought up in a housing estate often seem to feel unworthy, even inferior and their aspirations are often severely limited. Add to this the fact that many fail to obtain any kind of educational qualification and it is easy to understand why so many children brought up in one class estates find it difficult to break the mold.

Children brought up in poor surroundings are at an immense disadvantage. It has been found that traffic noise and the absence of greenery contribute to poor scholastic achievement. Their peers with less innate intelligence soon overtake them educationally. Education is not the only public service re-enforcing social exclusion and disadvantage. Dorling[227] has found that the majority of children living on or above the fourth floor in English tower blocks are black or Asian. The fact that Asian children attain a high level of educational achievement indicates that social disadvantage is many-faceted and that potential social disadvantage can be overcome by parental attitudes.

It has been a matter of choice for wealthy people to live apart from those who help to generate their fortunes. In the nineteenth century, rich industrialists were driven in their carriages everyday from their homes in Edgbaston to the smoky town centre of Birmingham where they made their money. Similarly, wealthy merchants and ship owners would be driven from Sefton Park to Liverpool docks. As transport systems improved they moved further afield, divorcing themselves even more from their work-people. Frances Peck, General Secretary of the Liverpool Personal Service Society from 1940 to 1965 expressed concern that ship owners and wealthy merchants who made their money in Liverpool largely spent it in the greener pastures of the Wirral. She saw it as important that they should spend time, energy and money helping poor citizens in the city which generated their wealth. As a way of emphasising her point she would sometimes say that volunteers were more important for who they were than what they did.

Unscalable walls have always oppressed the poor and disadvantaged whether they are inside looking out or outside looking in. In the dark ages, vagabonds, lunatics, thieves and those infested by disease lived outside fortified walls to subsist as best they could. Then it became more convenient to confine them behind high walls so that their superiors could safely travel the countryside. Now the wheel has turned full circle and the wealthy are entrenching themselves once more behind high walls in gated communities. They cross their drawbridges in 4 x 4's, reminiscent of army tanks.

Much the same process is occurring in parts of China. It is reported[228] that gated villages have, for years, been symbols of affluence enabling wealthy people to enjoy private schools, swimming pools and other superior facilities. But, to combat crime, authorities near Beijing are building fences round low-income villages where immigrant labourers are housed. Gates are closed at night and a rigid pass system severely restricts movement to and from the villages.

In the UK there have been significant transfers of land and property from the public sector to private ownership. Large areas of our cities, including streets and open spaces are now owned by property companies that are entitled to outlaw activities that have been an accepted part of town life for generations. They can ban skating, the taking of photographs, begging, demonstrations and the distribution of political leaflets. Residents can be forbidden to keep cats or dogs. It is easier for private companies to enforce such rules because they are not accountable to an electorate. The private citizen has no control over the rules and regulations imposed by commercial companies.

Volunteering in disadvantaged areas

Dorling describes what he calls the "Inverse Care Law" which says that in unequal societies, areas with the most ill and unhealthy residents are least well served by care services – despite attempts by government to redress the balance. By re-working 2001 census figures, he and Mary Shaw found a striking co-relation between locations where the population had great care needs and the willingness of local people to provide substantial amounts of voluntary assistance. Moreover, they found that many of the carers and many of the sick were living alone, that carers were likely themselves to suffer from poor health and that, often, there was no evidence of family ties.

Dorling says this evidence "changed what I believed about people". He continues:

> I know that many of us are kind but I was shocked to find that so many were so kind and caring as to give care when it is needed in almost perfect proportion to that need, free, not just at the time of delivery but, apparently, forever (p. 147).

The nature of volunteering in disadvantaged areas remains radically different from that in leafy suburbs. Research in the north of England confirms[229] that informal volunteering has a major impact on disadvantaged communities Some researchers have coined the term, "below the radar" to describe activities and organisations that do not appear on data-bases held by local authorities, the Charity Commission or Companies House. By definition it is difficult to know how many such organisations exist or the number of people involved. Estimates vary between 600,000 and 900,000 organisations[230]. A generous definition of the word "informal" suggests that the true number is very much higher and that most of us invest time and energy in organisations and networks that are under the radar. Researchers at Southampton University suggest that there are more such groups in disadvantaged neighbourhoods than elsewhere[231].

A Conservative Party report[232] unwisely described disadvantaged areas as "social deserts", where volunteering barely existed. There is more to volunteering than membership of an organisation and working within an administrative structure. It can be about offering help freely and informally to friends and neighbours in need. Such acts of kindness are not always recorded and cannot be readily colonised by organisations or recognised by people with clipboards ticking boxes but they are very real. Moreover, cuts in public expenditure are unlikely to reduce this area of voluntary enterprise.

Volunteering that does not fit the philanthropic template constructed by Lady Bountiful's descendents should not be ignored. What seems to be a social desert to outsiders may be socially active to people who live there. Like searching for tribes in the Amazon forests, explorers must know what they are looking for. Something that is out of sight still exists. It is not lost – it has simply not been found. Perhaps the greatest danger is that when voluntary activity is discovered in a disadvantaged neighbourhood it will be unwittingly destroyed by a missionary zeal to organise, improve and control it.

It needs great sensitivity, patience and understanding to build on the strengths that already exist in local communities and draw more people into community activities. Appendix 1 describes the work of RSVP in a disadvantaged neighbourhood of north London and shows the importance of local residents remaining in control.

Informal volunteering and self-help are empowering inasmuch as they are reciprocal and, unlike philanthropy, imply no stigma; power and authority are in the hands of local people. The Southampton researchers who studied a disadvantaged neighbourhood in South East England identified the modern equivalent of the "lady brigades" and "rival charitable eagles" that swooped on deprived areas in the nineteenth century. They described large, well established charities as essentially paternalistic and predatory which identified opportunities in 'deprivation funding' to run short term projects with no effective exit strategy. This left, "the deprived community with a distrust of new projects that are helecoptered into the area"[233]. Volunteer projects that are not embedded in the communities they serve are in danger of weakening community structures. There is a lesson here for funders. In disadvantaged areas - small is beautiful.

Social Cohesion
In the twenty first century large numbers of citizens in the UK suffer poverty, are confronted by racial abuse, racial taunts or overt discrimination. Some live in fear of intimidation from neighbours or teenage gangs. For

them, the social environment is oppressive – not supportive. It represents a hindrance to their aspirations that they cannot overcome.

These communities bear the brunt of unemployment, poor housing, and unsatisfactory schools and contain significant numbers of new immigrants. A House of Commons report[234] has indicated that regeneration schemes have sometimes led to resentment among indigenous white people who feel that they are being marginalised. Some believe that the lessons of the past are being ignored and that housing now under construction is as undesirable as the slums being replaced[235].

In 2001 Burnley and Oldham ignited with street violence between rival gangs, attacks on the police and damage to property. This exacerbated existing divisions and created further tensions.

An independent review team under the chairmanship of Tom Cantle[236] prepared a comprehensive report on the street violence. Its terms of reference emphasised the importance of consulting formal organisations and representative groups. But, for young people on the streets, these were, and are, irrelevant. The groups making up their world, giving them a sense of identity and self-esteem are not formal organisations with chairmen, secretaries, agendas and minutes. They are friends and family who meet in the street, pubs, clubs and one another's houses.

Like most committees of enquiry set up by bureaucracies, the committee consulted formal organisations and offered solutions that fitted a bureaucratic mould. But residents in disadvantaged neighbourhoods live in a parallel world to members of official committees. When they come together they may discuss the same issues but their words have different meanings. They employ different concepts and identify different solutions over different timescales. The values and characteristics of people who lead formal organisations are usually quite different from those who riot on the streets. No one can represent rioting residents except rioting residents themselves.

The challenge facing official enquiries is to understand the nature of disadvantage and how deprivation gnaws away at self-confidence and self-esteem so that daily humiliation and despair easily slip into violence. Few outside poor communities understand this. People like Attlee and Beveridge who spent part of their formative years living and working in poor areas had an instinctive understanding of the issues. So has President Obama who was a community worker in a disadvantaged area of Chicago before embarking on a political career. All three, not only worked among disadvantaged people but counted them among their personal friends. Sadly, most leading politicians today have been well insulated from the sharp end of society and fail to understand the hand-to-mouth existence led by so many people. They have not seen the strengths and resilience displayed by people facing the most gigantic odds.

Peggy, wife of Douglas Jay who was Economic Secretary to the Treasury in Attlee's government told the story of how Attlee once said to her husband, "Douglas, do you know that if you slip a piece of cardboard into your shoes it will help to keep your feet dry in wet weather?" Both politicians followed lifestyles that were not much different from many of their constituents. If a period of community service were included in the curricula of public schools whereby young people undertook tasks in socially deprived areas we might again breed politicians with a better understanding of the lives of their electorate. Only by living in a poor neighbourhood, making friends locally and sharing the joys and disappointments of local life is it possible to appreciate the toughness and the spirit of self sacrifice often present in these areas. National Citizens Service is commonly advanced as a means of helping children from poor backgrounds to improve their understanding of the world but affluent young people have the same need. As a colleague once commented, why not community service for toffs?

The Cantle committee's report listed a number of attributes it considered were present in a cohesive society. These include common values and civic culture, absence of general conflict, informal social control, tolerance, equal access to services and benefits, an acknowledgement of social obligations, a willingness to help others, a high degree of social interaction within communities and families, civic engagement, a strong attachment to place and an inter-twining of personal and place identity. This was an interesting academic discourse but offered little to rioting teenagers.

The report was a brave effort to understand factors that contributed to street rioting. It emphasised how local grievances were re enforced due to multi-faceted divisions caused by culture, language, religion, education and housing. It identified a challenging agenda for schools in disadvantaged areas, recognising that they need to extend their reach to influence parental attitudes. But it had few messages for the rest of society apart from policy makers and community leaders who were enjoined to open-up a public debate. Current divisions in society were not created by debate and require more than an extended dialogue if they are to be healed.

Rioters are not motivated by intellectual argument but by feelings of anger, resentment, alienation and frustration. They are desperate to express their sense of hopelessness about their day-to-day experiences of deprivation. To bring about change, their engagement with the rest of society must be tangible, offering hope, and support; it must give them a sense of belonging and a belief that they have something to contribute to the betterment of their own and other people's lives. Their experience of daily humiliation and despair can easily slip into open hostility and violence if they are provoked.

The Cantle report left far too much to politicians and community leaders who have had little success so far in creating cohesive communities. It failed to consider how to provide real empowerment and fulfillment to people whose aspirations, although modest, have largely been ignored.

The report failed to consider the position of older people. People over the age of 50 years make up about a third of the population. The proportion will rise to 50%

within 20 years. Trying to build cohesion by ignoring them is like launching a boat with a third of its hull missing. It will sink. Community cohesion is nothing unless it embraces the needs, aspirations and talents of everyone.

Rioting young people were front line troops providing the shock and awe. Behind them were substantial numbers of people of all ages who were discontent with their lot. Few older people march to the barricades but their sense of grievance is no less real. In stressing education Cantle confused symptoms for the disease. Older people are part of the problem but also part of the solution. Sadly, older people were omitted from the Cantle Report, referred to only in appendices prepared by others.

Social disorder in the summer of 2011 demonstrated the extent to which many people, especially those who are young and jobless, are alienated from society. As always, the police were targeted but the venom was largely directed towards industry and commerce – not nearby government and local government offices. Although some students and employed people took part, overwhelmingly participants appear to have been unemployed. They feel they have no stake in society and see little hope of influencing the world around them. Rioting and looting was an opportunity to experience empowerment in their own way in their own neighbourhoods and many clearly found this exhilarating.

There is general agreement that the 2011 riots were not racially inspired and, as shown in chapter one, research indicates that poverty is far more likely to create tensions among British people than ethnic diversity. Perhaps this means that the Cantle Committee's remit to investigate social cohesion following the Burnley and Oldham disturbances in 2001 was flawed.

Local newspapers frequently carry reports of mindless vandalism and casual crime. Letters columns are sometimes awash with references to yobbish street behaviour – often alcohol fuelled. It is common for older people to say they feel unsafe leaving their homes.

Most solutions proffered – and for which money has been available – have been designed to control, contain, punish and deter. They include antisocial behaviour orders, acceptable behaviour contracts, community wardens, harsher sentencing, volunteer patrols, more closed circuit television and higher police visibility. Although these measures have their place, they respond to symptoms not the fundamental malaise. Costly and confrontational, they re-enforce alienation and social division. They assume that the stick is more effective than the carrot.

At the heart of the problem is the lack of dialogue between young and old. The generations lead separate lives, insulated by different interests and organisations. They take possession of the streets and other public spaces at different times and have few opportunities for shared experiences which alone can develop understanding, mutual respect and trust. Many social organisations are insular and fail to reach out to others.

It should become the norm for organisations representing the interests of young and old – both statutory and voluntary – to develop joint activities. The young can benefit from the skills, knowledge and experience of older people while the energy and enthusiasm of the young can help relieve the practical problems and social isolation of frail and disabled people.

Volunteers have an important role in bridging the generational divide. Older people who assist school children to read or help in youth activities often comment that children greet them enthusiastically in the street instead of ignoring them. Young people helping to relieve the loneliness of frail, isolated people also develop new understandings. These are small but vital steps in building healthy, vibrant communities. Maggie Atkinson, the England Children's Commissioner said in 2010, "We have to find ways of getting the generations to talk to each other and break down barriers"[237].

Activities that cut across traditional organisational boundaries are difficult to achieve but communities should take up the challenge. It is common to hear complaints about the lack of joined-up thinking in government but an equally serious problem, is the absence of joined-up communities.

The curse of poverty
A key feature of disadvantaged communities is the high level of persistent unemployment which blights the lives of all age groups. Government money aimed at creating employment does not always produce the desired results because the money injected is spent elsewhere. Projects

aimed at regeneration have tended to appoint staff and consultants from outside the area, use construction companies that bus workmen in and send profits to shareholders far and wide. In these communities little of the money stays in the area to benefit local people. As one volunteer on an inner city estate observed, "The only people round here with flash cars are drug dealers and those working on the regeneration project." He regarded both groups with equal disdain on the basis that they thrived on the poverty of the indigenous population.

Supermarkets on the edge of the area similarly distribute profits widely; they buy their produce from afar and can only employ people with good transport links. Little of the money they generate finds its way into areas of disadvantage although they may attract significant sums from people living on public benefits. Public authorities are the biggest employers in poor areas but few health, housing education and social service professionals live locally and much of the public money invested immediately leaves the area.

The New Economics Foundation describes this phenomenon as "the leaky bucket" because, while government recognises the problem and contributes funds, the cash leaks out with very little reaching the pockets and purses of local people.[238] The Foundation goes on to describe how money injected into a community can have a multiplier effect if it circulates locally more than once. Actual figures will depend on many complex factors but the principle is sound – that money circulated in poor areas works harder for the local community than money spent elsewhere.

Let us suppose that a £100,000 contract for building repairs is allocated to a large company for work in a disadvantaged area. The only sum that will end up in the pockets of local people may be the money spent on lunches by workmen in the pub. If the contract is with a local business employing people from the area much more of it will be re-circulated locally. For example, after paying utility bills and rent, say, 60%, (£60,000) may be spent in the locality. If this money, now in the hands of local people is spent in the same way £36,000 is re-circulated, then £21,600 and so on. The original £100,000 puts more than £135,000 into the local economy as opposed to a few pounds for beer and sandwiches.

One study has shown how income from tourists staying in hotels mostly leaked away to non-local staff and shareholders whereas sums spent at guesthouses largely went into the local economy. Although hotel guests spent twice as much as those who stayed in guesthouses, less of the expenditure circulated locally. Local authorities can play an important role in channelling funds to disadvantaged areas by ensuring that local small businesses are encouraged to bid for contracts. Lambeth fast-tracks payments of invoices to small local firms. Southwark has donated surplus computer equipment to local voluntary organisations, making a huge difference to their viability.

The New Economics Foundation outlines ways in which local communities can work with public services to ensure that more public money benefits people living in disadvantaged areas. The wisdom of it is clear. It does not require increased budgets, just a different allocation of existing budgets. The financial regulations of public services are sometimes drawn so tightly that they prevent contracts being placed with available local businesses. It needs inspired leadership from local people who are passionate about their communities to challenge some conventional public policies that work against disadvantaged communities.

Some such communities suffer because they are seen as part of a larger area by major public services and the extent of their deprivation may not be recognised. Not only are the special needs of these areas overlooked but local people may be unwilling to bid for contracts to run services because they do not have the knowledge or inclination to operate in a wider geographical area.

Too often, large construction projects that profoundly affect communities are pushed through with inadequate thought given to their impact on the lives of local people. A topical example is the Olympic site in East London. Local residents live in some of the poorest neighbourhoods in Britain. They have suffered dust, noise and heavy traffic during the building of the London Olympic venue yet few of them have been offered construction jobs and not many will be able to afford tickets. They were promised that the Marathon would pass through their streets and angrily took the authorities to court when the decision was reversed. They will see little or nothing of the £400 million ticket money brought into the area by the Games.

Faith

In former times, religious belief was a powerful force for community cohesion. It relied for its effectiveness on a near universal belief system and a widely respected church hierarchy; religious display was an important part of the lives of the Victorian middle classes and aristocracy. Advancement in public life depended on being seen to observe religious practices. Being engaged in charitable work was perceived as an indication of religious devotion - although probably less than 25% of people in England and Wales attended weekly church services in the 1850's[239]. Many people did not understand the services or felt their clothing would be found unacceptable. Others saw it as a rich man's club.

The social status of church attendance created its own casualties. Non-believers seeking social advancement could feel like outcasts in their own country. With church and state united it was difficult to achieve civic office or a senior teaching post without at least adopting a form of religious practice. This persisted until recent times. In a witty autobiography[240], Jackie Kay, a woman of mixed race, describes how she was adopted by a communist Glasgow couple who had found it difficult to be accepted as adoptive parents because they were unwilling to lie about their religious beliefs. The adoption society found it easy enough to identify children for them when they said they would accept two of mixed race.

The unifying effect of religious beliefs that helped to build strong, cohesive communities has been lost as more and more dissenters have run up their flags and become bolder in announcing their separateness. The Christian religion is now one of a number of faiths claiming to offer a moral compass.

Community leaders come from a variety of faiths and none. For all the emphasis on church unity and interfaith relationships, few organisations see their role as developing cross-cultural activities as valued objectives in their own right. Despite genuine attempts to open their doors to the wider community and to extend a welcome to all there is anecdotal evidence that non-believers feel uncomfortable joining activities sponsored by religious groups and that the determination of church hierarchies to be inclusive is not always matched by their supporters at ground level.

To be true to their beliefs, faith-based organisations attempt to instil the notion that their central tenets are more worthy than those of other faiths. This promotes the very opposite of community cohesion. Indeed, some believers with extreme views deliberately set out to destroy cohesion. Events in the Middle East and Northern Ireland demonstrate how children, brought up in segregated communities accept stereotyped views of others and only meet on opposite sides of the barricades.

In the face of declining religious practices there is a noticeable tendency for religious organisations to claim common ground with other faiths rather than with agnostics as though any faith is better than none. For example, in analysing problems of family breakdown, poverty, addiction and homelessness the Salvation Army[241] declared that forgiveness was only found in faith.

Faith-based groups make an important contribution to social life in most communities. Their work is desperately needed. As a non-believer I argue that their deeds and mine are far more important to society than our personal belief-systems.

Comments by two volunteer organisers and a resident in disadvantaged neighbourhoods:

I was confronted by widespread apathy and a sense that nothing worthwhile could ever be achieved on the estate.

So many people have a lack of expectation about their older years.

I am housebound and my mobility is poor. I was invited to go on a day trip to Kew Gardens by minibus. I thoroughly enjoyed it. Since then I have two volunteers visiting me on a regular basis. They took me out for my 80th birthday. It was a real treat. I felt lost and very isolated until RSVP came into my life.

CHAPTER TEN

Deploying Volunteers

Where there is no vision the people perish

Proverb

Much literature about volunteering indicates the need for good management. Under the heading, *Managing Volunteers and Volunteering*, Volunteering England's report, Manifesto for Change[242], refers, in the space of twelve lines, to effective infrastructure, adequate management, careful management, good volunteer management, good management and effective management. Nowhere in the document are these terms defined.

What does management mean in the context of volunteering? As with apple pie, the wholesomeness of effective management cannot be questioned; but if its ingredients are not revealed and their relevance debated we are being asked to sign-up to a concept that means different things to different people.

By making such strong assertions about management the report implies that the only way for volunteering to be successful is for someone to control and supervise volunteers. But is this invariably true? Residents wishing to improve their neighbourhood may not want to be controlled by a manager especially one who is imposed from outside and does not know the area. Nor do they necessarily want to work within a hierarchical structure where they are at the bottom. It is not clear why the report rejected the idea that volunteers might be in charge of their own destinies with staff involved if, and as necessary to advise. Staff and volunteers can work in partnership without one controlling the other.

In a rare foray into voluntary work – including informal volunteering - the International Labour Office declared that, "what is not counted cannot be effectively managed"[243]. This statement betrays a yearning to manage volunteers. Yet to manage volunteering, especially informal volunteering may change it. Would the world be a better place if we knew exactly how many disabled people were helped by their neighbours? If I dig my neighbour's garden is this anyone else's business? More importantly, would the cost to collecting such data and keeping it up to date serve any useful purpose? If it is necessary to manage volunteers, is it also necessary to manage writers, artists and entertainers?

Services that start from the bottom up are more likely to gain the confidence and respect of local people and engage volunteers who are sometimes difficult to enlist – those who are poor, socially isolated or from minority ethnic groups. Provision that is devised, implemented and monitored locally is more likely to be sensitive to local needs and to be championed by local people. There is no reason to prevent volunteers from controlling budgets and staff although they may need help to gain the skills needed to do this effectively. When local people retain control of local services they have a greater incentive to make them succeed. They encourage more people to become volunteers and to take responsibility for activities in their neighbourhood. This is not to deny that some volunteers prefer to be organised by others but to attract as many people into volunteering as possible it is important to offer volunteering in a variety of different ways so that volunteers have a choice.

Where volunteers are supervised by paid managers, are the techniques needed the same as for managing staff? Could captains of industry grow volunteering like they grew manufacturing industry in the 19th and 20th centuries? If, on the other hand, managing volunteers requires specific skills or management arrangements that are not found elsewhere, what are they and does the management of older volunteers raise particular issues? Although studies of volunteering commonly criticise the quality of management, does that mean there should be more management, less or a change of style?

Vision

All organisations have objectives although small informal organsations may not write them down. Sometimes they are expressed in the form of a vision for the future or a mission statement. A clear vision, shared by all stakeholders helps to unify an organisation and is a valuable aid for getting across its message to the public. It is the beating heart of the organisation explaining what it is for, what it is trying to achieve, what distinguishes it from other organisations and how it will know when its work has been accomplished.

The following are statements of some leading charities taken from their websites:

A world where every older person has the opportunity and choice to get more out of life. WRVS

A society where everyone can participate to build healthy, enterprising, inclusive communities. Community Service Volunteers

(Our mission is to work to) break cycles of violence, hatred and despair by providing psychological, emotional and educational support to those affected by conflict. (We focus our) activities on children and young people, who have the greatest capacity to transcend the conflicts of their communities and to bring about change in the future. Action for Children

(We work) to improve later life for everyone by providing life-enhancing services and vital support. Age UK

(We help) people resolve their legal, money and other problems by providing free information and advice, and by influencing policy makers. Citizens Advice

All these organisations deploy volunteers in their work. It is noteworthy that, apart from Community Service Volunteers, they describe their mission as the provision of services: their volunteers are a means to an end, a way of enabling them to achieve their vision. In CSV, recruiting and deploying volunteers is the purpose of the organisation; it is seen as a way of enriching community life and, at the same time, providing services to people in need.

The WRVS statement is ambiguous because an older person might get more out of life by becoming a volunteer. Some do; the average age of a WRVS volunteer is 66 years. However the WRVS distinguishes in its literature between older people who receive help and volunteers who provide it by saying, "Our volunteers and staff work together to support people in need who might otherwise feel lonely and isolated, whether at home, in hospital, or in times of crisis." There seems no good reason for separating the sheep from the goats.

Values
Values refer to the way in which an organisation operates. Does it support diversity, respect confidentiality and encourage self-expression? Are service users, staff and volunteers consulted about the services provided? Are efforts made to ensure that volunteers have the best possible experience to develop their potential?

Some organisations regard it as important to articulate their values. The Red Cross, for example, lists its values as compassion, courage, inclusiveness and dynamism.

Speaking to older volunteers who have had an unsatisfactory volunteering experience, it appears that among the most important values they look for in organisations seeking to deploy them are honesty, openness, transparency, integrity, inclusivity and diversity. They look for an organisation that engages them in a dialogue about their role. For a significant number of volunteers, being consulted about changes and having the facility to influence policy are important indications of the value placed upon them. Equality of status between staff and volunteers also appears important. As we saw in earlier chapters these are all values that baby boomers have sought to make their own.

Many volunteers feel more comfortable in an organisation in which there are no rigid boundaries between what is regarded as work for staff and work for volunteers. Indeed, they look for shared leadership where volunteers are as likely as staff to take a prominent role depending on the skills required for a particular task. Studies in Northern Ireland suggest that the demarcation between the roles of staff and volunteers have been becoming more rigid[244]. This probably arises as paid managers replace volunteer organisers. It is an unfortunate development which could make it more difficult to persuade volunteers to take on organising roles.

Management Tasks
However well an organisation is managed, situations arise where the behaviour of a volunteer gives rise to concern making it necessary to investigate events or to confront him or her with the need to change. Where the volunteer is directly responsible to a member of staff this may be undertaken privately although if other volunteers are involved it may be necessary to consult them. Where a Volunteer Organiser stands between the errant volunteer and staff it is important that he or she is

included in the investigating and decision-making process so that, if possible there is agreement about the action to be taken. Volunteer organisers are not always happy to be involved but it is the only fair way to resolve a problem.

There is barely a limit to the extent to which responsibilities can be delegated to competent volunteers. It should be possible for those who are not stretched by the work provided to switch to other activities that better suit their needs. Managers should constantly ask themselves, "What am I doing that could just as well be done by one of my volunteers?" and "What help do my volunteers need to accept more responsibility?" Given the right environment, volunteers can provide the impetus and drive for services that money – even if it were available - cannot buy.

Volunteer managers must think outside the box. In any organisation there are always tasks waiting to be done, opportunities waiting to be seized and ideas that no one has found time to develop. At the same time there may be volunteers whose talents are not being fully utilised or who, with some encouragement, would acquit themselves well undertaking a more demanding task. Gifted managers identify possible openings for their volunteers and ask them to undertake tasks that make better use of their talents. Some volunteers may doubt their capacities making it necessary to provide extra help but it is probably true that more volunteers resign through boredom because they are offered only simple tasks than who resign because too much has been asked of them. Hoggart[245] quotes Bishop Wilson as saying,

"The number of those who need to be awakened is far greater than those who need comfort." The same probably applies to volunteers.

Managers and organisers should bear in mind the need for succession planning so that when vacancies arise tasks can, if necessary, be rearranged and current managers and organisers redeployed. In an organisation relying heavily on voluntary organisers it may be difficult to fill a vacancy with responsibilities for four or five hundred volunteers. However, a well managed organisation will have a network of volunteer organisers, some of whom may be prepared to accept greater responsibilities. A volunteering structure can divide and grow like an amoeba.

Volunteers who have a keen sense of ownership of a project or organisation display a greater willingness to accept responsibilities. Their commitment gives them a vested interest in its success. At this level, volunteering is more than wanting to be fulfilled. It is about a belief in the values that underpin the organisation and a willingness to make sacrifices for a good cause.

Managers sometimes find it more convenient to do things themselves than to delegate. They may rationalise this by saying that it saves time or that it is safer to keep all decision-making in one place. In an uncharacteristically harsh comment, Lady Reading said that managers who failed to delegate were selfish and that they probably lacked self-confidence, wanting to prove themselves. Managers who see their job as empowering volunteers find it easier to let go.

Too often, managers cite external reasons for their inability to attract and retain volunteers. They commonly place the blame on the high cost of living driving older people back to work, more working women or the availability of part time work in the area. Doubtless, these factors play a part but their impact is difficult to measure let alone do anything about. They can become excuses for failing to examine the turnover of volunteers or the impact of management processes on volunteer recruitment and retention.

Most organisations deploying volunteers have a narrow remit. They may work with children or old people, give advice or hold events. Not every would-be volunteer will be suitable for every area of activity. Before commencing the recruitment of volunteers organisations should ensure that they have details of other bodies in the vicinity to give to applicants who are unsuitable for them or who choose to look elsewhere. It is bad practice to allow a potential volunteer to walk away without offering an alternative. Some organisations have a policy of finding an opening for everyone who crosses their threshold. But only multi-purpose organisations can do that.

Volunteer managers are usually required to play a supporting role. A theatrical producer does not usurp the triumphs of the actors although he or she may appear with them to take a final bow. They must often resign themselves to influencing events from behind the scenes. If they want public recognition they are in the wrong profession. Their satisfaction comes from engaging in a flawless performance and watching hesitant volunteers blossom into confident achievers.

In his autobiography, Barack Obama describes how, as a young community worker in Chicago, he arranged for a group of residents from a poor district to meet the Mayor. His last words to them as the mayor arrived were to remind them to invite him to a rally later in the year. In their excitement they forgot. Obama describes his intense disappointment. He turned angrily to complain to a volunteer who replied, "You need to lighten up... (This) was the most fun Angela and them have had all year. Ten years from now, they'll be bragging about it...You made it happen."[246] So the future President of the United States learned from one of his volunteers that volunteers pursue their own agendas despite the best endeavours of managers. Moreover, he found that the process of volunteering can be more important than its end product.

It is important for managers to ensure that volunteering does not become an end in itself, isolating vulnerable people still further from their families and local communities. For example volunteers who befriend isolated older people sometimes say, with pride that, for the past two years, they have regularly visited an isolated old person and that, during that time, no other visitor has entered the house. Whilst this may reassure volunteers that their befriending scheme is reaching people in great need, we should hope that somewhere within the organisation questions are being asked about whether the befriending exercise is helping isolated people or volunteers. The aim should be to integrate isolated people into their families and communities, not provide substitutes. Befriending schemes that do not include attempts at developing other linkages are failing.

Intermediate Bodies

Mostly, volunteers are deployed and managed directly by the organisations in which they work but a number of organisations have followed the lead of the Women's Royal Voluntary Service in which volunteers are managed independently of the host organisation. Hospitals usually appoint volunteer managers, thus integrating volunteers into a wider team serving the public. This can lead to difficulties if volunteers have a different perception of their role from that of the manager or paymaster. Someone who is not locked into the structure more readily thinks outside the box and brings different insights to bear on familiar problems.

Strong volunteer managers represent the views of volunteers and may secure change but if they are part of the structure they will be expected to obey instructions. Structures do not work unless there is loyalty within them. It is difficult for a manager employed by a hospital to stand fast against a professional earning five times his or her salary. Where there is conflict such a manager is likely to support the hierarchy. Staff have trades unions and staff associations to speak on their behalf. Volunteers have no one to champion their cause if their immediate manager feels unable to do so and direct action can lead to uncertain and unwelcome results.

As we have recently seen with the Roman Catholic Church, when under pressure there is a tendency for even worthy individuals and organisations to protect the organisation rather than the principles on which it was founded. As a rule of thumb, the bigger the organisation and the more authoritarian its approach, the more there is a need for vigilance to ensure that bad practice is not condoned or concealed. It is no accident that the people most likely to blow the whistle on a failing organisation are students, junior staff and volunteers who have not absorbed the prevailing ethos and have less to lose than others by drawing attention to unsatisfactory behaviour and practices.[i]

Volunteers working in hospitals, hospices and care homes, as well as those in residential children's services, see much of the interplay between staff, patients/residents/children and relatives. They are well placed to judge the impact of domestic routines on residents. If they are managed by an intermediate organisation like the WRVS or RSVP they may be better able to draw attention to malpractices.

Intermediate bodies also benefit volunteers who are in membership of an organisation that has experience in a range of settings enabling them to switch between different work and different locations as their experience develops.

In the steps of Voltaire
Volunteers generally strive to reach the highest possible standard. It is unacceptable to provide something less because, "we are only volunteers". But in every field of service, if the best is not available it may be necessary to

---

[i] I have been told that at one time, volunteers operated in almost all of Islington's children's homes but they were gradually frozen out by staff. This was not fully understood until the child abuse scandal in 1992 revealed widespread abuse going back to the 1970's.

settle for something less. The barefoot doctors in China were usually farm workers taught enough to offer basic health care and served communities in rural areas where there were no doctors. There was no pretence that they offered the same services as a medical officer but they provided the best possible alternative at the time.

When Chad Varah began The Samaritans in 1953 there was widespread concern among mental health professionals that volunteers would be hopelessly out of their depth in responding to mentally disturbed people who were contemplating suicide and that they might even exacerbate problems. But mental health services were (and are) thin on the ground and difficult to access. Samaritans volunteers were instantly available at a time of crisis. No other service could provide that; they filled gaps in service provision, not by offering a watered-down mental health service but by offering human warmth and comfort when it was needed and easing the path into professional care.

It is important that we do not leave needy people without a service because we cannot offer the perfect package. As Voltaire said, *Le mieux est l'ennemi du bien* - the best is the enemy of the good.

Unless a defibrillator machine is on hand, a patient suffering heart failure is likely to survive no longer than eight minutes. Lives are saved at places like airports where machines are available but not in rural villages where it can take 20 minutes for an ambulance to arrive. For a modest cost, local communities can provide their own defibrillator at community centres and other places where people congregate. The principle is no different from the provision of life-belts on river and canal banks. Instructions for their use are clear and simple and machines can be programmed so that a voice tells the user how it operates and what to do. Experts say the machine is safe in the hands of amateurs.

Nevertheless, professionals and others have raised objections to the public availability of these machines on the basis that they are dangerous and should only be used by professionals. Yet, if any of us has heart failure and has less than eight minutes to live, who will object if an untrained passer-by attempts to save our lives? It should be recognised too, that the availability of a defibrillator is the surest way of gaining the interest and concern of local people. Every community group in the surrounding area asks for training in its use.

When a resident in Stourton, Wiltshire had heart failure it was an hour before an ambulance arrived. Villagers decided to take over a redundant public telephone box and installed a defibrillator. It is estimated that survival rates for heart failure victims in the village have increased by 80%[247].

Volunteers must be clear about their role and understand the limits of their competence. They are not shadow professionals but serve more as family friends helping out in emergencies, ensuring that the needs of the patient, client or user are understood and that his or her views are taken into account. By default, they may also find themselves ensuring that different services are coordinated

Task centred and volunteer centred management

Volunteers need leadership, someone who inspires them and ensures that they are focussed on the vision and values that brought them together. Management is not the same as leadership. An organisation may be headed by a pedestrian bureaucrat who ensures that t's are crossed and i's are dotted and leadership may come from elsewhere in the organisation. Too often, bureaucratic thinking blocks innovative developments and inspirational ideas get no further than the drawing board through lack of leadership. Successful organisations have the right blend of bureaucratic caution and entrepreneurial flair.

There are two extreme positions between which volunteering tasks fall. Firstly, there are tasks with precise functions, allowing little or no room for volunteers to influence policy or practice. A good example is a meals on wheels service. A volunteer may feel that he or she should be able to spend more time with recipients who are isolated and lonely but is likely to be told that any variation in the system will lead to delays and meals will be delivered cold. Hopefully, it will be possible to discuss other ways of alleviating loneliness among meals on wheels recipients but the volunteer can have only a marginal influence on the way the meals service operates.

This is task-centred volunteering but, it should be noted that the views of volunteers on the style and quality of meals should be considered. Other task-centred activities include those requiring great skill – like marriage guidance, counselling and advocacy where volunteers may learn complex skills and require close supervision. Volunteers who work in partnership with professionals also need to adhere to agreed forms of behaviour and there may be little room for them to influence the arrangements.

At the other extreme is a volunteer-centred approach where the purpose of the organisation is to enable volunteers to determine their field of activity and the tasks they will undertake. Such an organisation may include task-centred volunteering but there are likely to be more opportunities for volunteers to select from a range of activities and discuss the form that their involvement will take.

All organisations deploying volunteers lie somewhere between these two extremes. At one end of the spectrum are organisations in which volunteers agree to undertake specific functions; at the other end emphasis is placed on the empowerment of volunteers and their communities as a means of meeting the needs of local people.

An outside observer may not detect much difference in the service provided but for volunteers, a volunteer-centred service can be a much more exhilarating experience with opportunities to take greater responsibility for their work, to supervise others, to negotiate with partner organisations and to have a greater say in policy and practice. Not all volunteers want to take advantage of this expanded role but the fact that it exists draws-in and retains some exceptionally talented volunteers. In disadvantaged areas it can attract articulate and enthusiastic local people who wish to play a positive role in their communities and want to be regarded as part of the solution rather than part of the problem.

Complaints by Volunteers

Given the strong motivation among some volunteers it is not surprising that there are sometimes conflicts between volunteers and organisations that deploy them. Organisations established to meet specific service objectives are not always in tune with volunteers seeking fulfillment. As organisations increase in size and volunteers become remote from strategic decision-making there are increasing risks of misunderstandings and friction arising. Board members and the chief executive focus on the organisation's primary objectives and less thought may be given to the needs of volunteers who help achieve them.

There have been a number of well-publicised disputes between volunteers and organisations deploying them. In 2008 28 volunteers resigned from their organisation in York in protest at the treatment of a colleague who they felt had been dismissed unfairly. An independent review said there had been a failure of management and that trustees were guilty of a shortcoming in governance . The report recommended that the 28 volunteers should be given a formal apology and invited to return. The director and nine of the ten trustees resigned[248].

In another part of England a volunteer won an 18-month campaign for an apology from the organisation that dismissed her without warning. She said she had been given no right of appeal and that Board members refused mediation. Matters came to a head when she obtained national publicity. An independent enquiry found in favour of the volunteer saying that her dismissal was inappropriate, that it was not conducted properly and that the organisation did not provide an environment in which the volunteer felt respected or valued. It argued that an apology should be sent to the local MP who had been given false information about the circumstances of the dismissal[249].

In response to these and other incidents, Volunteering England set up an inquiry into the rights of volunteers. The inquiry team sought evidence from volunteers about their dissatisfactions and a dossier was prepared about bullying, intimidation and verbal abuse[250]. It is clear that some volunteers have good reason to complain but there are also some serial complainers who would test any system to the limit.

Conflict often arises between volunteers and organisations deploying them, not necessarily because of incompetent management but due to lack of clarity by governing bodies of the mission and values of their organisation, leaving both managers and volunteers trying to reconcile the irreconcilable. If volunteers searching for fulfillment join an organisation which recruits volunteers primarily to save costs, conflict may follow and services will suffer. More or different management training and codes of practice will not solve the problem unless there is a determination by Board members to change underlying values. It may be necessary to amend instruments of governance and make one trustee responsible for driving through improvements to the volunteer experience.

Possible solutions proffered in the Volunteering England report included legislation and statutory controls of volunteering as well as better management arrangements. There has been serious discussion of an official Ombudsman service for disaffected volunteers but it is difficult to believe that this would find favour with any government or that agreement could be reached about how the costs would be met. A Third Sector that cannot resolve its own internal problems is unlikely to cut much ice when advising government on social policy. One comment made to the enquiry team was, "The government should keep out of this altogether".

Volunteering England accepted that advice and invited organisations[251] to sign a document committing themselves to raising standards by following guidance on good practice and listening to the concerns of volunteers as well as agreeing that a trustee would have responsibility for monitoring complaints from volunteers. For the time being, the threat of more bureaucracy to counter complaints by volunteers has been held at bay but the ferocity with which demands have been made for government intervention suggests that we have not heard the last of it.

What do we mean by "well managed volunteers?"

The first paragraph in this chapter asked what the Commission for Volunteering meant by "well managed" volunteers. We can gain some idea of their thought processes by studying a horse from the same stable. The group responsible for preparing the Manifesto included three trustees from Volunteering England together with its former and present director. Volunteering England also manages the application of *Investing in Volunteers*[252] in England. This is described as a UK quality standard for organisations that involve volunteers and it is therefore reasonable to assume that *Investing in Volunteers* represents the views of the Commission for Volunteering on managing volunteers.

Investing in Volunteers has undergone many changes. A version issued in 2008 listed ten indicators that had been, "developed to cover all aspects of volunteer management". It was addressed to organisations deploying volunteers. A revision in 2010 was headed *Investing in Volunteers for Employers* and made slight modifications to the wording. It omitted the preamble about covering all aspects of volunteer management. Later in 2010 a further version was issued reinstating the original title and preamble. This version reduced the indicators to nine and deleted ten references to employers. By 2011 there were other changes to the document and it also incorporated the logo of the Wales Council for Voluntary Action

An undated version on the Internet in the autumn of 2011 with ten indicators contains the logos of Volunteering England, Volunteer Development Scotland, the Wales Council for Voluntary Action and the Volunteer Development Agency, Northern Ireland. It is headed, "Investing in Volunteers for Employers". It is clear that the authors struggled to establish both the purpose and the content of the document.

Indicator 2 says that the employer must commit "appropriate resources" for its work with volunteers. But some of the most impressive volunteer schemes have arisen from ideas formulated by local volunteers who then raise the necessary funds. It is often local people who know of friendly shopkeepers who might be willing to offer funds, who are aware of local charitable trusts and know neighbours in grant-making organisations like Rotary.

Some volunteers become experts at writing applications to charitable trusts, large companies, government departments and the European Union. Their role in fundraising can be crucial and this should be recognised in any document about volunteer management. Volunteers do not have an opportunity to use their abilities and skills if projects are presented to them only when the planning is complete and the funding is in place. Some potentially outstanding projects will never leave the drawing board if staff time must be found to raise funds before work commences.

Indicator 4 tasks the employer with promoting "appropriate opportunities for volunteering in line with its values which are of benefit to volunteers and the community. No reference is made to the need to take into account the wishes of volunteers about the work they will do.

Investing in Volunteers is an essay on controlling volunteers. It locks them out of key decision-making. Under these circumstances, they cannot be expected to take full ownership of projects in which they work. For that to happen there must be a co-ownership approach.

The document does not say that volunteers should be helped to develop their interests, talents, creativity and self expression. Managers and volunteers are not presented as partners working together and exchanging ideas. Unmistakably, a stratified structure is described that does not envisage employers or managers standing back to allow volunteers to take control. Volunteers are depicted as hewers of wood and drawers of water. They are passive players in a game in which the rules are made and applied by others. In practice it advocates the disempowerment of volunteers. This is not what substantial numbers of would-be volunteers want or need and will not necessarily deliver satisfactory services.

No reference is made to the vision or values that underpin successful volunteering. We are offered mechanistic, tick-box management. Nothing is offered to the potential volunteer who has his or her own ideas about how to solve local problems or who wants to play a key role in finding solutions. The process it describes is likely to deter some people, including those in disadvantaged areas, who are weary of outsiders parachuted into their midst with ideas and money, expecting local people to embrace them. No one should expect to colonise the social capital of a community unless they offer empowerment and self-determination in return. Managers must be able to help social entrepreneurs to blossom. Without this, formal volunteering will not reach its full potential and many baby boomers will be lost to volunteering forever.

Volunteering England's report, *Manifesto for Change,* was widely acclaimed by the volunteering industry although there was faint praise from some organisations that, presumably, were reluctant to swim against the tide of adulation. A letter from me published in "Third Sector" was the only expression of criticism I identified[253]. It said:

"The report is about process, not purpose, and does not satisfactorily address the imbalance of power between managers and volunteers. Unless those who earn their living by the efforts of volunteers make empowering them their number one priority, they merely encourage the use of cheap labour and fail to attract or retain some of the best volunteers.

The first duty of managers is to unlock the potential of their volunteers. A report that does not scream this from its pages misses the most important ingredient in revitalising volunteering for the twenty first century".

What are the values that underlie an organisation managed in the way envisaged by *Manifesto the Change* and *Investing in Volunteers*? Essentially they appear to be:

- Centralised decision-making and control.
- Risk avoidance at the expense of flexibility.
- Conformity prized more than flexibility.
- Volunteers are highly dependent on paid managers irrespective of their skills and talents.
- A clear separation of the roles of volunteers and staff.
- One-way learning - from staff to volunteers.

These values appear to exclude discussion, debate, criticism, argument or differences of view. Issues are presented as black and white. Signing-up to volunteering implies an acceptance of them.

But these are the brittle and uncompromising values of a reincarnated Lady Bountiful and her relationship with the poor. They bear no relation to David Cameron's vision of the Big Society in which power is devolved to communities and individuals within them. Nor, fortunately, do they represent the way in which the vast majority of volunteer managers operate. If managers in training are not encouraged to inquire into the way things are run, question traditional assumptions about management and debate alternatives how will they and their volunteers be equipped to challenge the way in which public services are delivered or to initiate change?

Manifesto for Change is a recipe for controlling volunteers, not releasing their talents. Management is about motivating people, not applying procedures. By failing to explore management issues the report is helping to sleepwalk volunteering into a morass of its own making.

> **Scottish athletics has the commitment and dedication of volunteers who support events 365 days of the year, over 80% of whom are over the age of 50. More than 70% are over 60. They provide a huge amount of technical and operational knowledge.**
>
> **Education and Development Manager, Scottish Athletics.**

CHAPTER ELEVEN

Is "management"
the right word?

Every profession has its secrets.
If it hadn't it wouldn't be a profession
H. H. Munro

There is little information available about the quality of the relationship between managers and volunteers and, as we have seen, although the word "management" may be used freely its meaning in the context of volunteering is not always clear. An otherwise useful report by the Department for Social Development in Northern Ireland[254] tells us that "good volunteer management should not be overly bureaucratic". By definition, all organisations are bureaucratic; only an organisation governed by a clear vision and agreed values is in a position to evaluate whether it is overly or under bureaucratic.

Octavia Hill who did so much to stimulate volunteering in the nineteenth century could be patronising towards the families she helped but was well ahead of her time in understanding the needs of her volunteers. She once said, "You cannot get the full benefit of heart and head and active will unless you give those who serve you responsibility, freedom of action and the opportunity of forming and striving to realise their own ideal"[255]. This is a lesson that is just as applicable 150 years later.

Meijs[256] argued that conventional management techniques need to be modified for highly motivated volunteers who perform well and feel more comfortable if they are virtually autonomous. He speculated whether management is the right word in these circumstances.

A manager once told me with unconscious irony that, among his most valued volunteers were several who refused to be managed. Discussion revealed that his habit was to keep volunteers on a tight rein but he had recognised that it was necessary to give some of them more freedom or he would risk losing their services. He negotiated individually with them and was unsure whether this was good management practice. Unwittingly, he had stumbled on the best way to work with volunteers.

After a lifetime's work older volunteers are often reluctant to place themselves in a position reminiscent of employment where they take instructions from others. They may have more life experience and relevant expertise than their paid manager and will only come forward if they can be sure that managers will feel comfortable with them. Some are not. It takes personally secure, well-balanced managers to work with volunteers with superior intellect or skill. Yet only in rigidly hierarchical organisations are managers expected to be omnipotent.

We shall never know how much untapped talent is lost to volunteering because managers find it difficult or impossible to work with talented volunteers. Observation suggests that older volunteers who have been employed in senior positions can quickly adapt to volunteering where they are treated as equals by people they respect. They have nothing to prove. It is no accident that the motto of the American Association of Retired Persons, is, "To serve, not to be served". AARP is the largest membership organisation in the United States after the Catholic Church, with 39 million members.

Some potential older volunteers are simply not attracted to offer their services to an organisation, which narrowly defines volunteer responsibilities and does not expect them to use their initiative. They may wish to stretch their wings, use their full talents and take on new challenges. They want to experience the thrill of achievement. They want to see a task through from start to finish. They do not necessarily want to be protected from the risk of failure or be treated like fragile porcelain.

The word that most closely defines the kind of management that is likely to motivate volunteers, particularly older volunteers, is "empowerment". This is a process of minimising the extent to which control is exercised, enabling volunteers to take the fullest possible responsibility for the work they do thereby unlocking talents that may otherwise not surface. This style of management motivates volunteers to achieve more, releases their creativity and heightens their sense of achievement. A good school tries to discover the potential of every pupil and then develops it whereas a mediocre school aims to mould pupils into a uniform product. Good practice for teaching children is also good practice for managing volunteers.

A study that considered the impact of older volunteers in government-funded projects in three disadvantaged neighbourhoods concluded that organisers must work towards the empowerment of volunteers. It went on, "This does not feature in orthodox management lexicons"[257].

Paid staff tend to borrow from the language of employment. Managers are expected to control what happens so their stock-in-trade tends to be rules and regulations. It is commonly asserted that volunteers should be provided with a written statement of their role or task. But borrowing this arrangement unthinkingly from employment practice can be unsatisfactory.

A job description provided by an employer is more than a statement of expectations. It is part of a contract, in return for which, the employee is remunerated. In volunteering, the organisation may set out guidelines about what is entailed in the work but the detail should be a matter for discussion and agreement with each individual volunteer. A description of the tasks to be performed should be jointly written, not mass-produced and handed down from above. Each volunteer has his or her own unique experiences, qualities and aptitudes and these must be reflected in the expectations of the organisation. If volunteers are to be more than numbers in an annual report they must be treated as individuals. Experienced volunteers are often in an ideal position to prepare task descriptions with and for new volunteers.

Job descriptions for staff are regarded as essential by human relations specialists because, among other things, they are indispensable for disciplining staff who underperform. However, some organisations would collapse altogether if every staff member adhered rigorously to the job description supplied.

Volunteers helping school children with their reading frequently identify other activities within the school that can benefit from their services and, in consultation with teachers, help with sports, gardening and cooking – all tasks that are labour intensive. Some of the most impressive volunteering schemes have developed haphazardly simply because there were no hard and fast task descriptions and volunteers determined how projects should develop in the light of their experience and in discussion with colleagues. Written task descriptions can be a straitjacket, preventing such volunteers from developing their talents and enthusiasms. Nevertheless, if a volunteer feels happier with a task description there is no reason why one should not be prepared. A study in 2008[258] found that just over half of organisations deploying volunteers issued task descriptions.

Organisations sometimes report that they can recruit no more volunteers because their management capacity is fully stretched. But in services where managers are constantly searching for ways of empowering their volunteers, a new recruit is not necessarily another individual to be managed but may be someone who can help manage the service. There are circumstances in which there is a finite limit to the number of volunteers an organisation can manage but by utilising the administrative, management and leadership skills of volunteers, that limit can often be further extended.

There is no agreement about staff/volunteer ratios that vary enormously even for similar work. Managers with five hundred volunteers are required to delegate and develop the capabilities of volunteers as fully as possible. They have no time to manage in any other way. Yet a manager with far fewer volunteers may be more stressed because he or she will have more oversight of day-to-day minutia and feel it essential to be aware of everything that happens. In their 2008 study, the Institute for Volunteering Research[259] found that 24% of volunteer managers were responsible for five or less volunteers and 53% for between six and fifty. It is clear that the single word, "management" has an elastic meaning if it is to be applied to managers who have both 5 and 500 volunteers reporting to them.

Experience suggests that contrary to expectations, higher staff/volunteer ratios can result in less responsiveness to the needs of volunteers. The bigger the bureaucracy, the busier staff are likely to become. In one organisation where I volunteered the insertion of an additional tier of management to respond to a rising workload delayed some decisions by up to three weeks; there was no discernable difference in the quality of decisions and the new manager constantly complained of overwork.

There is a tipping point where the staff/volunteer ratio changes the balance of power from top-down and staff-controlled to bottom-up and volunteer led. That point varies depending on the nature of the work undertaken but if more than about two-thirds of volunteers in an organisation are supervised by fellow volunteers that can be described as a volunteer-led organisation. Research is needed to increase our understanding of these issues.

The aim of some organisations is to raise enough money to convert from a volunteer-led to a staff-controlled body; but the acceptance of core funding to appoint paid staff has its dangers when a substantial proportion is contributed by one donor. What is given can be taken away leaving the organisation floundering. Any organisation accepting more than about 15% of its core funding from a single source risks being left stranded when funding comes to an end – as it always does. It takes considerable skill to divert offers of funding into acceptable channels and a strong nerve to reject money altogether but this can sometimes be necessary.

Some organisations are expressing concern about whether they will be able to respond to an increase in the number of volunteers as the boomer generation retires. Johnson[260] has suggested that some US organisations will choose not to engage older volunteers because funding will not be available. A more important question is whether baby boomers will tolerate the kind of structures that are being created for them.

We cannot know the number of would-be volunteers who are deterred or the number that give up in frustration when attempts are made to organise them like school children at a Sunday school outing. Nor do we know the extent to which volunteers who stay would have their experience enhanced by a different concept of management.

We know that, in disadvantaged neighbourhoods formal volunteering is at a low ebb and that, consequently, these areas do not attract the financial resources that are available elsewhere, impoverishing them still further. Residents often have a great suspicion of local politicians and public services. It may be that they do not wish to be colonised by middle class and middle-income outsiders. The solution lies in providing residents in these areas with the skills and confidence they need to take control. They need practical help, not direction.

Community Work

We saw in chapter four how two separate strands of volunteering developed in the nineteenth century. Lady Bountiful was the forerunner of the great Victorian philanthropic organisations in which volunteers were – and still are – deployed to meet the objectives and targets of a governing body. The term "management" which is commonly used by philanthropic organisations implies a power relationship in which volunteers are regulated and controlled. On the other hand, self-help organisations, which derive from the collaboration of groups of people protecting themselves from adversity create and run their own services and more often use the term "community work" to describe the skills needed to achieve cohesion and maintain discipline.

Government and other reports commonly refer to "the voluntary and community sectors" recognising that they represent two strands of voluntarism. They have different antecedents, lay different emphasis on the needs of volunteers and are structured and managed differently. They also have separate umbrella bodies.

There is no good reason for volunteering to remain divided in this way with one group eulogising traditional management skills as the way forward and the other identifying community work as the primary skill required. The fact that some organisations such as settlements and RSVP (see appendix 1) straddle both sectors suggests that the two strands can be combined with advantages to both. But, like the two communities in Northern Ireland, they have centuries of division and mutual suspicion to overcome.

The Big Society has already provoked clashes between the two camps. This may be helpful if it forces various factions to face up to the problem but the Big Society will fail to achieve its potential without a constructive dialogue. Lord Glasman is on record describing the body selected by the government to train 5,000 community workers for the Big Society as having a "paternalistic, eat your greens, don't smoke, don't swear approach". He said it lacked experience in working-class communities and was comprised of well-intentioned busybodies[261]. This is a caricature but neatly describes the relationship some philanthropic organisations have with their volunteers; it also represents the fears of some would-be volunteers about the organisations seeking to recruit them.

If they are to attract and retain baby boomers it will be necessary for philanthropic organisations to identify the talents of their volunteers and empower them in ways which are familiar to community workers. Volunteers mostly need facilitators, leaders and catalysts for change, not controllers or managers. Community workers manage situations, not people. They bring citizens together, promote discussion, pose questions and list possible solutions but decision-making is in the hands of local people. They help communities articulate problems but do not solve them. A community worker cannot empower others unless he or she is empowered.

Key tasks of the community worker are to ensure that local people articulate their own needs, that no one loses face, no one is manipulated and no one is bullied. During discussion it may be helpful for a community worker to draw on previous experience to identify what has worked and what has not worked elsewhere. If there is trust this will be accepted by the group as a valuable contribution. Progress can be slow and one task of the community worker is to bolster the optimism and confidence of the group by drawing attention to small gains as they occur. As one study of volunteers observed, "People want to see their participation makes a difference"[262].

The atmosphere should be one of mutual learning. The community worker knows the questions but only the group knows the answers that are right for them. They may need help to discover what answers suit them and to reach a consensus. Some volunteers need advice on composing letters or completing forms but this should be a learning experience so that less help is needed in future.

Community work encourages self-belief, releasing volunteers from a lifetime in which their self-expression may have been stifled and their spontaneity suppressed. For some, it provides a unique opportunity to develop their capacity to form personal relationships with people from many different walks of life. "Manager" is not only the wrong word but the wrong concept for most forms of volunteering.

The successful deployment of volunteers requires a cocktail of enablement, management, administration and teaching. The proportion of each ingredient depends on the volunteer and the task to be undertaken but enabling and teaching should always be more than half the total. A dash of humour is added and the mixture is topped up with genuine warmth and understanding. Some sprigs of leadership are essential to bring out the flavour. Appendix 1 shows how Community Service Volunteers' *Retired and Senior Volunteer Programme* (RSVP) has prospered by following this model.

Community work is a peripheral responsibility of several local authority services including those for children, adult care, housing and leisure. It has not been a core activity like teaching, social work or housing management and, until now, has not found a powerful champion to advance its cause. Perhaps the advent of the Big Society will bring a new impetus to its development.

Unless the purpose of volunteering is enunciated and the principles that underpin it are articulated, literature on the deployment and supervision of volunteers tends to be superficial. Critics may believe that the principles I have advanced are inappropriate and that, as a consequence, the style of management I favour is wrong. It is for them to show the principles and values that inform their preferred style so that judgements can be made about their merits. Volunteering cannot respond to the challenges of the Big Society until an agreed set of values is established.

> Fred Smith, a long-term unemployed man in his 50's lives in a disadvantaged area. He was advised to consider voluntary work and came to RSVP for advice. He became a volunteer driver taking frail people to hospital and GP surgeries and soon blossomed, becoming a Volunteer Organiser. Before long he had established three new transport schemes and recruited 37 drivers. They drive 2000 patients to medical appointments each year.
>
> This not only helps needy patients but helps to make the NHS more efficient as a family doctor can see six patients in his or her surgery for every home visit.
>
> **RSVP internal document**

CHAPTER TWELVE

The bureaucratisation
of volunteering

*The man who is denied the opportunity of
taking decisions of importance begins to regard
as important the decisions he is allowed to take*
C. Northcote Parkinson

In today's complex society, some level of bureaucracy is inevitable even for the smallest organisations engaging in voluntary work. This is particularly so if they wish to work in partnership with others. For example, local authorities may demand that health and safety and equal opportunities policies are in place, that there are robust accounting procedures and that the work undertaken is to their standards. Although bureaucracy is a creeping condition of modern society it is pleasing to note that the introduction of free bus passes for retired people has reduced form-filling and saves costs for volunteers and the organisations they serve. As one older volunteer told me, "When I am volunteering I am not spending money."

Organisations seeking funds for voluntary activity frequently complain of the complexities involved.

Application forms may require many hours of labour to complete by the most senior and experienced personnel. If matching funding is required, applications to more than one organisation may be necessary and subsequent reporting may be arduous.

Public authorities and charitable trusts feel more confident about providing funds for an organisation that is headed by staff, has a track record of achievement, works from an office and has the names of local worthies on its notepaper. It is not unusual for a group of volunteers providing a local service to be asked to join an established organisation if they wish to work alongside a statutory service or receive financial assistance. Although this can prove advantageous, it may entail a level of control that is not acceptable to the group which is required to choose between struggling to remain an independent, self-help organisation or accepting control within a larger philanthropic body.

Commercial businesses argue that, to prosper, they need financial stability that enables them to plan ahead. Many voluntary organisations rely on donations and other income that can fluctuate wildly. Any grants and contracts they have are likely to be short term with no certainty of renewal. Their staff are often on short-term contracts and likely to leave if a more secure post becomes available. When funding decisions or payments are delayed it may be necessary to issue redundancy notices that are rescinded if and when the blockage is cleared. This is a time-consuming and stressful exercise and is not the best way to provide top rate services.

Until recent years there have been no government regulations about the engagement of volunteers but growing concern about paedophilia has led to an expensive, complex and time consuming mechanism for checking the criminal records of staff and volunteers working with children and vulnerable adults

Whilst few people object to the principle of criminal records checks, this added a layer of bureaucracy, hindered spontaneity, created delays between the time a volunteer came forward and the time that volunteering could commence and demonstrated to volunteers that their enthusiasm to right wrongs was not entirely trusted. In any case, Criminal Records checks only reveal information about people who are known to the authorities so a clear record does not necessarily mean there is no risk.

In February 2011 the government announced new arrangements. In future checks will only cover those who have regular or close contact with vulnerable groups, defined as "regulated activity". But employers can, if they wish, obtain criminal records checks for others who work, paid or unpaid, with vulnerable people. Information in the checks will be continually updated and will not need to be renewed as staff or volunteers change jobs.

These changes remove some of the complexities in the system and ensure, once more, that responsibility for safeguarding vulnerable people lies with employers and individuals rather than the State. As the review document stated, "It is the effective management of risk rather than aversion of risk which is most likely to protect vulnerable people"[263]. It is the clear responsibility of the organisation concerned to make a judgement about an applicant's suitability as a volunteer.

Children's' charities report that too few men volunteer. According to research by charities, Action for Children and Chance UK, 17% of men surveyed who did not want to work with children, were unwilling because they did not wish to have a criminal records check. A further 13% said they were afraid of being suspected of paedophilia if they said they wanted to work with children[264]. Would Dr Barnardo agree to have a criminal records check if he were alive today?

Sharp increases in the number of fatherless families in the past thirty years mean that many children are brought up in households with little contact with men. It has sometimes been said that, for this reason, the most popular member of staff in a day nursery is the caretaker. He provides one of the few opportunities for some young children to enjoy any kind of relationship with a man. The engagement of more men in volunteering projects with children is a means of addressing this issue. Less intrusive checking procedures may allay some fears expressed by would-be male volunteers.

Older men probably find satisfaction in less formal pursuits than joining formal organisations and after a lifetime in the employment market they are less inclined to accept the real or imagined constraints that accompany any kind of supervised work. They look for freedom to do their own thing, perhaps to experiment and to work in an environment where their associates are equals. This makes it more necessary to reduce barriers that prevent men volunteering.

Legislation on equality is so complex that a specialist solicitor is required to give a definitive ruling if a charity wishes to restrict its services to certain groups of people. The legislation aims to prevent discrimination on grounds of age; disability; gender reassignment; marriage and civil partnership; pregnancy and maternity; race; religion or belief; sex; or sexual orientation. These categories are known in the Equalities Act 2010 as "protected characteristics" and charities may only restrict benefits to people so defined under certain conditions. The Charity Commission's summary guidance to the Act covers eight pages[265]. Other guidance has been issued by the Government Equalities Office, Volunteering England and the Equality and Human Rights Commission.

Although managers will wish to ensure that their organisations comply, it is quite possible that, on grounds of conscience, a group of volunteers will decide to discriminate against paedophiles, transvestites or some other category on the protected characteristics list. To avoid breaking the law they could try to form themselves into a religious cult. Another solution would be to remain an informal group. It would be understandable if someone who had been sexually abused as a child refused to work with a paedophile.

The desirability of anti discrimination policies are clear but legal requirements not only add to the cost of government but add costs to voluntary organisations, inhibit spontaneity and deter small community groups from providing services.

Guidance issued by the United Kingdom Border Agency indicates[266] that asylum seekers can volunteer in the voluntary sector but not in the public sector. This means that they can volunteer in a hospital canteen that is run by a charity but not one run directly by an NHS Trust.

Volunteer drivers commonly use their own cars to drive frail patients to hospital appointments. Some of them report that insurance companies demand a business insurance premium which prompts them to withdraw their service. After much lobbying by voluntary groups, the Association of British Insurers announced[267] in 2011 that companies representing 85% of the motor insurance market would not, in future increase premiums for drivers using their cars for local voluntary work.

There is uncertainty in some Jobcentres about volunteers claiming Jobseekers Allowance and it is reported[268] that some centres cut benefits on the assumption that fraud is taking place.

Many forces are weakening the position of volunteers. Carnivals, fetes and festivals, once common occurrences in local communities, are increasingly surrounded by health and safety issues as well as police and fire regulations. Four different licenses, registrations and consents can apply where food is prepared and served. Regulatory frameworks have tightened for doing almost anything; a volunteer tidying a verge or roundabout on a public highway outside his or her house is liable to be instructed to wear a florescent jacket and engage a second volunteer as lookout.

Almost any public event requires knowledge of licenses. The local licensing authority may need to give approval for playing music, for dancing, sporting events, theatrical performances and bingo. The Performing Rights Society will have an interest if copyrighted music is played and it may be necessary to have a separate license to play recorded music. The supply of alcohol has its own network of notices and licenses. Where events are held on public land it is necessary to obtain permission from the authority concerned. If a festival or other event requires the closure of a street, ample advance notice must be given and a license is required from the local authority.

Depending on the circumstances there are nine separate licenses concerned with showing films, videos or television programmes. Raffles and lotteries may have to be registered with the local authority or the Gambling Commission.

Each regulation originates from a sensible desire to protect the public but together they create an insurmountable barrier to many neighbourhood groups wanting to organise community activities. There is little doubt that the rules and regulations are widely flouted. As we have seen, totalitarian regimes closely regulate charities to ensure they do not usurp the power of the State. In the UK our regulatory framework is light until charities actually begin to do something. The effect is stifling. There may be a case for waving some of the regulations for small local voluntary groups and for the appointment of enablers to lead charities through the labyrinthine paths of the bureaucratic process. If there are no changes and attempts are made to fully enforce the law, community activities will decline still further.

In 2011 Lord Hodgson's Task Force on how to cut red tape for small charities, voluntary organisations and social enterprises reported.[269] A number of committees had already considered how some of the bureaucracy could be removed from volunteering but solutions had been difficult to find. Alas, although Lord Hodgson threw some light on a range of issues, he failed to identify a golden bullet that would release volunteering from its shackles. His one positive recommendation on volunteering was that posters should be displayed in job centres reminding visitors and staff of the benefits of volunteering. Other recommendations asked the Attorney General, the Law Commission and the Government to consider technical issues about the liability of volunteers and for a working party to further consider matters relating to insurance. In its White Paper on Open Public Services the government announced its intention to simplify health and safety regulations[270]

High insurance premiums are the other side of the coin, pricing some long-standing events out of existence. Those that remain are often run by large organisations employing staff. Local neighbourhood volunteers are being progressively disenfranchised and the essential glue that holds communities together is further weakened.

Organisations deploying volunteers are wise to protect themselves and their volunteers with insurance cover.

Public liability and employers' liability are virtually essential but personal accident cover is an additional protection. Insurance adds to costs and administrative burdens and can deter some small neighbourhood groups.

It is sometimes suggested that volunteering should be rewarded by tax breaks. The bureaucracy involved in such a scheme would be daunting, requiring charities and others to inform government of details of their volunteers and the work they do. Some volunteers would probably object to this, fearing that recipients of services might suspect they were volunteering merely for the tax benefits. If government is serious about tax breaks for volunteering it should consider how to reduce the costs of organisations that deploy volunteers.

Volunteering and trades unions
Voluntary action can be a powerful force in society and it is not surprising that attempts are sometimes made to curb the power that volunteers are believed to enjoy. An agreement between Volunteering England and the Trades Union Congress in 2009[271] included the following two principles for creating good relations between paid staff and volunteers:

- The involvement of volunteers should complement and supplement the work of paid staff, and should not be used to displace paid staff or undercut their pay and conditions of service;
- In the interests of harmonious relations between volunteers and paid staff, volunteers should not be used to undertake the work of paid staff during industrial disputes.

Volunteer Development Scotland and the Scottish Trades Union Congress have prepared a similar document[272].

It is understandable that trades unions are anxious to protect the jobs of their members and their bargaining position with employers. That is the reason for their existence. But their interests have to be considered alongside the interests of others.

One overriding principle that should govern the management of services is not included in the document – that they must provide value for money. The needs of taxpayers and service users should be at the heart of any consideration about the provision of services. Deviation from this basic principle will, sooner or later, require review, which may be accompanied by recriminations and accusations of bad faith.

The document underplays the role of volunteers by assigning their work to supplementing and complementing that of paid staff. This gives a false impression of the realities behind voluntary activity. Voluntary work can be pioneering and innovative. As we have seen, it does not need to hang on the coat tails of paid staff.

No one has the authority to sign away the right of members of the community to intervene if services are withdrawn from vulnerable people. If this kind of agreement is considered desirable it should include a clause to the effect that trades unions should not intimidate volunteers who wish to continue with their normal duties during an industrial dispute.

It has been the historic role of voluntary action to challenge people with authority. In industrial disputes, trades unions should not expect citizens to remain inactive if basic services are denied to people in need. Industrial action is usually depicted as a struggle between employers and employees, but others have an interest in the outcome when there is a dispute between a public service and its staff – namely, service users. They have no representation at the negotiating table and it should come as no surprise if volunteers choose to voice concerns on their behalf. They may believe it necessary to act as individuals if the agency that engages them declines to sponsor their actions

Local volunteers must determine what weight they place on the attitude of trades unions. It is totally unrealistic to believe that a group of men and women meeting in London can – or should – determine what is best for volunteers across the country. As the coalition government said in 2010, "cultural change can only be built and sustained from the bottom-up"[273]. Volunteers and trades unions are by no means always on opposing sides. During long industrial disputes, like the miners' strike in 1984, many groups not associated with the communities concerned raise funds for the families of strikers. Volunteers have the right to associate themselves with any cause that takes their fancy.

Voluntary action is part of a complex system of checks and balances that operate in a democratic and free society. It is an expression of popular will and a means by which ordinary men and women can make the intensity of their views known. The more that volunteering is bureaucratised and cedes authority to powerful institutions, the less effective it will become and society will be the poorer. It is not in the interests of volunteering for there to be rancour between volunteers and paid staff. Organisations representing trades unions and volunteers must work cooperatively, recognising and respecting one another's standpoint.

It is common for services pioneered by volunteers to be transferred to organisations employing paid staff. That is the history of our social services. There is no intrinsic reason why the reverse should not occur so that tasks currently undertaken by paid staff are transferred to volunteers. Changes in social need and in technology, together with the impossibility of public services meeting all needs make this inevitable. A Canute-like approach will not work. Yet the agreement assumes that there are clear and unchanging boundaries between paid and voluntary action. That has never been so. In many instances volunteers and paid staff work side by side and may be interchangeable with work allocated on the basis of who has the appropriate experience and skill, irrespective of whether they are paid or unpaid.

The agreement does not reflect realities on the ground and has already been overtaken by events. There are many examples of village shops and public houses being saved from closure by volunteers. Woodberry Down library in the London Borough of Hackney is one of a number of libraries across the country that is organised by volunteers. Other libraries are likely to follow. Hackney is not an ultra right-wing authority. Fifty of its 58 councillors are members of the Labour Party.

A recent government review raises a number of issues about the deployment of volunteers in public libraries[274]. It points out that library facilities can serve as a base for far more services than currently. It explains that in Essex, the service was concerned about people who were unable to reach the library because of disability, age or long-term illness. Volunteers deliver books, CD's, DVD's and information to customers in their homes and chat to them about reading. When asked what they got out of the home library service, people talked about the benefits of social contact, social stimulation and meeting new people. One person said, "Without it, life wouldn't be so interesting. I'd miss out on a good friend. I look forward to her visits". Another said, "I'd miss it greatly, his chats – it's a lifeline".

The report goes on to suggest that a greater use of volunteers would enable libraries to open longer, making them accessible to more members of the public and it argues for the joint management of libraries with community groups. This is a radical proposal but all political parties agree that authority for public services should be delegated wherever possible so that local people have greater control over the services they pay for and use. This has implications for the distribution of power and for the agreements reached by Volunteering England and Volunteer Development Scotland with trades unions.

Libraries could be the thin end of a very long wedge. Expert librarians, curators and horticulturalists are needed to run libraries, museums and public gardens but much of the day-to-day work can be undertaken by volunteers. If local people are in charge and have the authority to reallocate savings to services they regard as more important, there will be added pressure to utilise volunteer labour. Perhaps the local community would prefer to see a rise in the home help workforce and leave the planting of spring bulbs to volunteers.

There are no easy answers to the moral dilemma of utilising volunteers to undertake work traditionally performed by paid staff but the public response will depend on the way it is reported. The *Museums Journal* published a story under the headline, "Volunteers could replace staff at four museums in Hampshire". Two days later it changed the headline to, "Volunteers could keep four sites in Hampshire open"[275]. Both were accurate but they conveyed radically different meanings.

This is not to advocate the wholesale sacking of staff in the public service. New inventions and new ways of working inevitable lead to difficult decisions and tensions. Compromises and long phase-in periods may be necessary. The principle at stake is whether it is right to ossify public services in their present form for all time or whether we should endeavour to get full value for every pound spent.

Changes in Control

Some volunteers can trace their organisations back to a time when they were almost entirely controlled by volunteers. The Alzheimer's' Society, Scope and Mencap began as organisations representing families in need. They raised funds, lobbied politicians, and created services which they ran, often at their own expense. They were motivated by a powerful urge for self-help among people who felt they and their families were neglected by public services and politicians.

As they developed, some services became main-stream and their constitutions changed; suddenly, some of the most passionate volunteers have found themselves edged out by men and women in suits drawing salaries they can only dream about. Their organisations have changed from self-help to philanthropic where volunteers and families who were once at the core of the work are now on the outside looking in. Some of them feel disillusioned. The personal and financial sacrifices they made to create something worthwhile have been forgotten and the services for which they once sold raffle tickets for fifty pence each are now paying for the superior lifestyles of a new elite who attend conferences at £400 a day.

The Alzheimer's Society ran into a storm of protests in 2011 when it replaced 240 branches with 49 regional centres. Some branches have broken-away from the parent body and are in dispute about the ownership of property. In Sunderland it is said the branch chairman of twenty four years who had steered the branch with an annual turnover of £400,000 found the locks on the premises had been changed and "everything ransacked and seized"[276].

It is difficult to believe that any organisation is so well endowed that it can afford to discard the experience, integrity, enthusiasm and passion of long serving volunteers. A spokesman for the charity defended the restructuring, not on the grounds that it would improve services but that it would "make us better at meeting the needs of the public sector and better at winning contracts [277]. Volunteers had not realised that the mission of the Society had changed from pressing the government for improvement in services and filling gaps to competing for government contracts. In military terms, this is mission creep which is marginalising volunteers, pitching charities against one another and exposing them to financial risk. In hard times to come the volunteers may be welcomed back.

This is one more example of the trend identified in chapter eight in which philanthropic organisations are slowly abandoning volunteers and adopting a brazen business model.

Volunteers who serve as trustees make strategic decisions with the guidance of paid staff but volunteers are seldom given responsibility for staff at local level. Several national voluntary organisations have restructured with the declared intention of competing for contracts to run public services. Their contracts are likely to require them to provide services to the standards set by commissioners with the danger that, if they are successful, they will face more stringent financial controls in future. By embracing the contract culture they compromise what was once their strongest asset – their independence - and it will become more difficult for volunteers and the Society to criticise government policies.

Recent governments have emphasised the value of voluntary organisations competing with public and private agencies for providing public services. There appears to be no direct evidence of the benefits of such arrangements. A House of Commons Committee[278] could find no evidence that voluntary organisations provided improved outcomes for service users although there have been numerous claims that such services are more flexible and user friendly. Macmillan[279] examined 48 pieces of research about service delivery by voluntary organisations and found that, predominately, they paid greater attention to the voices of and concerns of staff than of volunteers or service users. It is simply not known whether, as widely supposed, voluntary organisations make any difference to the quality of services. That is an uncomfortable thought.

We can be sure we have not reached an ultimate point in the provision of public services. Given time there are likely to be complaints about extra costs arising from the fragmentation of control, the difficulty of strategic planning and the way in which some users fall between gaps in provision. There will then be pressure to return services to greater public and centralised control.

Voluntary organisations that contract to run services with public funds may be inhibited about criticising their pay masters. In the past, voluntary organisations have jettisoned services when they found themselves publicly criticised for poor quality provision, criticism that undermined their role as advisers to government and leading exponents of quality care. Both Mind and Help the Aged have been in this position.

Increasingly, legislation and good practice require public services to consult communities about their services. This has had only limited success. Residents and volunteers seldom have control over resources so are unmistakably the junior partner when they meet service providers. Conventional consultation based on formal meetings appeals to only a small and sometimes unrepresentative minority of people. Gatherings are in danger of becoming a one-way conduit where complaints and ideas from representative groups are fed to service providers. In these circumstances, the power of providers is unaffected and residents take on the role of supplicant with all the emotional baggage and negative overtones this involves.

Representative forums sometimes become stale and narrow in outlook, focusing almost exclusively on funding. Particular individuals and pressure groups can hijack them. They easily become accusatory in tone and ritualistic in practice with procedures becoming more important than content. Recent research has found that, "People's experience of formal public consultations had almost always been negative and this affected their willingness to participate in the future"[280]. Local residents are better able to understand and influence services if they work alongside providers as volunteers.

Has volunteering become part of the establishment?

A government report[281] indicates that of people who do not volunteer, 49% say they are put off by the bureaucracy involved. This figure should be treated with caution because we do not know how many of the 49% have experience of formal volunteering. Nevertheless their perception is a matter for concern and arises in part from the close interest government has taken in the subject.

A substantial increase in funding from the public sector is placing the independence of some voluntary organisations in jeopardy. In the seven years from 2000/1 to 2007/8 statutory funding increased from £8 billion to over £12.bn. More than one third of voluntary sector funding now comes from the State with 23% of voluntary organisations receiving statutory funding.

For 27,000 organisations, state funding represents over three quarters of their income[282]. Three quarters of charities with incomes over £10 million a year receive state funding compared with only 8% of charities with incomes less than £10,000. The main role for nearly a quarter of 40.000 voluntary organisations studied was found to be the delivery of public services while less than a third considered voluntary donations to be their most important source of income[283].

Because of the importance of satisfying funders, some charities are more aware of the number of people served than the quality of services provided. Hard-to-reach volunteers, like those from ethnic minority groups may be ignored because they are more difficult and more expensive to recruit and disabled volunteers may be sidelined because of the possible additional costs involved.

With so much government funding for specific types of project there is a danger that organisations are tempted to change their mission to extend opportunities for receiving public money. Charities may also refrain from speaking out on matters of public concern to avoid upsetting government and other funders. The Independence Panel[284] plans to monitor these matters in the coming years but much of the pressure on small organisations is subtle and not easily detected or proved to outsiders.

Volunteering is now neatly packaged and labelled. Volunteers have become outreach workers for service providers, largely sharing their values, endorsing their policies and accepting their control. There is less room for independent thought and action by volunteers recruited, deployed and funded by huge bureaucracies, particularly if their funds come from the government.

Lady Bountiful would be horrified at the way her work has been reined-in, even nationalised. As the government persuades third sector organisations to run what were, hitherto, public services. Large numbers of volunteers are effectively under state control.

Many organisations deploying volunteers today are unmistakably professional bodies, which allow volunteers on board to undertake specific and limited roles under close supervision. Volunteers do not necessarily feel that they own the organisations in which they work or have much opportunity to influence policy. They experience a stratified organisation where they are at the bottom.

It is easy for even well-established professional groups and organisations to persuade themselves that their own self interest coincides with the interests of volunteers and those requiring services. Only by having clear and agreed values is it possible to ensure that practice is not corrupted by power

In large organisations, especially those with a wide geographical spread, judgments about the competence of local managers may be made by senior staff who are remote from the action and have little or no knowledge of volunteering. Compliance with food hygiene regulations, health and safety instructions, equal opportunities policies and data protection procedures may all eat into the time of local managers. Making sure the paperwork is up to date on these matters may be a more certain way to promotion than providing fulfillment for volunteers.

This dichotomy is reflected in national umbrella organisations like Volunteering England which seems uncertain whether its mission is to advance the interests of volunteers or serve as a trade association for organisations deploying them. It operates like the Trades Union Congress one day and the Confederation of British Industries the next. Volunteering England has helped organisations trying to represent the views of practicing volunteers but it has proved difficult to create suitable structures. Perhaps, together with its counterparts in Northern Ireland, Scotland and Wales, it could create advisory committees drawn from volunteers in various settings. This would help establish, over time, whether there is sufficient interest to form separate organisations. As ever, cost is likely to be the deciding factor. Another approach which would be cheaper to operate might be for organisations composed of volunteers to be offered a consultative role.

Volunteering has regularly found itself on the government agenda in the past forty years. In the 1970's

David Ennals introduced the *Good Neighbour Scheme*. John Major launched the *Make a Difference* campaign twenty years later and the Blair Government launched a series of reports about revitalising communities which made heavy references to volunteers. It also introduced the *Experience Corps* to increase volunteering by older people at a cost of £19.5m. David Cameron's *Big Society* should be seen in this context.

Volunteering is, or should be, the wild card of public service, like a wet balloon, it can be grasped for an instant but is always on the move, as capricious as the weather and as likely to surprise as a jack-in-the-box. It cannot be regulated to suit government, trades unions or other powerful forces. Long may it stay that way. Bureaucratic procedures can impede it but are unlikely to kill it off. It is indestructible unless democracy itself is destroyed but its effectiveness can be seriously impaired by the unintended consequences of government action and by power struggles within organisations that deploy them.

In a number of areas, including Hackney, Barnet and Durham, RSVP has arranged for mobile libraries to distribute the same title to eight or ten housebound people and then for recipients to discuss the book through teleconferencing.

A Tea Dance Is held for 2 hours each week at Trinity Centre, North Ormesby. It is attended by over 40 older people and organised by two RSVP

volunteer organisers who are dancing instructors. Refreshments are prepared by volunteers. A special celebration was held for the wedding of Prince William when over 75 people attended.

A dozen volunteers have been trained by the Crime Prevention Officer to visit the homes of vulnerable elderly people after they have been burgled. Then a volunteer undertakes to befriend them. Volunteer Organiser, RSVP

CHAPTER THIRTEEN

Helping volunteers to find themselves

*The best way to find yourself is to lose
yourself in the service of others.*

Gandhi

Given the uncertainty, even confusion, surrounding the mission and values of volunteering it is not surprising that organisations deploying volunteers and the staff in their employ are in disarray about the skills required to deploy them successfully.

Except in those rare organisations whose primary purpose is the recruitment and deployment of volunteers, managers will be judged, not by whether volunteers are fulfilled or even by what they do or how well they do it but by the extent to which they contribute to achieving the wider objectives of the organisation. A common complaint by volunteer managers is that their employers do not understand their work. Satisfaction for volunteers is profoundly affected by the way they are managed but the skills and dedication of managers are largely unrecognised. Some of them say that their hardest task is not managing volunteers but trying to influence their employer. The art of volunteer management is balancing the needs of volunteers with the needs of the organisation deploying them.

Some voluntary organisations are reluctant to invest in professional training for their managers. Not only is staff training expensive but, once qualified, staff become more able to obtain work elsewhere. From an employer's point of view, in-house instruction, concentrating on administrative procedures is much cheaper. It would be a mistake to assume that employers will be prepared to fight for the professional training of staff responsible for supervising volunteers.

Volunteers, almost by definition have a low status in any organisation where volunteering is not the main purpose. Consequently, their managers lack prestige and cannot compete with professional groups whose levels of pay and status are determined by length of training, clearly defined skills and the number of staff under their control. Moreover, research[285] in England suggests that 40% of volunteer managers work part time and 23% are themselves volunteers which further diminishes their status in the eyes of colleagues.

Few volunteer managers are personally concerned about status – they would not have chosen such a career if status was important to them – but being at the bottom of the heap makes it difficult to negotiate satisfactory working conditions for volunteers or to ensure that powerful professional groups understand what volunteers have to offer. Furthermore, they may be excluded from strategic discussions both within the organisation and with partners.

Less than one in ten volunteer managers spends all his or her employed time managing volunteers[286]. More than half of 1382 studied in England said they spent less than 25% of their time on the task. Another study found that just 14% spend more than three quarters of their time organising volunteers[287].

In the United States it has been estimated that only one in eight volunteer managers devotes 100% of his or her time to volunteer management[288]. Some managers have responsibilities for staff as well as volunteers and may find that this arises by default, no one being quite sure what is entailed but assuming that the deployment of volunteers is not a time-consuming or energy-sapping enterprise. Volunteer management is a temporary haven for some staff while they work to hone their skills and look for promotion in their "proper" job. This does a disservice to volunteers and creates the impression that volunteer management is a soft option, a sinecure for people who do not have the skills to undertake more important or complex work.

Pay levels largely determine power structures within employment and the status of individual staff is determined by their salary and place in the hierarchy. Managers may command respect through their personalities but their control over finance and other resources guarantee that they are treated with deference. They decide how work will be allocated, what staff will be paid and who will be promoted. In a workforce without the exchange of money, managers are bereft of the usual tools of authority and rely on interpersonal skills to galvanize the workforce into meeting objectives. The absence of different pay levels to determine degrees of deferment means that volunteers rely on personal judgments about the relative status of fellow volunteers.

Volunteers mostly expect to be treated as equals. Their volunteer status demands that they are asked, not told, thanked, not taken for granted and welcomed, not ignored. In short they should expect to be treated with courtesy. Managers must work to gain their trust and respect. It would be no bad thing if the employment market were run in the same way. Some employers get very close to it but money speaks a different language. Good personal relations are the key to high quality work in any organisation.

The successful leadership of volunteers does not depend on the trappings of authority and power. Where a door separates managers and volunteers it should be kept open as often as possible. Opportunities for informal conversations are invaluable as are occasions when staff and volunteers share common tasks. Every opportunity should be taken to demonstrate that volunteers and the workforce are on the same side.

The atmosphere in some organisations is not welcoming towards volunteers because volunteers and staff do not share the same goals or culture. Volunteers are quick to notice negative comments about service users. As a young student I found that the quickest way to discover the attitude of professional staff towards their clients was to join them for an informal lunch. Their comments were sometimes flippant but always revealing. Students and volunteers find themselves in a unique position to overhear comments that might better remain private. They quickly become aware of attitudes and tensions within organisations.

It can be difficult for junior staff to understand why volunteers are treated differently from themselves. They may even be jealous of the time their manager devotes to volunteers. Also, friction can arise between volunteers and administrative and clerical staff who may be uncertain how to relate to them. Simple matters like the use of desk space and telephones and who makes the coffee or washes-up can create tension. Managers must anticipate these problems. I once volunteered in an office where hostility from clerical staff was so intense and the chief executive so unresponsive that I would have walked out had it not been for the solidarity among volunteers and our joint determination to beat the system.

The needs of volunteers vary but most appreciate volunteering for the sense of belonging that it provides. This is particularly true for those leading isolated lives. Not only do they appreciate the companionship of others but, if they fail to appear when expected, someone is likely to enquire about them. For some, Christmas and birthday cards from colleagues and regular social gatherings are important.

In paid work, organisations are structured to suit the requirements of managers; staff are then fitted into it. In volunteering, the talents of volunteers can sometimes come first and determine what structures are required. Organisations with conventional top-down management structures find it difficult to accommodate a bottom-up structure for volunteers. This can lead to friction, the cause of which is seldom understood. Volunteers establish relationships that cut across existing power structures, creating uncertainties among managers and staff in traditionally hierarchical organisations. This can easily create animosity towards them. Volunteers are not a simple add-on that can be bolted on to existing structures. They impact on the entire organisation and thought must be given to how they are integrated within it. If volunteers do not change the nature of the organisation in which they work they are probably not reaching their full potential. Where staffing structures are incompatible with volunteering it may be better to give up the struggle and transfer volunteering to an intermediate organisation.

Because of their lowly status, volunteer managers may not be part of the senior management team and have little input in strategic policy-making in the organisations that employ them. Despite overseeing a huge front-line workforce which may be the public face of the organisation, volunteer managers may find that their views on policy are not routinely sought and that colleagues controlling finance, personnel and general administration are more highly paid and valued. This re-enforces the marginalisation of volunteers.

Where volunteer managers are fortunate enough to be part of the senior management team they should take every opportunity to explain to colleagues the value of volunteers to the organisation. When colleagues believe they must limit their objectives to conserve resources volunteer managers may be able to specify how volunteers can fill gaps. In particular, they need to emphasise the range of skills that can be made available.

Volunteer managers that operate outside the senior management team may still be able to arrange for reports of their work to be circulated to senior colleagues and trustees. To gain maximum impact, such reports should be short and avoid the pitfall of the *Well I never!* approach, describing extraordinary one-off events. It is better to remain silent than to give the impression that volunteers trade in gimmicks. Every report should show the link between the work of volunteers and the objectives of the organisation so that readers learn to appreciate the value they bring.

One seldom asked question is, "Why are we recruiting volunteers?" If the answer is, "Because we cannot afford to employ staff", we should have the honesty to explain this to volunteers. They should be told if they are not our preferred option. Whether they are told or not, they will soon realise the truth.

There are many reasons why volunteers may be preferred to paid staff for certain tasks. There is much anecdotal evidence of them successfully forming relationships with people who have spurned assistance from paid staff. Volunteers in schools point out that some of the most disturbed children relate positively to them simply because they are not teachers and not paid.

Some children are said to be intrigued that a total stranger, for no reward, is prepared to show a personal interest in them. It is clear that the reason why some children's reading improves dramatically when a volunteer is assigned to help them is that they prosper in a one to one relationship which is not judgemental.

Listed in Appendix 2 are some circumstances in which volunteers may have a particularly valuable contribution to make.

A community's own leadership can sometimes be more acceptable than direction from outside. The philosopher and Literature Nobel Prize winner, Albert Camus[289] presents the dilemma of townspeople who are confronted by a plague that strikes down hundreds of citizens, leaving the streets lined with corpses. Should they passively accept what is happening or do their best to ameliorate it? There is an acute shortage of manpower to improve sanitary conditions, disinfect premises, drive ambulances and dispose of the dead. A call from the town hall for volunteers is ineffective. An enlightened citizen realises that only local people like himself have the power to mobilise the community; they are unlikely to save many lives but it would be unthinkable to do nothing so he sets about creating "sanitary squads" of volunteers.

As we saw earlier, most organisations deploying volunteers do so to further objectives that are unrelated to volunteering. Their volunteers can easily be neglected and tensions arise unless there is an effort to ensure that their needs are understood and mechanisms are in place to meet them. Volunteers are used to being praised and patronised but in policy statements they are often depicted as shadowy, even marginal figures. It is as though there is some shame attached to admitting that volunteers play an important part in the work undertaken. Ellis points out that they are commonly noted in policy documents as "assisting" or "supplementing" staff, not as being "innovative", or "working in parallel with". She goes on to suggest the following as a description of the role they perform in some agencies:

Our agency encourages the teamwork of salaried staff and volunteers so that we can offer our consumers the best service possible. Volunteers contribute their unique talents, skills and knowledge of our community to provide personalised attention to consumers, enable the salaried staff to concentrate on the work for which they were trained and educate the public about our organisation and its cause[290].

This wording is suitable for a large number of organisations deploying volunteers. However, it is not appropriate for organisations that are led by volunteers. For some organisations, the following statement may better reflect their role and purpose:

We aim to marshal the enthusiasms, skills and talents that exist in our community to enhance the quality of life and extend the life chances of the population. Although our main resource is people over the age of 50 years, we work with any organisation or individual that shares our aims and welcome people from all backgrounds and creeds.

Some organisations fit neither of these two models and need to construct a statement that is unique for them. For example, the Royal National Lifeboat Institution deploys volunteers with exceptional skills and provides services that extend beyond a local community. Pro bono work by lawyers and financial experts also lie outside these definitions.

Boards of management responsible for volunteers should be clear about the role of their volunteers including:

- The preparation and training provided;
- How they can develop their talents, skills and enthusiasms;
- How they can influence the wider policy of the organisation;
- The payment of out of pocket expenses;
- Access to a grievance procedure.

Some may wish to prepare codes of practice with details about how some or all of these policies should be achieved although this is not necessary; the more rules and regulations that are issued the less likely are practitioners to heed them. If the principles are embedded in everything the Trustees and managers do and say, staff and volunteers will follow suit.

Funders shape the future of volunteering and it is important that they have well thought-out ideas about what they expect from the organisations they support. Although they usually pay great regard to financial probity and governance, they are often less skilled at recognising the key components of high quality volunteering.

It is good practice for organisations deploying volunteers to ensure that at least one Trustee is made responsible for ensuring that the needs of volunteers are met. Research[291] shows that organisations in the health service that allocate specific responsibility for volunteering to a board member have a higher than average number of volunteers.

The limits of volunteering

Social workers are commonly castigated for failing to identify child abuse or to solve other problems within families but the issues are far more complex than generally recognised. Some families are so disorganised that they have no idea how to cook, clean, budget or look after children. They lack understanding of the basics of household management and have a short span of concentration. Their spirits are low; they suffer from ill health, chronic anxiety and depression. They may exist on budgets that would challenge the capacity of much more able people. Relationships between parents are frequently tense, accompanied at times by open conflict and violence. Their lives are characterised by failure and this is underlined every time a social worker knocks on the door.

Such families live in fear of being found wanting. A social worker making a brief call once or twice a week can become another burden to be endured, another person to be placated adding to the sense of stress and bewilderment. Why should they admit their failings and risk criticism or worse, lose their children? A volunteer carries less threat and may be better able to build a relationship of trust, especially if he or she has something in common with the family, such as coming from the same ethnic group or having grown up in the same neighbourhood.

A family in Bromley, London, has been quoted by Community Service Volunteers as saying:

> We truly believe because of our volunteer we kept our children. She believed in us and she kept us together and supported us as a couple and a family. Because of her and the strength she gave us we achieved our goal and will be forever thankful to her[292].

It would be wrong to believe that because a volunteer may more easily gain the confidence of a family in need than a social worker that he or she will be more effective in solving social problems. Forging a working relationship is only the first step and does not signify that the volunteer has absorbed the skills of a social worker any more than a volunteer in a general practice surgery becomes a doctor or, in a school, becomes a teacher. But a volunteer working in partnership with a professional may achieve far more than either on his or her own.

There is a danger that, in their enthusiasm to make a difference, volunteers or those who support them, will take on challenges that overwhelm them leading to failure and disillusionment.

One early programme for helping families with multiple problems was developed during the Second World War by conscientious objectors who were excused duty in the armed services. They created "Pacifist Service Units" in deprived urban areas to serve, in their words, as "willing volunteers[293]" to assist families with the most extreme problems. In 1945 a book was published[294] about the services offered. A review in a national newspaper caught the eye of The Chairman of Lloyds Bank, Lord Balfour of Burleigh. He was so impressed that he helped to put the organisation on a permanent footing under the name, *Family Service Units*.

Family Service Units recognised that helping families with deep social problems required trained staff. Its pioneering work with disorganised families became well respected and its methods were copied by other voluntary organisations as well as by local authorities. In 2008, it ran into financial difficulties and went into administration.

Now move forward about ten years. *Working Families Everywhere* is a charity that appoints volunteers as family champions to act as key workers for families with multiple problems, brokering support from relevant agencies to help them find jobs. The government has asked the charity to assist 120,000 workless families by 2015[295]. It is ironic that so soon after its demise, *Family Service Units* is being re invented under another name. But instead of being funded locally with experienced staff and integrated into local services it now relies on volunteers and government funding. Furthermore, success is measured by whether or not volunteers succeed in placing unemployed people in work. Other problems like child abuse, criminal activity and family violence will take second place.

Any scheme that promises to utilise community strengths to tackle social problems is to be welcomed but if *Working Families Everywhere* is rolled out across the country it is in danger of duplicating work already in hand in some areas. By applying a single blueprint, it may alienate organisations currently in the field. Furthermore, unless there is a careful selection of volunteers and ample support from skilled professionals there is a strong possibility of willing volunteers being disillusioned and families being let-down. Volunteers with Community Service Volunteers who work with families where a child is at risk of serious harm are closely supported by professionals. A successful service is not cheap.

Evaluation

The tendency has already been noted for volunteering to be measured by reference to the number of volunteers engaged and the number of hours they work rather than by what they achieve which is more difficult to calculate. As funders move away from grants and towards contracts, it is necessary to be more precise about the outcomes desired and achieved. Funders are not the only interested parties. It is important for managers and volunteers to know what works and how improvements can be made.

Volunteering impacts on the services provided, on the organisation and on volunteers. Effective evaluation must take into account all three aspects. It can be useful for managers and organisers to ask themselves how volunteers are influencing their work. It is also instructive to ask volunteers what volunteering has taught them about themselves. A keen awareness by volunteers and managers of the dynamics of their interaction helps to build trust and can make volunteering more rewarding.

Studies into evaluation techniques and impact measures indicate the complexity of the task. The Institute for Voluntary Action Research[296] found that it was not possible to produce an approach that was universally appropriate for community organisations. Informal volunteering is particularly difficult to measure and evaluate. Close examination may change or even destroy it.

Evaluation can be time consuming and, unless they are involved from the outset, volunteers can feel threatened. However, some of them gain great satisfaction in applying evaluation techniques and their involvement can be greatly reassuring for those under scrutiny. Volunteering England has published what it calls "a toolkit" to assess the impact of volunteering on volunteers, the organisation, beneficiaries, and the broader community[297]. Charities Evaluation Services offers training, information and consultancy to charities about methods of evaluation[298]

Evaluation exercises can be a means of involving local colleges and universities as well as their students in volunteering activities. They may have staff or students with particular interest and skills in evaluation techniques. Their involvement could lead to other areas of cooperation and the recruitment of retiring lecturers as volunteers. Managers should always be searching for allies among local organisations.

There are indications that voluntary organisations are eager to see improvements in the way volunteering is measured. Agenda Consulting and the Association of Volunteer Managers have launched a benchmarking study to enable comparisons to be made between different volunteers and different managers[299]. That over eighty organisations have agreed to take part at a cost varying from £588 to £1176 suggests that there is a huge willingness to invest time and money to identify how to measure and, therefore improve, volunteering performance[300].

The "Does he take Sugar" syndrome
"Does he take Sugar" was the title of a long-running radio series in the 1970's which highlighted the tendency for some to communicate with disabled people by addressing their carers. This parallels the way volunteers are sometimes treated by those who work closest with them.

As a group, volunteers are not particularly articulate. More than any other substantial group in society, their views are expressed for them by others. National meetings about volunteering are attended overwhelmingly by paid staff. When volunteers attend they may find themselves the only people present meeting their own expenses. The cost of conferences on volunteering is so prohibitive that few grass roots organisations or volunteers can afford to be represented.

There is something faintly ludicrous abut eighty staff attending a day conference on volunteering at a cost of £350 each with little or no input from volunteers.

Organisations with 30 volunteers and a staff/volunteer ratio of 1/20 may be represented in significant numbers but not those deploying many hundreds of volunteers with staff/volunteer ratios of 1/400. A similar phenomenon arises in relation to conferences about social exclusion. They are usually priced in such a way that there is little danger of a socially excluded person attending.

Human nature being what it is, it is likely that, without evil intent, managers often represent the interests of themselves and their organisations rather than the interests of volunteers. As a volunteer languishing at the back of conferences being addressed by worthy people I have sometimes found comments about volunteers fatuous, sentimental and patronising. Unmistakably, power lies in the hands of non-volunteers. Like the poor and disadvantaged, the voice of volunteers is muted by machinery of governance.

These problems could be rectified if prospective speakers refused to accept invitations unless at least a quarter of the audience were volunteers. This could be secured if booking fees entitled an organisation to send a member of staff plus a volunteer on each ticket. The solution is in the hands of conference speakers and organisers.

Burgess[301] describes how a group of older volunteers arranged free seminars for other older volunteers in five English towns to discuss common problems but organisations deploying volunteers were, "loath to cooperate, either not responding to our initial approaches or, having responded, being unwilling to distribute information to their volunteers". A national conference for older volunteers funded by the Home Office was held in HM Treasury in Whitehall following the regional seminars. Burgess notes that although invitations were distributed widely through organisations deploying older volunteers, the take-up was low considering the venue and that a senior government minister was on the platform. In some cases, invitations reached no further than the chief executive's desk.

It is difficult to avoid the conclusion that even among organisations that welcome the contribution of volunteers there are some that do not see their role as helping them to extend their horizons and achieve their full potential.

Writers and lecturers on the subject of volunteering often betray their beliefs about the subject in the way they order their material. The general assumption is that the idea for developing a volunteering project begins with staff of an existing organisation and that volunteers will be recruited, trained and supervised to achieve goals established by staff. This is the assumption made in *Investing in Volunteers*, already described. But it is not the only way. It never was. Large numbers of volunteering groups are created by local people who want to do something about problems in their community. If staff become involved at all, it is only after the groundwork has been laid by volunteers.

Authors of learned papers and conference speakers on volunteering are almost invariably paid staff. They explain that they have experience of serving as volunteers - most people have – but they commonly write and speak from a management perspective, taking it for granted that managers have more skill and knowledge than volunteers and that volunteering cannot operate without paid managers.

There was a time when research into health and social care services seldom included references to the experience and views of service users; they have been pushed further up the agenda in recent years but, otherwise high quality research into volunteering is sometimes less useful than it could be because the views of every stakeholder except those of volunteers are included.

There are many unsung heroes and heroines in the squalor of inner cities who fight against almost impossible odds to improve the circumstances of people in their neighbourhoods. Others struggle to help people suffering extreme disadvantage through illness or unemployment. Perhaps they would achieve better results if they were part of an organisation with a manager at their elbow but they spurn help from what they regard as a suspect source. They instinctively distrust what they see as experts, remote from their community, taking over. One expressed the truth as she saw it, "If you have staff they tell you what to do". The correct riposte to such a statement is, "Yes, but not if you have a well trained and well experienced community worker". Sadly, until volunteer managers have an improved image, they will be rejected by many who need them most.

Much of the success of volunteering is a matter of chance. It depends on the abilities of those who come forward to volunteer, on the capacity of organisations to uncover the abilities of volunteers and on the availability of funds. With so much outside the control of managers and organisers it is tempting for them to abandon strategic thinking and leave the future to look after itself. It is precisely because the future is uncertain that they need to be clear about the direction they intend to travel both in relation to the organisation they represent and volunteering generally. They must be ready to nudge events in their favour. Everyone with a management role should have a plan for the future, however slender, so that they can recognize and seize opportunities as they present themselves.

Believe in volunteers

As we have seen, volunteering should unlock the skills and talents of volunteers and empower them. This cannot be achieved unless volunteers feel they have some control yet they are frequently held at a distance from levers of power. As Rousseau might say, "Volunteers are born free but why, everywhere, are they in chains?

A commitment to volunteering can be fragile. Volunteers vote with their feet. If they feel they are not appreciated they may move to an organisation which they find more congenial or, sadly, are lost entirely to volunteering. Burgess found that where committed volunteers resigned from one organisation to join another, the reasons given were generally that managers had been too insensitive and bureaucratic[302].

The director of a Settlement in London recently announced her intention to spend a government grant by appointing an administrator to ensure a consistency of approach to volunteers[303]. She saw volunteers as a means of achieving established priorities. But what about the priorities of local people?

The unique strength of a Settlement is its ability to empower its community so that it can determine its own priorities and identify ways of improving lives. If baby boomers are to volunteer in large numbers they must be at the helm, helping to formulate policies and setting the pace. It is difficult to criticise the editor for the headline he provided – *Taking volunteers in hand* – but it is a good example of the way volunteers are patronised. They want to be liberated, not taken in hand by administrative staff. It is also an example of government rhetoric not being matched by its actions. While grants supporting skilled community work are being reduced or withdrawn, £27,000 has been provided for an administrator.

Government and lottery funding for volunteering projects often leave community workers questioning how decisions have been reached. There appears to be no consistent framework for evaluating applications; grants are at times offered to organisations with values which conflict with those of the Big Society. It sometimes seems that funds are denied to organisations that are embarking on space travel in favour of those that are subscribers to the Flat Earth Society.

The scale of public funding for volunteering projects makes it imperative to ensure that government and lottery grants promote best practice. Decisions about funding should be informed by people with appropriate knowledge and experience, preferably with an understanding of local issues.

The potential of older volunteering is enormous but, unless volunteer managers and organisers and the organisations that deploy them understand how to release that potential, much of it will be wasted. It is easy to blame the government for failing to offer adequate support but there is an urgent need for the volunteering sector to put its own house in order.

Anyone can become a volunteer manager or organiser without specific training. Perhaps, one day, there will be regulation but that appears to be a long way off. In the meantime steps can be taken to distinguish between the good, the bad and the indifferent by asking them to accept the terms of a statement of intent. Some kind of Hippocratic Oath would help to cement the concept that volunteer management has values that are not necessarily in the forefront of those who provide volunteering opportunities. It would push volunteers higher up the agenda.

My first draft is as follows:

Proposed Statement of Intent
for Volunteer Managers/Organisers

I will work in partnership with volunteers to:

1. provide the highest possible quality of service to the public within the resources available;

2. enable them to have as much freedom and choice as possible about the work they do and how they do it, compatible with 1 above;
3. provide a range of opportunities so that they can engage in activities that, are compatible with the time they have available and are of sufficient complexity to challenge them if that is what they wish;
4. encourage them to accept maximum responsibility for their work;
5. ensure they are offered suitable training and that their personal development is encouraged;
6. welcome their contribution to changing policies, procedures and practices.

Such a statement of intent, displayed in the office of a volunteer manager or organiser would, in a life of competing pressures, help remind him or her of their key responsibilities. It would also assist volunteers to understand what they can expect from their manager or organiser and provide a firm anchor for discussions and dispute-resolution with employers.

In the aftermath of the street rioting in August 2011, residents in several communities that were worst affected gathered up brooms, shovels and buckets to clear away the debris. They wanted to demonstrate that did not approve of what had happened. This is just one example of groups of people spontaneously seizing the initiative to do something positive for their communities.

The Frome Times (29th September 2011) tells us that, earlier that week when the projectionist opened the doors of the local cinema, black smoke billowed out. A plastic radio had been placed on a cooker which had been left on. The projectionist sent out a call for people to help him clear-up the mess. Thirty local residents armed with shovels and brushes arrived the following morning to help.

George described his retirement as "a time to write a new life specification" for himself. He decided to join RSVP because it offered him the chance to explore the needs of his community and to write his own agenda. To his surprise, he persuaded British Telecom to donate twenty answer-machines for RSVP organisers. This led to close collaboration with BT on a number of schemes including telephone befriending to combat social isolation.

Appendix 1

The Retired and Senior Volunteer Programme

If any voluntary organisation can be described as unique, the word must apply to RSVP. It is a national organisation of volunteers over the age of 50 years providing services to local communities and is largely organised and led by older people themselves. They choose what volunteering they will do, negotiate with public services about how they will be organised and provide the leadership to see it through. In areas where it operates it usually provides a range of services and boasts that no volunteer is rejected.

RSVP is a free-standing programme within Community Service Volunteers working in many different types of communities across England, Scotland and Wales. It currently has over 16,000 volunteers[304] with a staff/volunteer ratio of 1 to 450. In 2010 it was estimated that RSVP volunteers provided about 2.4 million hours of service each year benefitting 70,000 people delivered through over 400 projects. If these hours are costed at the median weekly pay, this represents over £33 million for an outlay of less than £2 million. Each of 17 regions has a regional coordinator post filled by a volunteer responsible for coordinating activities and advising organisers. These coordinators are each responsible for the work of up to 500 volunteers.

RSVP volunteers are active in schools, hospitals, clinics, surgeries, day centres, libraries, prisons and children's homes. They run transport schemes and visiting services for people in need. They are involved in a great many environmental projects, fit fire alarms and security devices to the homes of older people and advise on energy efficiency. They support young offenders, helping them learn literacy and numeracy skills. About 4,000 volunteers belong to knitting groups providing clothing and other items for mothers in need, refugees and disaster relief round the world.

The concept of RSVP was born in the USA where it was launched in 1971 with $500,000 from the federal government. Its aim was to provide useful activities for older people. It grew rapidly and, by 1974, it had 666 projects nationwide. In 1988 it had 400,000 volunteers and was still growing.

RSVP International was created in 1984. Based in New York it was headed by the late Arthur Garson a successful businessman who sought to encourage the development of RSVP projects across the world. In a visit to the UK he talked to a number of organisations. The British government showed little interest although the visit caught the imagination of some voluntary organisations in England as a result of which two or three pilot schemes were set-up.

The matter may have rested there but for the subsequent interest of Community Service Volunteers which Mora and Alec Dickson had created in 1962. They believed passionately that young people could make an important contribution to community life and that, in doing so they would learn lessons that would be valuable to them throughout their lives. They were to turn traditional youth work on its head by demonstrating that, if challenged, young people would respond by serving others. The Dickson's were prepared to accept risks when they arranged for Borstal boys and others with records of challenging behaviour to embark on community service.

Elisabeth Hoodless, a qualified medical social worker, was appointed to assist Alec and Mora Dickson in 1963 as the only paid employee. She became Executive Director of CSV in 1975 and was made Dame Commander of the British Empire in 2004, retiring in 2011.

When Elisabeth's father retired in 1972 he joined with neighbours of a similar age in the Lake District to offer a friendly visiting service to frail elderly people in nearby villages. Members of his group drove them to surgeries and clinics and generally assisted wherever there was a need. The new service was successful but it was difficult to raise funds to support active older people. Eventually the Joseph Rowntree Trust provided funding but the project remained a local initiative.

During the 1980's redundancies and early retirement became more common in the UK. Elisabeth decided the time was right to create a national service dedicated to the recruitment and deployment of older volunteers. She raised sufficient funds to pay for a full-time Development Manager and appointed Edith Kahn who was retiring from the post of head at Woodbury Down School in the London Borough of Hackney. Arrangements were made for an official launch of RSVP in the House of Commons. Sadly, Edith died suddenly the night before.

Janet Atfield was now appointed RSVP Development Manager. Aged 52, she had been trained as a youth and community worker and currently worked for CSV in Bristol having previously held youth worker posts in London. It was essential to her plan to locate volunteer organisers who could be enthused to set-up new projects, raise funds and recruit older volunteers.

One of her first appointments was to accompany Elisabeth to Canterbury to meet Muriel Jennings, a volunteer whom Arthur Garson had interviewed on his visit to the UK some years before. Muriel agreed to set up an RSVP group in the city. It was the first of many to be established across the UK.

Janet knew the kind of experience newly retired executives were looking for – challenging opportunities to extend their horizons, to accept responsibility in a cause they knew to be worthwhile. Some good secondees and volunteers came forward and Janet was largely able to entrust the building of RSVP's administrative structure and systems to them while she made contacts in different parts of the country to set up local volunteer groups.

Janet wanted to secure the support of influential people in and around government and created an Advisory Committee under the chairmanship of David Gibbons MBE., chief executive of Abbott Laboratories. He gathered round him a group of industrialists and Members of Parliament who met regularly at the House of Lords. They opened doors for RSVP. Once, when a local trades union official raised objections about an RSVP activity, Lord Murray, formerly General Secretary of the Trades Union Congress and a member of the Advisory Committee invited him to lunch at the House of Lords. There is no record of the conversation but the objections were withdrawn.

In 1997, Alan Michael, a Home Office Minister, launched the Older Volunteering Initiative to create more and better volunteering opportunities for older people and for them to become more involved with their communities. Alan Michael was familiar with youth and community work and this led to a free exchange of views between him and RSVP.

Paul Boateng MP, who became a junior minister in the Health Department, took a particular interest in RSVP when it launched a flagship project in his constituency. Through his good offices and those of Lord Levy, the President of CSV, RSVP volunteers were invited to contribute to an Anglo-French conference on volunteering at the British Embassy in Paris.

A senior civil servant at the Home Office Voluntary Service Unit with whom Janet negotiated for a grant was sufficiently impressed by RSVP to become a volunteer when he retired. His knowledge of government and his organising ability were invaluable. At a meeting of the Advisory Committee he explained that he felt like the man in the television advertisement at the time who was so impressed with the product that he bought the company.

He became an effective advocate for RSVP and had a special interest in volunteers working with general practitioners. He described to doctors the value of having volunteers based in their surgeries and, once he had explained that their staff would not be expected to recruit, train or manage volunteers they readily signed-up. His work led to the creation of several dozen primary care projects across Britain, each with its own organiser.

The enthusiasm of volunteers knew no bounds. With a grant from BT information about eight telephone befriending schemes was collected and published[305]. The report was launched at the BT revolving tower in London. Following a meeting of RSVP volunteers involved in partnerships with primary health care teams it was decided to publish a booklet about the issues surrounding partnerships[306]. This was launched at the Department of Health in Whitehall.

A close association with Whitehall led to an RSVP volunteer being asked to prepare a manual for managers of older volunteers[307] which was launched in the Cabinet Office by Lord Falconer in 1999. Janet was invited to take along a group of older volunteers to meet him. She knew that some of them would be overawed by the occasion and tension was lifted a little by a surprise encounter with John Major in the foyer as he bid the group a cheery good day while he elbowed his way past.

Many aspects of volunteering were discussed that morning including funding, publicity and relations with statutory services. Janet ensured that each volunteer had an opportunity to contribute to the discussion.

Doubtless, she would have liked to contribute herself but knew that some volunteers would be pushed to the margins unless she stuck to the task of choreographer-in-chief.

Volunteers joked that Janet could persuade volunteers who fainted at the sight of blood to work in a blood transfusion service. New ideas tumbled out of her head. She worked with a group of volunteers with management skills who helped mould her ideas into practical projects and reminded her when she was about to commit funds she did not have. Not that she was deterred by the absence of funds. As an eternal optimist she believed that if she started a project she would find someone to continue funding it. The division of labour she oversaw ensured that she could concentrate her time and energies on matters at which she excelled.

Janet firmly believed there must be room for volunteers to express their creativity and spontaneity so that they left an impact on the culture of the organisations with which they worked. They were not expected merely to absorb and conform to the culture and values of the workplace but to alter them. Volunteers had to be themselves. When she was accompanied to a meeting at the Home Office by a Jamaican volunteer there was surprise all round when the woman produced a bottle of double strength rum and some glasses. Volunteers left an indelible imprint on the Home Office that day.

When asked in later years how she had adapted to the change from working in small, local organisations based in church halls to a national role where she negotiated in board rooms with leaders of big business and with government ministers in Whitehall, Janet said she learnt from her volunteers – which was undoubtedly true.

Janet was awarded the OBE when she retired in 2000. RSVP membership stood at 9,000. This was a modest number but RSVP was not a national name and there were no funds to embark on a massive advertising campaign. In any case, there were limits to the pace at which it could grow. Local surges in membership required the recruitment of organisers, a training programme and fundraising. It was also necessary to have capacity at headquarters to respond to their needs. The aim was for a slow, sustainable and steady growth.

Denise Murphy became the next RSVP director. At the time of her appointment she was Head of Residential and Day Services for the London Borough of Hackney Older People's Service. The transition was smooth. Denise had previously served with volunteers as a community worker and her easy manner meant that she had no difficulty gaining their support. Her knowledge of public services and how they operated meant she was a shrewd negotiator.

Many of the early HQ volunteers stayed with RSVP, developing their roles for the next 15 years. They persuaded others to join their ranks and no important meeting took place about fundraising or the provision of services without at least one volunteer present. On one occasion Denise was leading an RSVP delegation at a meeting in Strasberg and someone remarked that she looked remarkably calm, bearing in mind that she was to host a two-day RSVP conference the next week in Coventry with delegates from across the country and overseas. Was she not needed back in the office to deal with last-minute hitches presented by speakers, civic dignitaries and delegates? "No", she shrugged confidently, "We have a competent team of volunteers at HQ who are attending to all that". This reminded one onlooker of Francis Drake's response when the Spanish Amada was spotted in the Channel.

Denise recognised the importance of identifying and articulating a clear strategy for development. She gathered together a Policy Group composed of staff and volunteer organisers. It became a sounding board for new ideas and commissioned studies into various aspects of RSVP's work. One of its first tasks was to prepare a business plan which helped to secure national funding. Another group, headed by a volunteer with specialist knowledge formulated a strategy for new technology and developed training for volunteers.

Among the headquarters volunteers was one who was well connected with people in big business and, unusually, he was willing to make use of his contacts for fundraising. In the course of 15 years he raised about a million pounds and advised many struggling volunteers how they could locate funds in their areas. This enabled RSVP to embark on projects that would otherwise be impossible. He was particularly successful in obtaining money for national gatherings of organisers. These two-day meetings were held in various locations and were greatly appreciated by volunteers.

RSVP had a unique style of management. It was largely undertaken by organisers who were themselves volunteers. As far as possible, new recruits were able to determine the tasks to which they set their hand. If a volunteer wanted to help in a school, RSVP's role was to help him or her to make the necessary arrangements. Some recruits were very clear about what they wanted to do – like sing in a concert party, repair old bicycles for young people in a poor area or set up a service for cancer sufferers. If there was no service locally in which to place such volunteers, headquarters volunteers, staff and organisers helped to find like-minded volunteers so that they could establish a new service. If particular expertise were required it could normally be found free of charge.

Informal groups of volunteers already active in their locality would sometimes join RSVP, recognising the benefits that membership of a national organisation could bring. Others defected from established organisations complaining that their work was not valued by managers. RSVP levied no membership charge. As well as providing free expertise and, occasionally, money, it insured every volunteer.

Membership steadily grew and the search for funding widened. Some large organisations approached for assistance had difficulty understanding how RSVP worked and doubted the wisdom of relying so heavily on volunteers. When Denise told them that a ratio of 450 volunteers to one member of staff was manageable and that to replace organisers by paid staff would jeopardise the principles behind RSVP, they were sometimes speechless. The subsequent course of events shows that, had RSVP adopted the policy of replacing volunteers by staff, it would have proved to be a Faustian pact with disastrous results.

As indicated below, RSVP recognised the need for staff to kick-start projects in disadvantaged areas and had some success attracting funds for this purpose. However, in general, it found that such areas needed intensive help over an extended period and funding for this was difficult to secure.

To demonstrate that a volunteer-led organisation could reach the highest standards, Denise set about proving it. In December 2003 she received the prestigious *Investor on People National Standard* for RSVP, awarded by the Training and Skills Council to organisations achieving a high level of good practice for the training and development of people. The assessor visited RSVP projects and spoke to many volunteers before concluding that the award was merited.

In the year before she retired, Denise recognised that income from CSV was diminishing and that, to remain viable, local projects must aim to be self-supporting, raising income for themselves. She worked hard with regional coordinators to achieve this.

On retirement in 2009, Denise had 13,500 volunteers and problems of size had begun to emerge. The organisation had become too large to be managed as a single entity and regional managers were appointed with delegated authority. But fundraising for these posts was particularly difficult. Money was still being raised for specific pieces of work but few people were interested in funding a regional manager post. There was also a difficulty of ensuring that volunteers and managers across the country felt they were part of the same team when there were few opportunities to meet.

Rachael Bayley became director in 2008. Almost immediately economic storm clouds gathered across the country and it was her task to respond to dramatic cuts in funding. Inevitably, the only way to make meaningful reductions was to dismiss staff. While the government was advocating the "Big Society", some skilled and experienced staff who had been championing the idea for many years found themselves looking for new jobs.

Europe

RSVP played a leading role in bringing together organisations from across Europe that promoted older volunteering. Tentative links began in 1991 when Janet spoke at an international conference in Stockholm. She met a number of people from key voluntary organisations in Europe and her networking skills were put to good use. The following year, RSVP joined with a voluntary organisation in France and an exchange was arranged between older people in residential care in Canterbury and Paris.

During the 1993 European Year for Older People and Solidarity Between Generations there were several European conferences attended by RSVP volunteers. Janet used the events to identify suitable organisations with which RSVP could run joint projects and made informal soundings about creating a network of older volunteers. She was particularly concerned to ensure that the organisations selected in each country were willing to engage volunteers in the project and that it did not become an elite group of European managers.

At a meeting in Paris in 1994 the European Network of Older Volunteers (ENOV) was born with RSVP providing the secretariat. Modest funding came from a French trades union. Participating organisations included Finland, France, Germany, Ireland, Italy, the Netherlands, Spain and the UK. From the start, organisations in a number of Eastern European countries became closely involved particularly from the Czech Republic and Hungary but they had even less access to funds than organisations in Western Europe. Sometimes it was possible to persuade the European Union to meet their conference expenses although, at that time, they were not in membership of the EU.

A working group of ENOV members undertook a study of volunteering patterns among older people in Europe[308]. In 1996, an ENOV conference was held in Empoli, Italy where particular interest was aroused by a project, Filo d'Argenti (Silver Thread) a telephone befriending scheme. As a result of what was learned, similar schemes were launched in the UK and in Summerhill, near Dublin. The Dublin scheme was later rolled out across Ireland.

When Help the Aged received a request from ex patriots living in Spain for help in meeting the pressing social needs of older British citizens, part of its response was to arrange for RSVP and an ENOV member from

Germany to discuss with them how they might organise volunteer services.

An international event hosted in Summerhill was particularly memorable. Delegates from nearly 20 countries were bussed from their hotel to the community centre. As they entered the car park the Police Band struck up and about fifty children rushed forward to greet their guests. There was a good deal of singing and dancing before the guests were ushered inside to start their meeting. During the next three days, whenever conference delegates appeared in the streets they were greeted enthusiastically by children.

ENOV enjoyed good links with the European Union which funded research, publications and conferences. The latter were attended by delegates from across Europe and fraternal delegates from the United States. Representatives from ENOV also worked inside other European organisations concerned with older people to ensure that the potential of older volunteers was recognised.

In 1998 the EU provided substantial funding to enable information to be gathered from six member organisations about ways in which the use of new technology and telecommunications by older volunteers combated social isolation. Particular attention was paid to projects which could be replicated in other countries. A report[309] about this research, in three languages, was published the following year and discussed at an international conference in London.

Other projects included a Newsletter in English and French and a video about older volunteering in Europe with different soundtracks for each language. ENOV also enjoyed fruitful links with volunteer organisations in the US and hosted a number of events in London for visitors from across the Atlantic.

In the new century, as a result of pressure from member governments, EU funding for ENOV fell away. Exchange projects tailed off and the bi-lingual newsletter ceased publication. There was fierce competition for EU funds and ENOV members found themselves meeting under the aegis of other organisations. An ENOV meeting was held in Bristol in 2006 funded by the UK government as a contribution to the Year of the Volunteer and ENOV was revitalised. Its name was changed to the European Network of Older Volunteering Organisations, ENOVO. There followed a programme of exchange visits which were entirely financed by the EU under the umbrella title of "Life-long learning" This programme has been ongoing.

Both Janet and Denise saw international links as a way for volunteers to learn about the many facets of volunteering and to develop new approaches to their work. Those who participated, learned a great deal about how volunteering fared under different political systems. In parts of Eastern Europe they found there to be little appreciation of the role of formal volunteering but discovered how oppressed people forge informal links to support one another in time of crisis. Additionally, in describing and explaining their own activities they broadened their own understanding.

Disadvantaged Areas.
On a cold, grey morning in April 1995, workmen were tracing a water leak in a block of flats on the Stonebridge

Council Estate in the London Borough of Brent. Water was dripping from an upstairs flat to which the workmen were unable to gain entry. They forced open the front door and waded through a two foot high pile of post and newspapers. On the kitchen floor they found a jumble of bones belonging to the tenant, 69-year-old John Sheppard, who had been dead for three and a half years. The Council asked Help the Aged to investigate what had gone wrong.

The Help the Aged report[310] found some incompetence but no villains. As in most housing and social services departments, staff were overworked, under-resourced and prioritised their work accordingly. The Council had no obligation to inform itself of the death of a tenant – only to cause a body to be removed as soon as it was discovered.

In painting a picture of the estate from the point of view of older tenants the report demonstrated that it shared the attributes of many inner city disadvantaged areas. Drug dealers dominated the area, vandalism was rife, violence flared from time to time, lifts often did not work, young people and drunks took over stairwells and muggings were common. Older people were reluctant to leave their homes, especially after dark.

There were few opportunities for older people to make social contacts; they made little or no contribution to community life, being surplus to the needs of the rest of the estate. Their lives were their own. Like shadows, they were ever present but seldom noticed by the rest of the community. Often, they had been left behind as younger relatives moved to more congenial areas. Like most of their neighbours they led impoverished lives. The report outlined the need for opportunities to be available for them to serve their community. The work of RSVP was highlighted as an example of how older people could be engaged with minimal cost to the public purse. An appendix in which these issues were discussed was subsequently reproduced in *Policy Studies*.[311]

At a conference to discuss the report, chaired by newspaper columnist Polly Toynbee, Help the Aged announced that it would provide £22,500 to set up an RSVP project on the Stonebridge Estate. This was a new departure. Hitherto RSVP had relied on organisers coming forward. It had never tried to arouse interest in an area where it had no volunteer leader but now, it decided to appoint a part time member of staff to recruit volunteers and establish a presence on Stonebridge.

It was difficult to explain the concept to older people on the estate. Traditionally, those over retirement age were regarded – and regarded themselves – as passive recipients of services, grateful for any help offered. RSVP saw them as important players with the capacity to influence events and change attitudes. Some older people were not sure that this was right and voiced the view that, at their age, they should be able to sit back and receive help from others. Some were clearly intrigued by the idea of volunteering. Many had led active lives and some did not welcome the role of wallflower that society has assigned to them.

On the other hand, there was an air of resignation among residents. Judging from their experience, they did not believe that anyone would listen to their views let alone take any notice of them. They found it difficult to envisage a way of life in which they could influence events around them and make choices about their lifestyles. They were also timid about taking on leadership roles. A great deal of discussion took place between headquarters volunteers and Stonebridge residents. Training on leadership and teambuilding was provided.

An office was rented to the group by the Stonebridge Housing Action Trust where meetings could be held. Volunteers were encouraged to discuss the estate's problems and to identify how they could help resolve them. An Advisory Group was formed which was attended by representatives of local statutory and voluntary services and about 15 volunteers. It was chaired by a local resident who had retired from London Transport. He was well liked and proved to be a good organiser.

The first task selected for attention was the loneliness and isolation of frail and housebound people. Several small, local charitable trusts were approached and money was raised to enable volunteers to hire coaches to take otherwise housebound people to the shops, parks and to the seaside. Police cadets were persuaded to join some of the activities and provided the brawn needed to push wheelchairs. Another project which commenced soon after was one in which volunteers helped slow readers in local schools. Later, a very successful service was a lunch club for older people.

Regular meetings of volunteers kept them all informed and helped them to feel part of a worthwhile organisation. These meetings, which included both black and white volunteers, were happy events where there was a lot of good-natured banter. At meetings with volunteers from other parts of London, Stonebridge volunteers shared their knowledge and learned about projects elsewhere. Any excuse would be used to hold a party where the aroma of exotic West Indian dishes filled the air.

When the short-term contract for the project director expired the group felt unable to continue without a member of staff on the estate. Some money was still available and a new appointment was made but, this time, the staff member was made responsible to the volunteers. Later, the group became self supporting although, as for all groups, staff and headquarters volunteers were available to assist when required.

Because of its proximity to central London and interest shown by government ministers the Stonebridge project received a steady flow of official visitors, including senior civil servants, members of parliament and the Housing Minister, Angela Eagle. Foreign dignitaries received included the Deputy Prime Minister of the Czech Republic. On each occasion, care was taken to ensure that local volunteers took the limelight and the credit. This sometimes led to embarrassment with local civic dignitaries who were not sure it was correct etiquette for a local resident with no civic office to host meetings with government or foreign ministers.

Funding organisations had their own mysterious rules. Some applications for small sums of money were accepted only when application forms were signed by the chief executive of CSV and accompanied by national accounts. Sometimes charitable trusts refused to provide funds on the grounds that CSV was too large, not understanding that RSVP Stonebridge was a self-supporting organisation with its own accounts. In the first years of the new century RSVP Stonebridge had an annual budget of about £1,500 to cover telephone and postage costs, photocopying and room rental. The only practical help it needed from paid staff was to negotiate funding applications with local public services and charitable trusts. It was estimated that, in staff time, this cost RSVP the £1,500 that was raised.

Perhaps the biggest problem faced by local volunteers was to be taken seriously by service providers and potential funders. There was a deep prejudice about the trust-worthiness of people living in disadvantaged areas. Even when it was made clear that the group had the backing of an advisory body which included local professionals there was a reluctance to negotiate with residents on the estate or to believe that they could be trusted to handle money. Yet even while senior local public officials refused to meet them, volunteers were being fêted by government ministers and senior civil servants. One volunteer was invited to an event at number 10 Downing Street. Eventually, with reluctance, it was agreed that, to ensure that a dialogue continued with its major funder, the volunteers would be fronted by the secretary of the local Age Concern Group.

Janet had recruited a partner organisation in Madrid for ENOV. This worked in an area of disadvantage – Pan Bendito – similar to Stonebridge. Run by older volunteers, it had undertaken a number of projects to improve community life. With EU funding, exchange visits were arranged between volunteers in Stonebridge and Pan Bendito. Not only were some firm friendships made but it proved to be a good learning experience for volunteers from both countries.

Much of the success of RSVP Stonebridge was due to the enthusiasm and tenacity of the chairman, a man who was born in the West Indies. When he died some years later the local church was filled to capacity for the funeral service. Among the mourners were just a handful of white people – his friends from RSVP and officials from local services with whom he had worked. No individual volunteer is indispensible but he was keenly missed and, for a time, the future of the group was in the balance. As so often happens, volunteers raised their game and the work continued.

Projects based on the Stonebridge experience began in other parts of London but it was difficult to secure funding. Then the Home Office Older Volunteers Initiative provided funds for RSVP to launch similar projects in Coventry, Middlesbrough and Sheffield where the model was developed further. The Welsh Assembly and the Scottish Executive funded similar schemes. Staff in the Cabinet Office project, *Better Government for Older People*, took a great interest in this programme which led to a close partnership between RSVP and BGOP.

Older volunteering is undoubtedly difficult to sustain in disadvantaged areas. Close support can be required from staff over a long period and the challenge is to provide it in such a way that volunteers remain in charge. It is encouraging that the government announced in 2011[312] its intention to set aside £80 million to encourage social action in neighbourhoods with significant deprivation. The plan is that new and existing neighbourhood groups will work to improve the quality of life locally. They could do worse than learn lessons from Stonebridge.

Wider Lessons

Although RSVP wants to grow it is not prepared to do so at the cost of quality. Expansion is only acceptable when volunteers can be offered the backing they need to undertake satisfactory work. Only by steady, organic growth is it possible to minimise the risk of volunteers finding themselves unsupported or waiting interminably for volunteer tasks to be presented to them. That is why, in 2003, a number of people associated with RSVP opposed the creation of the Experience Corps, a vehicle through which government pumped nearly £20 million into older volunteering. Its emphasis was on recruiting hundreds of thousands of volunteers irrespective of the capacity of the available infrastructure to deploy them and to offer long term support.

The money spent by the government on the Experience Corps to increase older volunteering made little impact on RSVP. Nor would the unspecified sum recommended by Lord Warner[313] in 1999 for creating a cadre of paid managers to increase the number of volunteers working alongside public services. This was a proposal to boost volunteer numbers in preparation for the International Year of Volunteers.

Other major government projects like ChangeUp, Capacitybuilders and Futurebuilders that have channelled substantial government funds into voluntary organisations have also passed by RSVP. It has not been tempted to modify its principles or its objectives to attract funds or please government agencies. The integrity of volunteering has always come first. RSVP's foundations are the dedication of local people, not the quick sands of government funding that can disappear as quickly as it appears.

It is undoubtedly easier to develop volunteering projects if funds are available to appoint staff to manage them but many in RSVP believe this is not the best way to create long term, self-sustaining projects. When funding is withdrawn, worthwhile schemes collapse unless thought has been given to developing leadership roles among volunteers.

The cost of volunteering projects rise substantially when they are required to bear the cost of paid staff. Volunteers are always in the front line when public sector cuts are under discussion. They cannot offer a consistent service to the community if they pursue stop-go policies in line with the changing priorities of public services. Modest and stable funding from a wide base, including local communities, is needed so that gains made can be sustained even during an economic downturn. RSVP has grown modestly but steadily each year, irrespective of public spending policies because it has its own momentum.

Looking back, it is clear that managers employed by RSVP have always been fully engaged supporting existing projects. There has been no time or money to develop a presence in new areas. Somehow, despite considerable investment by governments in older volunteering, RSVP has failed to convince them or other major funders that investing in one or more development managers for RSVP would enable it to develop projects in new areas that could become self sustaining.

Appendix 2

**Circumstances in which volunteers may have a
particularly valuable contribution to make.**

- Some members of the public are suspicious of people
  in authority but are willing to speak to a volunteer.
  This is especially true if the volunteer has faced the
  same difficulties. People in need often resist the
  notion that they are a patient or a client but have no
  difficulty opening their heart to a volunteer.
- Volunteers sometimes have greater knowledge of
  local living conditions than a professional from
  outside the area and, for that reason, may be more
  acceptable to residents and be able to offer more.
- Volunteers help to "de-institutionalise" residential
  homes and hospitals, undertaking tasks that may not
  be in staff job descriptions like talking with residents
  and writing letters for them.
- Some activities are labour-intensive over short
  periods of time making it impractical to hire staff. For
  example, managing fetes and carnivals. The Calgary
  Stampede lasts ten days and is largely run by about
  2,500 volunteers.
- Volunteers can be powerful allies for any organisation
  seeking to influence public opinion. A campaign
  spearheaded by volunteers may achieve more than one
  led by professionals who may be seen as having a
  vested interest.

- It may be important to find someone with special experience – a particular religion, racial background or language. Volunteers can provide a wider pool of people making it more likely that someone with appropriate knowledge or experience can be identified.
- A volunteer may have skills or expertise that are not otherwise available. For example, horticulture or knowledge of football for children's homes and schools.
- Patients in hospices and other long-stay institutions sometimes welcome discussions with volunteers because they are not professionals. They know that staff are short of time.
- Volunteers understand administrative processes from the recipient's point of view and can sometimes indicate how services can be improved.
- Professionals and volunteer managers are part of the power structure of the organisation in which they work. Volunteers are not. They are therefore freer to blow the whistle on bad practices if that is the only practical way to secure desirable changes.
- Volunteers can provide individual attention in situations where professionals find this impossible or impractical. For example they can offer a one-to-one reading experience for children who, for whatever reason, have fallen behind in class.
- Volunteers sometimes appear to be more effective fundraisers because, unlike staff, they are not seen to benefit directly from the funds raised.
- In the same way that auditors are seen as independent, volunteers can be seen to act independently if they provide advocacy services or assist with evaluation exercises.

- Where volunteers serve their communities by meeting social needs they help create cohesive communities and encourage self-help.
- Volunteers often have extensive knowledge of the local community and how to approach those who might provide skills or other resources.
- Many social problems extend beyond the administrative boundaries of existing statutory or voluntary services and a volunteer can sometimes offer a new approach to them.
- As community leaders, volunteers may be able to influence the attitudes or behaviour of local groups that are causing concern to the community.
- Volunteers can often respond quicker than formal organisations to sudden needs arising from illness, accident or other emergency.
- Volunteers are the best advocates of volunteering and make effective recruiters.
- Volunteers have an important role as mentors, passing on their unique knowledge and expertise to others.

References

[1] Oborne, Peter. *The Rise of Political Lying*. The Free Press. 2005.

[2] Simey, Margaret. *From Rhetoric to Reality*. P143. Liverpool University Press. 2005.

[3] Levitt, Tom MP. *Trustees are the unsung heroes of the charity world* E Politix 2010.

Chapter One. The Challenge

[4] Institute National d'Etudes Demographiques. *Infant Mortality Rate*. 2009.

[5] Davies, Charlotte. *ADHD linked to premature birth*. BBC News. 4th June 2006.

[6] Hope, Jenny. *National scandal of 11 stillbirths a day means Britain has one of the worst survival rates*. Mail Online. 14th April 2011.

[7] *Euro-Peristat indicators for the year 2004*. European Prenatal Health Report. 2008

[8] Observatoire Demographique European. *Life Expectancy at Birth*. 2006.

[9] Devlin, Kate. *Women's life expectancy among the poorest in Europe*. The Telegraph. 16/11/2008.

[10] Johnson, Simon. *Scots to have Europe's Lowest Life Expectancy*. The Telegraph. 17th November 2010.

[11] *Increase in Scottish Life Expectancy*. General Register Office for Scotland. 2010.

[12] Pro Life Campaign. *Latest Comparative Abortion Rates in Europe 2006*. 2008.

[13] *Statistics by Country for Sexually Transmitted Diseases*. Wrong Diagnosis. 2010.

[14] *New UK Abortion and STD Statistics*. LifeSite News. March 2004.

[15] Unicef. *A League of Teenage Births in Rich Nations*. 2001 updated 2010.

[16] Health Improvement Analytical Team. *Health Profile England*. P. 61. Department of Health. 2010.

[17] *Doing Better for Children. Country Highlights*. OECD. 2009.

[18] Royal College of Psychiatrists. UK and Spain top league for common psychological disorders in European Study. Press Release 2008.

[19] Table DRD-5. *Percentage of drug-related deaths to all deaths*. EMCDDA. 2006.

[20] Ghodse, Hamid et al. *Drug-related deaths in the UK*. St George's University of London. 2009.

[21] EMCDDA Op cit

[22] Doughty, Steve. *Britain now official drugs capital of Europe*. Mail online. 7th November 2008.

[23] *Alcohol deaths. UK rates increase in 2008*. Office for National Statistics. 2010.

[24] *Scotland's drinking habit*. The Scottish Government. 2009.

[25] *Alcohol, smoking and drugs*. NHS Greater Glasgow and Clyde. 2011.

[26] Changing Scotland's Relationship with Alcohol. Annex B. The Scottish Government. 2008.

[27] Statistics on Alcohol: England. The Health and Social Care Information Centre. 2009

[28] *Rise in prescription items dispensed to treat alcohol dependency.* NHS Information Centre. 2011.

[29] Row, Stephen, Coleman, Kathryn, Kaiza, Peter. *Violent and Sexual Crimes* in Statistical Bulletin 2008/9. Home Office. 2009.

[30] Patton, Bob. *Alcohol Problems in A & E.* National Addiction Centre. 2004.

[31] Nationmaster.com. *Obesity Statistics – countries compared.* OECD Health Data. 2005.

[32] Martin, Daniel. *Britain sickest country in Europe with worst rates of obesity and teenage pregnancy.* Daily Mail. 27th January 2009.

[33] Levy, Andrew. *Crisp kings of Europe: Britons are the biggest snack eaters.* Mail Online. 11th June 2011.

[34] *Information and Statistics.* Anorexia and Bulimia Care. 2008.

[35] BBC. *Low self-esteem leads to obesity.* 11th September 2009.

[36] Mental Health Foundation. Self-harm. Ce alcohol 2006.

[37] Erlam, Rebecca. *Self-harm figures "set to rise" in Manchester.* BBC News Manchester. 7th August 2010.

[38] Gray, Louise. *Scots teenage girls Europe's worst for inflicting self-harm.* The Scotsman. 21st May 2005.

[39] Mental Health Foundation. *Mental Health Statistics: Suicide.* 2011.

[40] *Britain top of European Crime League.* Daily Telegraph. 6th February 2007.

[41] *Alcohol and Crime Factsheet.* Institute of Alcohol Studies. 2010.

[42] Bellis, M. A. Hughes, K. Anderson, Z. Tocque, K. And Hughes, S. *Contribution of Violence to health inequalities in England.* Journal of Epidemiol Community Health. 2008.

[43] Hope, Jenny. *NHS staff report rise in attacks*. Mail Online. 9th February 2011.

[44] Brooks, Cameron. *Over 28,000 assaults on public service workers*. Argyll 2010.

[45] Rowe, Mark, Pyke, Nicholas. *Britain is Road Rage Capital of Europe*. The Independent. 14th May. 2000.

[46] *The World Prison Population List* (fifth edition). Home Office. 2003.

[47] *Compendium of reoffending statistics and analysis*. Ministry of Justice Statistics Bulletin. 2010.

[48] Prison Factfile. *Bromley Briefings*. P. 9. Prison Reform Trust. 2006

[49] Morris, Nigel. *Record numbers of women imprisoned*. The Independent. 2nd November 2009.

[50] Hartney, Christopher. *US rates on incarceration: a global perspective*. National Council on Crime and Delinquency. 2006.

[51] Travis, Alan. *Prison leaves 17,000 children separated from their mothers*. The Guardian. 30th September 2011.

[52] Fazel. S. et al. *Prison Suicide in 12 Countries During 2003 -7*. Kriminalvarden. 2010.

[53] *Prevalence of Domestic Violence*. Women's Aid. 2008.

[54] *An overview of child well-being in rich countries*. Unicef. 2007.

[55] *Open Public Services* White Paper. HM Government. 2011.

[56] *Doing Better for Children*. OECD United Kingdom Country Highlight.s 2009.

[57] Beatbullying. *Statistics*. 2006.

[58] Harlin, Rebecca P. *Bullying and Violence Issues in Children's Lives*. Childhood Education. 2008.

[59] *The Bullying and Truancy Report*. Beatbullying. 2006.

[60] Bullyonline. *School Truancy*. 2006.

[61] International Obesity TaskForce. *Overweight children around the world*. 2010.

[62] Norfolk, Andrew. Who ate all the pies? The Times. 11th July 2009.

[63] *Nearly one in five children leaving primary school is obese*. NHS Information Centre. 2010.

[64] *Alcohol related hospital admissions double in last ten years according to latest official figures*. NHS Information Centre. 2008.

[65] Doing Better for Children. Country Highlights. OECD. 2009.

[66] Morris, Nigel. Almost 3.000 children now held in custody. The Independent. 19th April 2009.

[67] Prison Reform Trust report calls for councils to foot the bill for children in jail. Prison Reform Trust. 2006.

[68] Children with learning disabilities more likely to go to prison. Prison Reform Trust. 2010

[69] Civitas. Factsheet – Youth Crime in England and Wales. 2010.

[70] European Environment and Health Information System. Prevalence of asthma and allergies in children. World Health Organisation. 2007.

[71] Science Daily. Psychological factors implicated in development of asthma. 1st October 2001.

[72] Weil, Constance et al. The relationship between psychological factors and asthma morbidity in inner-city children with asthma. Pediatrics in Review. 6th December 1999.

[73] Migration Policy Institute. Foreign-Born Populations in Europe. 2005.

[74] Vaisse, Justin. Muslims in Europe: A short introduction. Center on the United States and Europe at Brookings. 2008.

[75] Pridd, Helen. Pope in Berlin. The Guardian. 23rd September 2011

[76] Randeep, Ramesh. Poverty is more likely cause of mistrust than race, says study. The Guardian. 28th November 2010.

[77] Chakrabortty, Aditya. UK; riots: political observers see what they want to see. The Guardian. 10th August 2011.

[78] Ponticelli, Jacopo and Voth, Hans-Joachim. Austerity and Anarchy: Budget Cuts and Social Unrest in Europe, 1919-2009. Centre for Economic Policy Research) (pdf) 2010.

[79] Clark, Laura. Divorce and Viagra blamed for soaring rate of sexually-transmitted diseases in over-45s. Mail Online. 24th July 2009.

[80] Child Population. The Health of Children and Young People. Office for National Statistics. 2004.

[81] Written Answers. House of Commons. 25th March 2009.

[82] Chapple, S. Child Well-Being and Sole-Parent Family Structure in the OECD: An Analysis. OECD Social, Employment and Migration Working Papers. No 82. 2009.

[83] O'Neill, Rebecca. Experiments in Living: The Fatherless Family. CIVITAS. 2002.

[84] Rodgers, Bryan and Pryor, Jan. Divorce and separation: The outcomes for children. Joseph Rowntree Foundation. 1998.

[85] Lexmond, Jen and Reeves, Richard. Building Character. Demos. P40. 2009.

[86] Ibid P. 38.

[87] NHS Greater Glasgow and Clyde Health Board Media Centre. General Facts and Figures. 2009.

[88] Wilkinson, Richard & Pickett, Kate. The Spirit Level. Allen Lane. 2010

[89] Putnam, Robert. Bowling Alone. P. 296. Simon & Schuster

[90] Gilligan. J. Preventing Violence. Thames and Hudson. 2001.

[91] The Equality Trust. Income inequality and violent crime. Equality Trust Research Digest. 2011.

[92] Op cit P. 33.

[93] Press Association. Income affects child discipline. 2011.

[94] Press Release. Processed food diet in early childhood may lower subsequent IQ. University of Bristol. 2011.

[95] Armistead, Louise. Vince Cable to launch fresh attack on pay gap. The Telegraph. 17th September 2011.

[96] Wales poorest areas given bad deal by lottery. Western Mail 27th July 2009.

[97] Ball, James. Camelot under fire for failing to say where national lottery cash is spent. The Guardian 4th October 2011.

[98] Op Cit. P.187.

[99] Field, Frank. The Foundation Years. Preventing poor children becoming poor adults. Cabinet Office. 2010.

[100] Mc Kenzie, Tom and Pharoah, Cathy. How generous is the UK? Charitable giving in the context of household spending. Centre for Charitable Giving and Philanthropy. 2011.

Chapter Two. The elephant in the living room

[101] Sigman. Dr Aric. Remotely Controlled. Vermilion. 2007.

[102] Curtis, Polly. England plunges in ranking for reading. The Guardian. 29th November 2007.

[103] Sigman. Dr Aric. Children Need Slow TV. Daily telegraph 14th December 2008.

[104] Clark, Laura. Middle-class parents too busy to teach children how to talk, say 'communication champion', Mail on Line. 1st January 2010.

[105] Huesman. L.R., and Eron. L.D. Television and the Aggressive Child; A cross-national comparison. Lawrence Eribaum 1986

[106] Hoggart, Richard. The Uses of Literacy. P 202. Penguin. 1963.

[107] Hoggart, Richard. The way we live now. P 259. Pimlico.

[108] Cleave, Van G. Unplugged: my journey into the dark world of video game addiction. Health Communications. 2010.

[109] Anderson, C. A. and Dill, K. E. Video Games and Aggressive Thoughts, Feelings and Behaviour in the Laboratory and in Life. Journal of Personality and Social Psychology. Vol. 78. No. 4. 2000.

[110] Alleyne, Richard Mobile phone text messaging is making children more impulsive claim researchers. Daily Telegraph. 11th August 2009.

[111] Van den Buick, J & Custers. K. Television exposure is related to fear of avian flu. European Journal of Public Health. August 2009.

[112] Boyland, Emma. Children Exposed to Food Ads Eat More The Medical News. 26th February 2007.

[113] Harris, Jennifer. TV Ads make children choose more junk foods. Journal of Health Psychology. The American Psychological Association. July 2009.

[114] Lehrer, Jonah. Science of Spending. RSA Journal. Spring 2009.

Chapter Three. The volunteering industry

[115] Cabinet Office, Commission for the Compact, Local Government Association. Volunteering Code of Good Practice 2008

[116] Saxton, Joe and Baker, Jonathon. How government definitions over-estiimate levels of volunteering. NfpSynergy. 2009.

[117] Young, Niki May. nfpSynergy pays staff to "volunteer" by watching World Cup. Civil Society Governance. 2010.

[118] Pharaoh, Cathy. How do the Public See Us? Third Sector. 11th May 2010.

[119] Machin, J. and Paine, Angela Ellis. Management Matters: a national survey of volunteer management capacity. Institute for Volunteering Research. 2008.

[120] Home Office Citizenship Survey 2003. Table 6.1. 2004.

[121] Scotland's People Annual Report. Results from 2009 Scottish Household Survey. The Scottish Government. 2010.

[122] Das-Gupta, Indira. Damn lies and volunteer statistics. Third Sector. 23rd January 2008.

[123] Conservative Party. A Stronger Society. Responsibility Agenda Number 5. 2008.

[124] 2010 -11. Citizenship Survey. Department for Communities and Local Government. 2011.

[125] Staetsky, L. Individual voluntary participation in the UK. Briefing Paper 6. Third Sector Research Centre. 2007

[126] UN General Assembly Report of the Secretary General. Follow-up to the implementation of the International Year of Volunteering. United Nations. 2005.

[127] Manual on the Measurement of Voluntary Work. I.L.O. 2011.

[128] Information Sheet. Volunteering England. 2008.

[129] Citizenship Survey. Helping Out: a national survey of volunteering and Charitable Giving. Cabinet Office. 2008 and Scottish Household Survey annual Report. Scottish Government.

[130] Wiggins, Kaye. V's Placements mainly on-offs Third Sector. 25[th'] May 2010.

[131] Home Office. Citizenship Survey 2003.
[132] Hunt, A. The Hone Help Service in England and Wales. P. 58. HMSO. 1970
[133] Avon County Council. Care and Commitment. 1982,
[134] Dekker-Committee. Willingness to change. The Hague, The Netherlands. 1987.
[135] World Values Survey. www.worldvaluessurvey.org
[136] Helm, P.J. Exploring Saxon and Norman England. P 73. Hale. 1976.
[137] Alinsky, Saul. D. Rules for Radicals. Vintage Books. 1989.
[138] Council of Europe. Expert Council on NGO Law. First Annual Report. OING Conf/Exp 2009.
[139] European Volunteer Centre. Volunteering in Russia. Facts and Figures Report. 2010.
[140] The World Fact Book. People. Central Intelligence Agency USA. 2011.

Chapter Four. Two centuries of volunteering

[141] Booth, Charles. Labour and Life of the People. East London. P504 -507. Williams and Norgate. 1889.
[142] Bryans, Shane. Martin, Clive. Walker, Roma. Prisons and the Voluntary Sector: a bridge into the community. P.56. Waterside Press. 2002
[143] Woodroofe, Kathleen. From Charity to Social Work. p23. Routledge and Kegan Paul. 1962.
[144] Charity Organisation Society. Thirteenth Annual Report 1882. p 20.
[145] Woodroofe, Kathleen, Op cit p32.
[146] Young, A F., & Ashton, E T., British Social Work in the Nineteenth Century. p108. Routledge and Kegan Paul.
[147] Ibid. p53.

[148] Report, Minutes of Evidence. Select Committee on the Friendly Societies Bill. 1849

[149] Rowntree, B. Seebohm. Poverty. A study of Town Life. P 359. Macmillan 1901.

[150] Ibid. P 360.

[151] Hutchins, B L. Women in Modern Industry. p253. Bell 1915.

[152] Asquith, Lady Cynthia. Diaries 1915-18 p34. Vintage Pimlico. 1969.

[153] De'Aeth, Frederic. Quarterly Report. Liverpool Council for Voluntary Aid. October 1928.

[154] Frere, Margaret. Children's Care Committees. King. 1909.

[155] Moxon, Frank. Some remarks, with statistics, on the treatment of 1,305 School Children. British Medical Journal. October 1912.

[156] The Committee on Local Authority and Allied Personal Social Services. Cmnd 3703. HMSO. 1968.

[157] Aves. M. Geraldine. (Chairman) The Voluntary Worker in the Social Services. Allen and Unwin 1969.

[158] Keeling, Dorothy. The Crowded Stairs. p141. The National Council of Social Service. 1961.

[159] Jennings, Hilda. Societies in the Making. p143. Routledge and Kegan Paul. 1962.

[160] Open Public Services White Paper. HM Government. 2011.

[161] Meiners, E. R. Disengaging from the Legacy of Lady Bountiful in Teacher Education Classrooms. In Gender and Education, Volume 14. March 2002. pages 85 –94.

[162] Simey, Margaret. Charitable Effort in Liverpool in the Nineteenth Century. University Press. Liverpool. 1951.

Chapter Six. The changing lives of older people

[163] Focus on Older People. Office of National Statistics. 2009.

[164] Ibrahim et al. Marital Status, change in marital status and mortality in middle-aged British men. American Journal of Epidemiology. p 834-42. 1995.

[165] Call in Time. Age UK 2010.

[166] Spotlight Report. Help the Aged. 2008.

[167] Mental health statistics: older people. Mental Health Foundation. 2011.

[168] Talking Incontinence. Help the Aged. 2005.

[169] Nowhere to Go. Help the Aged. 2007.

[170] www.continencefoundation.org.uk

[171] Good Practice in Continence Services. Department of Health. 2000.

[172] Foresight. Tackling Obesities: future choices, Government Office for Science .2007.

[173] Byham, William C. 70:the new 50. Development Dimensions. 2007.

[174] Walker, Alan. Active Strategies for older workers in the UK .In Foden, D &, Jepson Maria Active Strategies for older workers in the European Union. P 406 European Trade Union Institute. 2002.

[175] Smeaton D & Vegeris S. Older People Inside and Outside the Labour Market. Policy Studies Institute. 2009.

[176] Women in I T. Informatics Research Institute, Salford University. 2006.

[177] Jennings, Hilda. Societies in the Making. P.47. Routledge and Kegan Paul. 1962.

[178] Keep Trade Local. Federation of Small Businesses. 2008.

[179] Local Data Company. July 2011.

[180] Spotlight Report. Help the Aged. 2008.

[181] Future Communities: Re-shaping our society for older people. P7. Help the Aged. 2009.

[182] Ibid

[183] Death of the Petrol Station. BBC 24th March 2008.

[184] Hansard HC Deb, 9 November 2009, c13

[185] Walsh, Dominic. Eyes Down as Gala Coral mulls bingo hall closures. The Times. 15th June 2009.

[186] People who play bingo do better in mental tests. The Independent 12th July 2002.

[187] www.citizensonline.org.uk/publications.

Chapter Seven. The baby boomers' life cycle
[188] Harbert, Bertie. My Life: from horse bus to space travel. Edited by F W Harbert. 2005.

[189] Watson, John B. Psychological Care of Infant and Child. Norton. 1928.

[190] Yankelovich, Daniel. New Rules: Searching for self-fulfillment in a world turned upside down. Bantam. 1982.

[191] Steinhorn, Leonard. The Greater Generation. In Defense of the Baby Boom Legacy. P. 30. St Martin's Press. 2006,

[192] Jordan, Father Gregory. The 1960's Cultural Revolution from self sacrifice to self fulfillment. 2002.

[193] Willetts, David. The Pinch. Atlantic. 2010.

[194] Prescriptions have doubled in a decade. The Guardian. 11th June 2010.

[195] Harkin, James and Huber, Julia Eternal Youths. How the baby boomers are having their time again. Demos. 2004.

[196] Iyeng Sheena, S & Lepper Mark R. When Choice is Demotivating: Can One Desire Too Much of a Good Thing? www.columbia.edu/~ss957/whenchoice.html
[197] Fromm, Erich. The Fear of Freedom. P. 89. 1942.

Chapter Eight. Volunteering and fulfillment
[198] Freedman, Marc. Prime Time: How baby boomers will revolutionize retirement and transform America. P. 69. Public Affairs. 1999.
[199] Brodie, Ellie et al. Pathways through participation. Final Report. P 69. NCVS.,!VS., INVOLVE. 2011.
[200] Older people in the labour market. Office of National Statistics. 2011.
[201] Weeks, David. Eccentricity: The Scientific Investigation. Stirling University Press. 1988.
[202] Titmuss, R. M. The Gift Relationship. Allen and Unwin. 1970.
[203] Hamilton, David. R. Why kindness is good for you. P 4 Hay House. 2010.
[204] Ibid. P 117.
[205] Ibid. P 118.
[206] Modern Medicine. Seniors who volunteer outlive non-volunteers. 4th May 2009.
[207] Titmuss. Op cit. P 210
[208] Hamilton. Ibid. P 200.
[209] Titmuss. Op cit P 156.
[210] Plummer, John. Peers agree that payment of trustees might spread. Third Sector Online 23rd September 2011.
[211] Ostrower, Francie. Nonprofit governance in the United States The Urban Institute Centre on Nonprofits and Philanthropy. 2007.
[212] Putnam, Robert. Bowling Alone. P 28. Simon & Schuster Paperbacks. 2000.

Chapter Nine. Disadvantaged communities

[213] Hanley, Lynsey. Estates. An Intimate History. P 7. Granta Books. 2008.

[214] Open Public Services White Paper. HM Government. 2011.

[215] Plant, Martin. Young People and Alcohol; An International Insight. Alcohol and Alcoholism Vol. 36 No. 6. P 515. 2001.

[216] Gregory, James. In the Mix: Narrowing the gap between public and private housing. Fabian Society. 2009.

[217] Open Public Services White Paper. HM Government. 2011.

[218] Life Expectancy for Special Areas. General Register Office for Scotland. 2010.

[219] NHS Greater Glasgow and Clyde Health Board Media Centre. General Facts and Figures. 2009.

[220] Alcohol related deaths highest in Glasgow. Nursing Times. 17th September 2009.

[221] Information Services. NHS Scotland. Sexual Health. 2009.

[222] Leyland, A. H. And Dundas, R. The social patterning of deaths due to assault in Scotland, 1980–2005: population-based study. J. of Epidemiol Community Health. Vol 64. pp432-439. 2010.

[223] Hunt, Sally. In Gap Widening between Britain's best and worst areas for educational success, warns report. P 2. University and College Union. 2009.

[224] Curtis, Polly. Selfish, lying and cheating – that's just the parents. The Guardian. 3rd November 2009.

[225] Paton, Graeme. Warning over school admissions "theft", Daily Telegraph. 2nd November 2009.

[226] Housing Market Research Special Report. High Performing Primary Schools add vale to Property Prices. Nationwide Building Society. 2010

[227] Dorling,Danny. So you think you know about Britain? P 130. Constable. 2011.

[228] Mackinnon, Mark. Inside China's New Gated Communities. The Globe and Mail. Vancouver 19th July 2010.

[229] Mohan, John, Kane, David, Wilding, Karl, Branson, Julia and Owles, Fiona. Beyond flat-earth maps of the third sector.. Third Sector Trends Study 2010.

[230] McCabe, Angus et al. Below the radar activities and organisations in the third sector. Working Paper 29. Third Sector Research Centre. 2010.

[231] Lindsey, Rose. Clifford, David. Deprived areas have fewer charities and voluntary groups. Voluntary Sector Network. 2011

[232] Conservative Party. Voluntary Action in the 21st Century. 2008.

[233] Lindsey, Rose. Clifford, David. Deprived areas have fewer charities and voluntary groups. Voluntary Sector Network. 2011

[234] House of Commons Report Social Cohesion. London. Stationery Office. 2004.

[235] Hanley, Linsey. The Guardian 3rd February 2010

[236] Cantle, Ted Social Cohesion: A report of the Independent Review Team. London. Home Office. . 2001.

[237] Shepherd, Jessica. In their best interests. The Guardian. 4th August 2010.

[238] Ward, Bernie and Lewis, Julie. Plugging the Leaks. New Economic Foundation. 2002.

Chapter Ten. Deploying volunteers

[239] The Religious Census 1851

[240] Kay, Jackie. Red Dust: An Autobiographical Journey. Picador. 2010

[241] Salvation Army The Seeds of Exclusion. P59. London. 2008

[242] The Commission on the Future of Volunteering. Manifesto for Change. P22. Volunteering England. 2008.

[243] Manual on the Measurement of Voluntary Work. ILO 2011

[244] It's all about time. Volunteering in Northern Ireland. Volunteer Development Agency. 2007.

[245] Hoggart, Richard. The Uses of Literacy. Penguin. P317. 1963.

[246] Obama, Barack. Dreams From My Father. P226. Canongate. 2007.

[247] Riddle, Annie. Lifeline for Stourton. 26th August 2010.

[248] Director and nine trustees quit York CAB after volunteer walk-out. Association of Volunteer Managers. 2008.

[249] Plummer, John. Citizens Advice volunteer wins apology for dismissal. Third Sector, 27 October 2009.

[250] Volunteer Rights Inquiry. Interim Report. Volunteering England. 2010.

[251] Volunteer Rights Inquiry. Recommendations and call for action. Volunteering England. 2011.

[252] Investing in Volunteers. Volunteering England. 2011.

[253] Harbert, Wally. Volunteering report Makes Me Uneasy…. Third Sector 6th February 2008.

Chapter Eleven. Is *management* the right word?

[254] *Join in, Get Involved, Build a Better Future. A consultation paper on a volunteering strategy for Northern Ireland.* Department for Social Development, Northern Ireland 2009.

[255] Bell, E. Moberly. *Octavia Hill*. p123. Constable 1942.

256 Meijs, Lucas C. P. M. *Management is not Always the Right Word*. The Journal of Volunteer Administration. XIV No.3 1996.
257 Harbert, Wally. *Whose estate is it anyway?* P21. RSVP. 2001.
258 Machin, L. and Paine, A.E. *Management matters: a national survey of volunteer management capacity*. P. 6. Institute for Volunteering Research. 2008
259 Machin, J. Paine. A. E. *Management Matters*. pp22 &19. Institute of Volunteering Research. 2008.
260 Johnson. Christopher. *The strength of the infrastructure of volunteer agencies and its capacity to absorb "baby boomer" volunteers*. Harvard-MetLife Foundation. 2003.
261 Jones, Gareth. *Labour peer criticises Locality for paternalistic approach to Big Society*. Civil Society News. 25th May 20011.
262 Brodie, Ellie et al. *Pathways through participation*. Final Report. P 73. NCVS., !VS., INVOLVE. 2011.

Chapter Twelve. The bureaucratisation of volunteering
263 *Vetting and Barring Scheme Remodelling Review – Report and Recommendations*. P. 3. Department for Education, Department of Health, Home Office. 2011.
264 Caird, Jo. *Wanted Men*. The Big Issue. August 2007.
265 *Who can Benefit from Charities? Equality Act summary guidance*. Charity Commission 2010.
266 *Guidance for employers on preventing illegal working. Asylum seekers and refugees*. UK Border Agency 2010.
267 Association of British Insurers. *Motor insurers support Big Society and give green light to volunteer drivers*. ABI News Release. 2011.

[268] *Bureaucratic Barriers affecting volunteering.* Volunteering England. 2010.

[269] *Unshakling Good Neighbours. Report of the Task Force established to consider how to cut red tape for small charities, voluntary organisations and social enterprises.* Department of Business Innovation and Skills, Cabinet Office and Department of Communities and Local Government. 2011.

[270] *Open Public Services* White Paper. HM Government. 2011.

[271] *A Charter for Strengthening Relations between Paid Staff and Volunteers.* Volunteering England and the TUC. 2009.

[272] *Volunteering Charter.* VDS and STUC. 2011.

[273] *Giving Green Paper.* The Cabinet Office. 2010.

[274] *The modernisation review of public libraries: A policy statement.* Department for Culture, Media and Sport. 2010.

[275] Wilding, Mark. *Balancing staff with volunteers.* Third Sector. 20th September 2011.

[276] *Alzheimer's Society – a peculiar kind of charity?* Care in the UK. 18th March 2011.

[277] Wiggins, Kaye. *Alzheimer's Society to restruicture creating 100 jobs.* Third Sector Online. 1st December 2009.

[278] Public Administration Select Committee. 2008.

[279] Macmillan, Rob. *The Third Sector Delivering Public Services: an evidence review.* Third Sector Research Centre. 2010

[280] Brodie, Ellie et al. *Pathways through participation.* P7. NCVO, IVS, INVOLVE. 2011.

[281] Citizenship Survey. *Helping Out. A National Survey of Volunteering and Charitable Giving.* Cabinet Office. 2008.

[282] *The UK Civil Societry Almanac 2010.* NVCO. 2011.

[283] *2010 National Survey of Charities and Social Enterprises.* Cabinet Office. 2011.

[284] *Voluntary Sector Independence. Panel on the independence of the voluntary sector* The Baring Foundation. 2011.

Chapter Thirteen. Helping volunteers to find themselves

[285] Machin, J. and Paine, A. E. *Management Matters*: pp. 22 & 19. Institute for Volunteering Research. 2008.

[286] Ibid. P.5

[287] Brewis, Georgina. Hill, Mathew. Stevens, Daniel. *Valuing Volunteer Managment Skills.* P 19. Institute of Volunteering Research. 2010.

[288] *Volunteer management capacity in America's charities and congregations.* The Urban Institute. 2004.

[289] Camus, Albert. *The Plague.* Penguin. 2001.

[290] Ellis, Susan. J. *From the Top Down. The Executive Role in Successful Volunteer Involvement.* 3rd edition P 28. Philadelphia: Energize, Inc 2010.

[291] Sibley, Merlin. *Volunteering in Health Services.* In *Making a Difference Strengthening Volunteering in the NHS.* NHS Executive 1996.

[292] Annual Review 2010/2011. P 7. Community Service Volunteers. 2011.

[293] Starkey, Pat. *The feckless mother: women, poverty and social workers in wartime and post-war England.* Women's History Review Vol. 9 No.3. P 540. 2000.

[294] Stephens, T. *Problem Families.* Family Service Units. 1945.

[295] Higgs, Lauren. *Family charities say work plans are too narrow*. Children and Young People Now. 23rd August 2011.

[296] *Assessing the Impact of multi-purpose community organisations*. P 28. Institute for Voluntary Action Research. 2011.

[297] *Volunteering Impact Assessment Toolkit*. Volunteering England. 2010.

[298] Charities Evaluation Services at www.ces-vol.org,uk

[299] *Introducing Volunteer Management Benchmarking*. Agenda Consulting. 2011.

[300] *Volunteer Benchmarking*. Third Sector. P 6. 30th August 2011.

[301] Burgess. P. *Valuing Volunteer Voices*. P.6. Experience Corps. 2005.

[302] Ibid. P 2

[303] Colborne, Fenke. *Taking Volunteers in Hand*. Third Sector. P 21. 3rd May 2011.

Appendix 1. The Retired and Senior Volunteer Programme

[304] *Annual Review 2010/2011*. P 5. Community Service Volunteers. 2011.

[305] *Mrs Smith's Handbag*. RSVP and Community Network. 1995.

[306] *Part of the Team: Partnerships between professionals and older volunteers in primary care*. RSVP. 1996.

[307] *Lifelong Action: A Guide to Recruiting and Retaining Older Volunteers*. Home Office. 1999.

[308] ENOV. *Gone Out Europe*. RSVP 1994.

[309] ENOV. *Alone – but not isolated*. RSVP. 1999.

[310] Help The Aged/Brent Council. *A Lonely Death*. 1994.

[311] Harbert, Wally. *Isolated Elderly People: Reflections on Policy.* Policy Studies. Vol 16 No. 2. 1995.

[312] *Giving White Paper.* Cm 8084. HM Government. 2011.

[313] Warner, Norman. *Giving Time, Getting Involved.* Home Office. 1999.

Index

Also by the author

Welfare Benefits. Liverpool Personal Service Society 1968

The Home Help Service. (with Margaret Dexter) Tavistock. 1983. (translated into Japanese).

Community Based Social Care. (joint editor) Bedford Square Press 1983

Letters to My Staff: a manual of management. University of Bristol 1987

The Welfare Industry. Holhouse 1988

A Lonely Death. Brent Council and Help the Aged 1994

Child of the War. An evacuee in Devon. Third Age Press. 1995

My Life: from horse bus to space travel (joint editor) 2005

Bent Twigs. Blackie 2005

About the author

After a disrupted wartime education, Wally Harbert left school at 16 to become a messenger in a London office. He later worked as a junior clerk and as a builder's labourer before doing National Service in the Royal Air Force. He then trained in psychiatric social work and after working eight years in community mental health services became Chief Executive of the Liverpool Personal Service Society in 1965. In 1970 he was Hackney's first director of social services. He joined Avon County Council in the same capacity in 1973. In 1990 he became Help the Aged's UK Director, retiring in 1996.

He has served on government committees concerned with probation, children, community service orders, one parent families, mental illness and transport. He has drafted publications on volunteering for the NHS Executive and the Home Office. He has served as Hon Policy Adviser to the Retired and Senior Volunteer Programme (RSVP) of Community Service Volunteers. He is author of two biographies and six books on the social services including one translated into Japanese. He is a former President of the Association of Directors of Social Services, has lectured in many countries and undertaken assignments in Europe for the United Nations, the World Health Organisation, the European Union and HelpAge International. He was awarded the O.B.E., in 1985.

He lives in Somerset with his wife Sue. They have five adult children.